Mindfulness-Based Supervision and Mentoring

Using an embodied dialogue to support learning and reflection

Alison Evans and Pamela Duckerin
With a Foreword by Rebecca Crane

Mindfulness-Based Supervision and Mentoring

© Pavilion Publishing & Media

The authors have asserted their rights in accordance with the Copyright, Designs and Patents Act (1988) to be identified as the authors of this work.

Published by:
Pavilion Publishing and Media Ltd
Blue Sky Offices, 25 Cecil Pashley Way, Shoreham by Sea, West Sussex, BN43 5FF

Tel: +44 (0)1273 434943
Email: info@pavpub.com
Web: www.pavpub.com

Published 2025

All rights reserved. No part of this publication may be reproduced, stored in a retrieval system, or transmitted in any form or by any means, electronic, mechanical, photocopying, recording or otherwise, without prior permission in writing of the publisher and the copyright owners.

A catalogue record for this book is available from the British Library.

ISBN: 978-1-80388-375-5

Pavilion Publishing and Media is a leading publisher of books, training materials and digital content in mental health, social care and allied fields. Pavilion and its imprints offer must-have knowledge and innovative learning solutions underpinned by sound research and professional values.

Authors: Alison Evans and Pamela Duckerin
Editor: Graham Russel
Head of Publishing: Darren Reed
Cover design and layout: Tony Pitt
Printing: Independent Publishers Group (IPG)

Praise for this book

"Mindfulness has become mainstream. This landmark book ensures its integrity and supports its evolution. Richly informed by theory and research, steeped in lived experience, and eminently practical, it offers a comprehensive and embodied framework for supervision and mentoring. Alison Evans and Pamela Duckerin bring clarity and depth to the important work of supervision and mentoring, articulating a model that supports teachers' learning and development. In so doing, it strengthens the potential of mindfulness-based interventions to promote mental health and human flourishing.

Mindfulness-Based Supervision and Mentoring uses the metaphors of warp and weft and dance. More than poetic devices, they are nuanced ways of understanding how supervision can meet people where they are, adapt to different needs and circumstances, and respond to wider systemic and cultural issues.

The authors' embodiment, extensive training and experience manifest in the book's depth, rigour, inclusiveness, compassion, humility and wisdom. This is a book that every mindfulness teacher and supervisor should read – and reread. I have a shelf where I keep a small set of seminal mindfulness books – this book has taken a well-earned space there."

Willem Kuyken, Ritblat Professor of Mindfulness and Psychological Science, University of Oxford, UK

"This text is a must read for mindfulness supervisors, teachers, and serious practitioners alike. The MBS framework provides a much-needed comprehensive structure that can be applied in any setting, from academia to workplaces, traditional and secular, and even to personal practice. Each part of the framework reveals and expands on hidden layers of contemplative practice, and demonstrates how teacher supervision is a key aspect to improved outcomes for participants of mindfulness programs. Alison Evans and Pamela Duckerin have taken key findings from research in the discipline of mindfulness, getting at the heart of the dynamic process of supervision that integrates and complements teacher competency models. Their masterful synthesis of the MBS framework enriches both mind and heart in the ongoing evolution of the supervisory relationship."

Ted Meissner, mindfulness teacher, supervisor, and science communicator, Mindfulness Voyage

"Since Jon Kabat-Zinn's introduction of Mindfulness-Based Stress Reduction (MBSR) in the 1970s, many mindfulness professionals have started to teach Mindfulness-Based Programmes (MBPs) and/or key elements and exercises from MBPs in secular domains, such as health care, education and management. I am very grateful to the authors of this book for sharing their deep and genuine interest and understanding in an area that hasn't had much attention to date – namely, how to support mindfulness professionals in developing and deepening their mindfulness-based practice and work with supervision and mentoring.

I can wholeheartedly recommend *Mindfulness-Based Supervision and Mentoring* as a 'jewel of richness' to all MBP teachers and professionals working with mindfulness as a profound source of inspiration, for deepening your own understanding and for improving skills in sharing the gems of wisdom and compassion with others."

Frits Koster, certified MBSR and IMP teacher, co-developer of the Mindfulness-Based Compassionate Living programme, co-author of several books

"The relational space in which one can safely reflect, explore, learn and grow is at the heart of mindfulness-based supervision and mentoring. Drawing on their extensive experience, knowledge and passion, Alison and Pamela have developed a framework that creatively draws these aspects together. A beautiful balance between containment and spaciousness permeates this offering, and this sense is further conveyed throughout the book. Their work rests on the foundation and ethics of mindfulness, is underpinned by practice, informed by research and infused with the warmth of compassionate care and wise counsel.

We are invited to reflect, inquire and practice along the way, while skillfully being guided through the different components and applications of the framework. Relevant examples add a sense of aliveness. Personal bias, prejudice and blind spots are respectfully considered. Diversity, inclusivity and trauma-sensitivity are foregrounded, and adaptations honouring different contexts and communities are encouraged.

Alison and Pamela have gifted mindfulness-based teachers, trainers and supervisors with an invaluable and inspiring resource. This contribution will greatly assist in raising awareness of the significant role that supervision and mentoring can play in supporting the teaching of mindfulness in these challenging times."

Barbara Gerber, Supervision Lead, Senior Teacher, Trainer, Institute for Mindfulness South Africa (IMISA).

Contents

About the authors 1

Acknowledgements 3

Foreword 7

Introduction and welcome 13

Part One: Introduction to Mindfulness-Based Supervision 23

    Chapter 1: Overview of the Mindfulness-Based Supervision Framework 25

    Chapter 2: The Theory Informing Mindfulness-Based Supervision 37

Part Two: The Mindfulness-Based Supervision Framework 59

    Chapter 3: The Container 61

    Chapter 4: Mutual Inquiry 83

    Chapter 5: The Space 111

    Chapter 6: The Petals 121

    Chapter 7: The Belt 133

Part Three: Using the Mindfulness-Based Supervision Framework 155

    Chapter 8: Using the Mindfulness-Based Supervision Framework with Culture in Mind 157

    Chapter 9: Using the Mindfulness-Based Supervision Framework within Workplace Mindfulness 181

    Chapter 10: Using the Mindfulness-Based Supervision Framework Through the Developmental Journey 199

    Chapter 11: Using the Mindfulness-Based Supervision Framework to Respond to Challenging, Complex and Sensitive Issues 221

    Chapter 12: Using the Mindfulness-Based Supervision Framework in Group Supervision 241

Chapter 13: Using the Mindfulness-Based Supervision Framework within Supra-vision 259

Chapter 14: Using the Mindfulness-Based Supervision Framework with *You* as a Mindfulness-Based Supervisor in Mind 273

Appendices

Appendix A 289
Mindfulness-Based Supervision Contracting Conversation Checklist

Appendix B 291
Sample Mindfulness-Based Supervision Contract

Appendix C 296
Sample information sheet for recording supervision

Appendix D 298
Sample consent form for recording supervision

Appendix E 299
Mindfulness-Based Supervision Self-Report Competency Checklist

Afterword 309

The resources to accompany this book can be downloaded by visiting the link or scanning the QR code

www.pavpub.com/mindfulness-based-supervision-and-mentoring-using-an-embodied-dialogue-to-support-learning-and-reflection-resources

About the authors

Dr Alison Evans

Alison (she/her) originally trained and worked as an occupational therapist in mental health. In 2004, she moved into the mindfulness field. She led a master's programme in Mindfulness-Based Cognitive Therapy (MBCT) at Exeter University, UK. Developing a supervision process and building a group of supervisors was key to the programme's success. During this time, she studied mindfulness-based supervision (MBS) as the topic for her MSc, resulting in the publication of the paper 'A framework for supervision for mindfulness-based teachers: A space for embodied mutual inquiry'.

She joined colleagues at the Centre for Mindfulness Research and Practice (CMRP) at Bangor University, UK, developing MBS training and refining the MBS framework. Alison centred her doctoral research around MBS, resulting in a peer-reviewed paper, 'What do supervisors and supervisees think about mindfulness-based supervision? A grounded theory study'. She was also first author of the paper, 'Using the Mindfulness-Based Interventions: Teaching Assessment Criteria (MBI:TAC) in supervision'.

Alison is currently the Supervision Lead for the Mindfulness Network (MN). Since its beginning in 2012, supervision has been a strong part of the charity, which Alison co-founded. The role includes leading the internationally renowned supervision team and developing and continuing to facilitate an MBS training pathway. Alison has a wealth of experience offering supervision to mindfulness-based practitioners worldwide. She nurtures the growth of many supervisors through supra-vision.

Much of Alison's working life is being immersed in MBS.

Pamela Duckerin

Pamela (she/her) has been working in the clinical field of mental health since 1984, originally in public services as an occupational therapist, then as a dialectical behaviour therapist, and later as a cognitive behavioural therapist. Since 2023, she has worked freelance as a psychological therapist. She has provided clinical supervision for clinicians and mentoring of students since 1985, acting as an ambassador for supervision. Gradually, supervision became a more substantial part of her clinical work, including specialist clinical supervision in psychological therapy, in a 1:1 context and through group supervision. Through this time, she developed a strong interest in what best supports therapists in doing their work, supporting their clients' well-being whilst also looking after their own well-being.

Pamela joined the Centre for Mindfulness Research and Practice (CMRP) training team in 2015, working on the master's in mindfulness programme and delivering training and supervision in the Mindfulness Network (MN). Since 2019, Pamela and Alison have co-facilitated MBS training and the development of the supervision training pathway. Pamela also wrote a chapter, "Professional Practice", in a book for mindfulness teachers.

Much of Pamela's current working life is dedicated to supervision, offering supervision to mindfulness-based practitioners and mindfulness-based supervisors worldwide, and to clinicians and clinical supervisors within the UK.

Acknowledgements

We wish to acknowledge the many people who have generously contributed, both directly and indirectly, to the creation of this book.

We thank Rebecca Crane for her beautiful foreword. Within it, we see how deeply she understands mindfulness-based supervision (MBS) and its immense and transformative contribution. Becca is a beloved friend, peer and mentor, and a steady guiding influence, who inspires and encourages us. We are indebted to her for the consistent support of supervision over the years.

Our grateful thanks to our interviewees, Uz Afzal, Debbie Hu, Jem Shackleford, Martin Summerfield, and Ted Meissner, for our conversations and their generosity in sharing their experience which has shaped the book immeasurably.

We owe much to our supervisors and mentors over the years who, through these unique relationships, nurtured our growth and development, and inspired our desires to follow in their footsteps in making supervision part of our life's work. We also wish to honour the people within three key organizations for holding this work – it's like they are the container or vessel within which the work can flourish.

We are particularly grateful to Cindy Cooper who touched both our lives in the most profound way. For me, Alison, she was a kindred spirit in her enthusiasm and energy for MBS. I am so grateful to have had precious years with her as a close companion and collaborator. Her commitment to raising the profile of supervision and her generosity in relation to this endeavour remains with me. For me, Pamela, she was a steady support and influence throughout my mindfulness-based journey, from being my first teacher on a 1:1 course, through to teacher training, becoming my first supervisor, then later the privilege to call her a peer when I became part of the training and supervision team at CMRP and MN.[1] Cindy's influence and presence has been strongly with us during the creative process of writing this book. Cindy, you are much missed.

---

1 The Centre for Research and Practice (CMRP) at Bangor University; the Mindfulness Network (MN) charity

Acknowledgements

I, Alison, am honoured to have been supported and nurtured by colleagues at Exeter University where I first began this work – Willem Kuyken, Christina Feldman and Jenny Wilks – all of whom have mentored me in different ways. Willem, for your guidance, mentoring and supervision for my MSc, my first foray into exploring MBS, and for co-founding the Mindfulness Network (MN) which has provided a home for MBS since 2012 and continues to do so. Thank you for believing in me. Christina, for your skilful and pithy teaching and mentoring over the years. And Jenny, a dear friend, colleague and mentor from whom I have learned so much. My early appreciation of the value of MBS began when teaching on a research trial at Exeter University, supervised by Willem Kuyken, Rebecca Crane, John Teasdale and Trish Bartley – no wonder I quickly developed a love of supervision.

Our thanks to the CMRP team, especially Cindy, Jody Mardula and Eluned Gold, for their foundational work in supervision. Jody, you will be much missed. Thank you to Gemma Griffith and Trish Bartley for their guidance and encouragement to write this book. We are grateful to all the past and present trainers who have shared their skills, wisdom and good company.

We would like to give a big shout out to the MN for hosting MBS over the years in many ways – keeping it at the core of the work of the charity. They have also been the catalyst for connections with colleagues – our fellow teachers, trainers and supervisors. Waving the flag for MBS, and trusting and believing in us to bring it into the mindfulness field. We wish to give a special thanks to the amazing past and present supervisor team. Your love, dedication and care for MBS is deeply touching. Thank you for the connections.

I, Pamela, offer my sincere gratitude to Grace Sewell and Shirley Kelly for the companionship and support when we began establishing our personal practice at the same time we moved into offering dialectical behaviour therapy as part of our clinical work. I have fond memories of sharing round Grace's copy of the book, "Full Catastrophe Living" and a set of audio cassette tapes of the practice guidance. Without any access to an eight-week course in our part of Canada at that time, creating support for each other was essential. I also express my deep appreciation to Barbara Reid for her gentle and encouraging mentoring when I first joined the CMRP training team. I learned so much from your approach to learning and development and I think of you often as I engage with my own learning and that of others.

I would like to honour my dear friend and colleague, Jan Bloor, for the many years of peer MBS. Our deep explorations into our MB work and personal practice highlighted what is possible within a safe yet challenging space. My gratitude to Domenica Lopane, my current peer supervisor. I am always inspired and stimulated by our explorations into our MB work. I so value your kindness and clarity. Within my clinical supervision work, I'd like to thank Bijal Desai for all

I learned from our experiences within peer supervision and our lengthy peer reflections around our experiences of offering clinical supervision. To Mhairi Stewart and Munya Chigwada, thanks for your friendship and your enthusiasm and dedication to your craft. I so value our stimulating conversations and explorations around our clinical work that helps keep my learning fresh and influences how I am in my role as a clinical supervisor.

I, Alison, express my gratitude to my supervisors and mentors. Robert Marx, for our supervision together, thank you for your consistent compassion and wise words. To Domenica Lopane and Nicky Mouat, for our peer supra-vision group, especially the opportunity to step into the observer role and witness the intricacies of live MBS and for your feedback to me about how I am as a supervisor. To Niki Buckingham, thank you for your generous guiding and practical support in creating this book and taking care of myself. To Catherine McGee, for the incredible bodily based inquiries and encouraging me to get creative with my personal practice. Thank you to John Teasdale for your steadiness and encouragement to get *really* interested in my personal practice in the early days.

We wish to thank all our supervisors over the years; each and every one of you has gifted us something unique which we treasure. We are also indebted to all of our supervisees and supra-visees. It's through the reciprocal process of engaging in supervisory and supra-visory relationships that we have honed our craft. This constant feedback loop nourishes our energy and enthusiasm. Do not under-estimate how much these meaningful cross-cultural connections fire up our learning.

To all our MBS trainees and retreatants across the world, we offer our appreciation for all that you so generously bring to these spaces. You have deeply shaped this book. May you continue to be ambassadors for MBS. We value the ongoing connections.

To Steve and Ashley, our respective husbands, we thank you for your patient understanding with our absorption in this book project. We so appreciate the practical support offered through the design and printing services, gorgeous soups, curries and cakes, and your un-ending trust that we could do this.

To all of you we have acknowledged, please know that there is something of each of you in these pages.

Our thanks go to Pavilion Publishing and everyone who has been involved in bringing this book to print. A special thank you to Darren Reed and Graham Russel.

And how could we forget each other. What a ride! Deep hugs for the collaboration, companionship and creativity, and for the many moments of fun within the midst of the hard work.

Foreword

Over the last 40 + years mindfulness has increasingly been integrated into multiple disciplines including medicine, psychology, leadership, and education. There is a rapidly expanding body of empirical and theoretical literature examining the effectiveness of mindfulness-based approaches in a range of mainstream contexts including health care, schools and workplaces, as well as with a vast range of different populations. Mindfulness is no longer a fringe engagement. It is embedded into mainstream practice. Yet, bringing mindfulness into mainstream practice in ways that ensure its integrity and transformational potential are fully available requires care and attention. It calls on us to navigate the creative tensions and nuances inherent in an approach which draws on ancient contemplative practices and integrates paradigms of non-fixing, non-duality and non-striving with those of our outcome-focused mainstream institutions.

The resource book you now hold in your hands is a deep dive into one vital element that supports the integrity of this process of 'mainstreaming' mindfulness – Mindfulness-Based Supervision (MBS). MBS is a way of getting alongside and proactively supporting the mindfulness professional,[2] to give them the best possible conditions for being a skilled vehicle for communicating mindfulness to others. The book is a treasure trove of resources on how to bring mindfulness into the world in skilful ways, and it compellingly conveys how engaging a supervisor is a valuable underpinning support to navigating this territory. As we grapple with the multiple social and environmental challenges of our time, discovering engaging and impactful ways to offer mindfulness services in a diversity of communities requires creativity, thought and care. It is more needed than ever, that we have a trusted supervision space to resource ourselves for this work.

Over the years of guiding and nurturing the Bangor University mindfulness centre and the Mindfulness Network, I have been privileged to be part of an

---

[2] I use the phrase 'mindfulness professional' rather than 'mindfulness teacher' because some but not all of our trainees and supervisees are teaching mindfulness. Others are engaged in mindful leadership, mindful therapy, mindful coaching, mindful caregiving, or using mindfulness as an inner support to a range of working engagements including construction, legal services, sport, school teaching and many more.

extraordinary group of colleagues. Each member of our training team has pioneered and disseminated specialisms that they are particularly passionate about. There have been creative outpourings on mindfulness work with parents, with expectant couples, and with people who are dying, living with cancer, identify as neurodivergent, or who want to proactively contribute to addressing the climate crisis. Creative energy has dedicated itself to unpacking the pedagogy of mindfulness teaching, developing the Mindfulness-Based Interventions: Teaching Assessment Criteria (MBI:TAC) and its many offshoots, and examining how mindfulness can influence social as well as personal suffering.

For Alison and Pamela, it is the work of supervising mindfulness teachers that has called them. As described in these pages, alumni members of our team, Jody Mardula and Cindy Cooper, were the first to think deeply about how MBS could optimally take place. Alison has taken this work to the next level through a combination of her own personal engagement with supervision, academic research (including a professional doctorate on this subject), delivering multiple MBS trainings, and leading the internationally renowned supervision team within the Mindfulness Network (who are themselves a group of senior highly skilled creative pioneers in this field). Her recent collaboration with Pamela is the catalyst that has brought this book into being and provided stimulation to the ongoing iterative development to the MBS process. In addition to her valued mindfulness teaching and training skills within our team, Pamela brings over 40 years of clinical and supervisory experience in the UK and Canadian health services.

Before Cindy died in 2017, Alison and Cindy had four phenomenally creative and productive years of collaboration on MBS. Cindy is remembered with deep fondness and inspiration by her students and by us, her friends and colleagues. She cared deeply about the work of bringing mindfulness into the world. The very fact that she committed her last working energies to MBS is a testament to how vital she felt good supervision is. I wholeheartedly agree with her. It is an extraordinary enabler. Somehow, in the alchemy of this intentional relationship, we dig deep into ourselves and discover interior resources and potentials we didn't know we had and find ourselves making these available to others in ways we didn't know we could. I've been privileged to be a close witness to the emergence of MBS over more than 20 years and have deep appreciation and admiration for the hours of care, commitment and sheer love that has been poured into its development.

In the early years of formulating understanding about how to train mindfulness teachers in the UK context, we drew strongly from the supportive wisdom of colleagues at the University of Massachusetts Medical School in the US where Jon Kabat-Zinn first originated Mindfulness-Based Stress Reduction (MBSR). They were our primary teachers and supervisors. Over many years, I personally received periods of supervision from Ferris Urbanowski, Melissa Blacker and Pamela Erdmann, senior MBSR teachers from this centre. I would need a book to fully convey the depth and breadth of what I received from these inspiring women. I categorically know that without those deep intentional conversations, I would not have had the courage to do the work I did, nor the deep confidence they inspired in the potential of bringing compassionate awareness to experience. In the early 2000s, they, like us, were in process with figuring out how to scale up the numbers of mindfulness teachers to respond to growing demand, without scaling down the depth and transformational potential of the practice. In the early years, Jon had drawn in colleagues with long mindfulness practices to train as the first generation of teachers in his centre. As the field moved into training future generations of teachers, we had to think carefully about what experience, what training, and what ongoing support is needed to enable new generations of teachers who would come with a range of different life experiences to carry the work forward. We were essentially systematising what had initially been informal and beginning to lay down shared guidelines and expectations for this emerging professional field.

It was around 2006 when Professor Mark Williams and I convened a meeting of the leads of the UK training centres. At that time, there were five UK centres (now there are over 20!) – Bangor, Oxford and Exeter Universities, Breathworks, and an emerging teacher training for NHS colleagues in Scotland. Over the next years, we became an engaged working party, collaboratively bringing something new into being. Our challenge to ourselves was to find ways to align around shared principles of good practice in our work of training and supporting mindfulness professionals, and to create an atmosphere of collaboration rather than competition between us. We called ourselves the UK Network for Mindfulness-Based Teacher Training Organizations. We've never been good at snappy titles – but it has evolved into the more neatly named British Association for Mindfulness-Based Approaches (BAMBA).

Over the next few years, we aligned on Good Practice Guidelines for mindfulness teaching in the UK. They have evolved somewhat since those early days, but the basics are the same. The key recognition underpinning the guidelines is that mindfulness professionals are doing delicate and challenging work. They sit at a fulcrum point, bridging the paradigms of mindfulness with those of the mainstream contexts they operate in. They carry the integrity of the work. We therefore knew that the main purpose of these guidelines was to formalise structures and processes that would surround these precious colleagues with all that they needed to do the delicate and skilled work asked of them. Right from the beginning, we unanimously aligned around the importance of requiring every mindfulness professional to have an ongoing supervision process. Requiring supervision was a first step (and professional networks internationally now also include supervision as a requirement). Operationalising this required careful thought – What is supervision in a mindfulness context? Who can do it? What skills are involved? How do they get trained?

These questions and more are carefully and compellingly unpacked in this beautiful book. Alison and Pamela are perfectly positioned to take you by the hand and support you in this immersive journey. Over many years, they have done the thoughtful work needed to join the theoretical and practical worlds of mindfulness and supervision, and to bring them alive in the exquisite encounters that take place in the relational intimacy of the MBS space. The depth and breadth of their examination of MBS is vast – from consideration of the nuances of cultural sensitivity, to a range of explorations of different kinds of supervision for different contexts. They illuminate the narrative by giving us 'fly on the wall' perspectives into the usually private world of MBS conversations, and then unpack the content and process to make visible and explicit what is often hidden and implicit.

Likewise, we get a window into Alison and Pamela's own personal stories, and the undercurrents of their lives that have motivated and guided them. In doing this they embody a key principle underpinning MBS – the undercurrents of our life are so often habitually 'off radar' and not accounted for, but in practice this personal patterning is unwittingly in the driving seat of how we engage in the world. The tender work of recognising and holding experience in compassionate awareness is a lifetime of work for each of us to do. It is particularly vital work for a mindfulness professional to undertake. How can we ask others to meet their vulnerable wobbly places if we are not willing to do that for ourselves? (I can hear Cindy's voice singing out – 'teach from your wobbles'!). Regular, mindfully and intentionally held relational connections with a supervisor are a vital support for this tender personal work. For many of us, including me, it is the enabling ingredient that releases our capacities to embody the fullness of our humanity when we take our seat as a teacher, offer mindful therapy, represent mindfulness within our organization, lead organizations in ways that are informed by mindfulness and so on.

At the heart of the book is a deeply thought through framework for offering and receiving supervision which names and holds all the elements of the process. The framework is infinitely flexible, enabling the relational engagement to be adapted to fit the range of contexts in which mindfulness is being applied. Some are using mindfulness implicitly within their own inner process to support their work as leaders, mentors, coaches or as therapists. Others are explicitly sharing or teaching mindfulness in a range of contexts. Some are teaching established curriculums, while some are adapting and tailoring workshops or courses for particular populations or contexts. The range of possibilities for bringing mindfulness alive in the world is vast and growing as the field continues to innovate. MBS is an anchoring thread of consistency through this diversity, offering a reliable relational space to reflect, resource and build skills and understandings.

Alison and Pamela's love of and enthusiasm for MBS is contagious. This book will be a resource and guide for those of you who are considering or already in supervisory, mentoring, leadership or training roles; you'll find yourself inspired to read it all in one go, as well as to return to key chapters for support, guidance and inspiration along the way. This book will help you recognise why supervision is so vital and how to be in that role in the 'best' way possible. The book is also a mindfulness journey – you will be invited to engage in the material in a participatory embodied way through practices and reflections on the material.

May the work of mindfulness-based supervision support mindfulness professionals across the globe to communicate mindfulness to diverse groups and communities. May this work support the flourishing of all living beings.

Professor Rebecca Crane, PhD
Centre for Mindfulness Research and Practice
Bangor University
December 2024

Introduction and welcome

Welcome to this book about mindfulness-based supervision (MBS). We begin by setting the scene: our intentions for writing this book, introducing ourselves, and the context and conditions that have influenced the content and process of writing. We are using the term *supervision* throughout the book, as this term is used in our context of supervising mindfulness-based (MB) practitioners. However, we are aware that in some contexts, the term *mentoring* is often used for a similar supportive relationship that allows for learning and growth. There are also connections with the practice of coaching, emphasising growth and development.

Our intentions

In writing this book we intend to inspire and share our passion for what is possible within MBS. We bring together what we and others have experienced and explored about MBS. We want to share the MBS framework with a broad audience to articulate what MBS is and how to supervise in this way. We aim to be current and relevant and appeal to a wide range of supervisors and mentors. We offer both structure and flexibility. The people we have in mind as we write are supervisors, potential supervisors, mentors and leaders, who are mindfulness practitioners with an established personal mindfulness practice, have experience teaching or conveying mindfulness in their work, and would like to support others through MBS. We have also written this book for trainers, training organizations and professional mindfulness associations to make MBS's process and importance visible. Finally, this book might appeal to practitioners who want to understand more about the process of MBS to support their engagement with it.

The overarching learning outcome for readers is to improve the practice of MBS. More specifically:

- To understand the MBS framework.
- To understand the linkage between theory and MBS practice.
- To use the MBS framework as a scaffolding for supervision, exploring and experimenting with bringing specific aspects of the framework into supervision from both a supervisor and supervisee perspective.
- To reflect upon one's skills as a supervisor and identify areas of strength and growth.
- To consider how best to use supra-vision to support development as a supervisor.
- To learn ways of bringing mindfulness practice into being a supervisor and directly into the supervision space.
- To be open and aware of cultural factors.
- To have a resource to return to when meeting new situations and challenges in supervision.
- To use the materials in the book as a companion to experiential learning accessed through MB supervision training, retreats for supervisors, supra-vision and working with peers.
- To be a resource for MB trainers and training organizations to support embedding MBS into training programmes for foundational training and the continuing professional development of MB teachers.
- To be a resource for professional mindfulness associations to refer to when embedding supervision into good practice within MB work.

It is not complete or set in stone; MBS will grow and develop differently according to cultural contexts and supervisors engaging with the material.

About us

I (Alison) locate myself as female, white, middle-aged, married, and the mother of two children who are now adults. Several aspects of my identity afford me certain privileges in the way society is constructed, such as being white, able-bodied, well-educated, heterosexual, and middle-class. I offer a brief overview of some aspects of my life that have shaped my social location and identity.

I live in a small village in southwest England with my dear husband and cats. Our two wonderful children are now adults and have left the family home. I was born in the East Midlands, where my parents, grandparents, and great-grandparents lived on my mother's side. My father's family were originally from further north in England. The roots of both sides of my family were working class, and this shifted as my parents became adults. I was brought up by both my parents, alongside my younger sister, in the west of England. I had a happy childhood with a loving family, a good education, and friends who all lived close by. Our neighbourhood was safe for us to have freedom to play. I was sometimes shy, bringing about teasing from a friendship group at times. I was brought up to be a Christian and went to a Church of England church until my teenage years when I opted out.

As I reflect on my early life, an interest in what I might call spirituality has remained alongside the reflective side of myself. There was a strong work ethic in our home, and I continue to carry this with me. It has led me to put much effort and energy into my work, and I would say that overall, I have loved it. There is, of course, an edge here and a need for me to balance. My nuclear and extended family are important, and I value them greatly. I have always been a 'productive' person and wished for my life to be fruitful and of service. I like to make and create. Being fair and kind are values I grew up with and hold firmly. I think a combination of some of these aspects of my upbringing led me to my work as an occupational therapist in mental health settings and then to an MB practitioner. During my education and working life, key teachers, mentors, and supervisors have significantly impacted me personally and supported my ability to learn and have self-confidence. I am grateful to all these individuals, and they inspire my love of what is possible through good supervisory/mentoring relationships.

I (Pamela) am a white female and am middle-class. My wonderful husband and I live with our pets in a small village in Wiltshire, UK. I have two beautiful adult children and two delightful young grandchildren. I was born in Scotland to working-class parents and have an older brother. My parents divorced when I was 9 years old and over the next 20 years, I only met my father again on four occasions. My mother's new partner was an alcoholic and addicted to gambling, and the next eight years were marked by poverty, violence and a chaotic lifestyle, with a brief period of homelessness when I was 12 years old. We lived in what were called 'troubled' neighbourhoods in Edinburgh, moving often due to eviction for non-payment of rent or to temporarily escape the violence, which significantly disrupted my education and friendships, as well as resulting in a long-term vulnerability around feelings of shame and self-worth. I had no contact with my father's side of the family from the age of nine, and on my mother's side, there were frequent rifts between family members that lasted for decades, so there was little support from extended family. I am deeply appreciative that my husband and I have been able to break the cycle and create loving and supportive relationships within our family.

As I reflect on my early life, I can see the hugely significant role that mentors played in my growth and development; I still recall two key teachers from high school who 'saw' me and took the time to nurture and encourage me. They have no idea how important this was for my education and, more importantly, my sense of self. At 18 years old, I began professional training as an occupational therapist, and again, here I can see how vital my tutor and early clinical supervisors were as I took these first steps towards having a sense of agency and purpose in my life.

I have spent over 40 years working in the mental health field, mainly as a psychotherapist, with an unwavering belief that being seen and nurtured are vital for people to flourish. Throughout my career, alongside the direct clinical work, I have taken on the role of preceptor and supervisor, hoping to contribute to the mentoring cycle, seeing and believing in other practitioners within clinical and MB work. My first MB teacher, supervisor and mentor, Cindy Cooper, talked about the role of the supervisor as 'catching the spark' of the other. I'm eternally grateful to Cindy for catching mine.

We could go on, but these are not our biographies; however, we do wish to set the scene of our cultural backgrounds and some of the experiences that have shaped us and the choices we have made in life. We also acknowledge how our respective cultural backgrounds and experiences shape our perceptions and views and how we need time to reflect and work with this both on our own and with others to aid in seeing what we can't see.

Why write this book?

Since Jon Kabat-Zinn introduced Mindfulness-Based Stress Reduction (MBSR) in the 1970s, there has been exponential growth within the mindfulness-based programme (MBP) field, with clearly demonstrable benefits. MBS is crucial to maintaining integrity within this expanding and evolving work. This book pulls together a body of work on MBS spanning over 12 years and explores the use of a mindfulness-based approach to supervision that is both framework- and practice-driven. Through extensive collaboration and expert narratives, drawing on a diverse range of theories and research, including specific empirical MBS research[3] and evolution through three iterations, we present our unique MBS framework, summarized in Chapter 1 and explored in detail throughout the book.

In brief, we would define MBS as:

A mindfulness-based embodied inquiry-led approach to facilitate the supervisee in reflection, understanding and development in relation to their mindfulness-based work.

The MBS framework describes the nature of MBS, the processes involved, what makes it mindfulness-based, the ethos underlying it, how it supports integrity in the mindfulness field, the context within which it is held, the depth and breadth of the

---

3   Evans et al., 2024

content of MBS, and the experience and skills required to be an MBS supervisor. Each framework element is explored in detail in Part 2, illustrated with stories, examples, metaphors, and diagrams.

The benefits of offering an articulated framework include:

- Using it as the underpinning for training of MB supervisors to ensure consistency and quality.
- Making the process transparent for supervisees, which may foster a more proactive and collaborative role within the supervisory relationship.
- Supporting the ongoing learning and development of MB supervisors.
- Supporting the learning and development of MB practitioners who also supervise/mentor within other contexts and who wish to bring a more mindful-based approach to their supervisory/mentoring work (this might include a range of settings such as psychology, counselling, business, education, coaching, social work, charity work, community-based projects).
- Supporting the professionalising of MB work, maintaining standards and ensuring integrity within the field.

A clear thread running through our collaborative conversations has been the expression of a deep passion for supervision. This love and commitment to enhancing the art and science of MB supervision is a primary motivator in writing this book. We have had the privilege of being in relationships with our inspiring supervisors and appreciating first-hand the value of this precious and unique partnership. Through our connections with supervisors and potential supervisors who attend MBS training and with our supervisees in our roles as supervisors, we continue to appreciate the reciprocal process of discovery and growth. As well as a potentially inspiring place, supervision can also be a tender place where we meet ourselves and the other in all our humanness. So, throughout the book, we highlight this combination of the crucial role of the supervisor and the value of a mindfulness-based approach.

The *fabric* of mindfulness-based supervision

While honouring literature on supervision that incorporates some mindfulness-informed practice into supervision, this book is clearly written from an MB perspective, where everything about supervision is steeped in mindfulness. Alongside their personal mindfulness practice, the MB work of the supervisor will be underpinned by specific training in mindfulness-based approaches (MBAs), and they will be engaging with an MB supervisor themselves. The work and title of 'Mindfulness-Based Supervisor' are not currently licensed, but it is a discipline, and we suggest that this MBS framework can act as a guide to navigating all that arises within the scope of this work.

Within the supervisor's personal practice, different dimensions of mindfulness are cultivated through many forms of mindfulness practice (e.g. formal practice – body scan, sitting, movement and everyday practice), understandings (e.g. through reading, talks, podcasts, own insight) and what we might call 'community' (being alongside others practising in this way). We suggest that MBS itself is a relational form of mindfulness practice, accessing all the dimensions of experience (body, thoughts, feelings, actions), being present with another in dialogue, practising mindful speaking and listening, cultivating mindful ways of reflecting, and providing a lens in which to see what is happening and having a broader perspective. Whenever we name something 'mindfulness-based', it needs a personal mindfulness practice underneath, alongside, and around it.

In their work as MB supervisors, supervisors may be offering supervision or wish to provide supervision for:

- Mindfulness practitioners and teachers/conveyors of mindfulness: so, the supervisee also has a personal mindfulness practice and understands the underlying theory and principles of the MB approach. The supervisee may be offering curricula-based programmes, e.g. MBSR, Mindfulness-Based Cognitive Therapy (MBCT), compassion-based curricula, or other innovative ways of conveying mindfulness.
- Practitioners within other contexts such as health and helping professions, workplace, education, or third-sector organizations engaged in social, environmental or cultural endeavours: these supervisees may have more recently developed or be in the process of developing a personal mindfulness practice, may know a little about the underlying theory and principles of an MB approach, and have a keen interest in bringing an MB approach into their lives and their work in some way.

We believe that the MBS framework is highly relevant in both situations. We will use a metaphor to help clarify and define how it can be used within these different contexts and settings. A seminal paper in the mindfulness field[4] uses a metaphor from weaving of the warp and the weft and we too find this a really helpful metaphor in relation to MBS: the warp contains the consistent threads that offer structure, and the weft includes the threads that are woven through the warp and have different colours and textures depending on what you wish to create.

We are also aware that MB supervisors could be drawing on elements of the framework in their other supervisory relationships, often in a more implicit way, as the supervisee is not engaged in MB work. For example, the MB supervisor might offer clinical supervision and draw upon embodied presence within the supervision session.

---

4 Crane et al., 2017

What it means to write this book now

We are aware of the context within which we are writing, from the macro to the micro: the unparalleled changes within our global world and changes within the field of mindfulness. Crane et al. call for MBPs to move beyond the focus on personal and individual well-being and instead consider what is called 'bigger-than-self' issues, wider relational and societal themes. They argue that social awareness must be embedded into MBPs if we are to *"truly increase access and build equity into the MBP field."*[5] This long overdue call for a new paradigm within MBPs requires collaborative conversations and working together with individuals and MB practitioners with lived experience that truly represents the diversity of our human species to explore the potential for a mindfulness-based approach to support all of us to live with ourselves and our planet in wholesome and sustaining ways.

Michael Carroll[6] speaks about the widening scope of supervision – that, as well as looking inwards, it also supports the supervisees to look outwards at the systems they are part of and work within. We see MBS as having a crucial part to play in the evolving landscape of MBPs: we need to examine the barriers that hinder MB practitioners from diverse backgrounds from moving into this work and moving into supervisory roles and places where they can influence the development going forward, and we call on all MB supervisors to explore for themselves their relationship to these bigger-than-self issues.

Carroll names the importance of assimilation learning, this ability to change in the light of the new. So, as supervisors, as well as drawing on the support of what has come before (including the nourishment and learning we have received from our supervisors, mentors and leaders in the field) it is essential that we embrace assimilation learning. We are committing to our own ongoing personal and professional learning and development, including moving into uncomfortable and unknown territory, and we are committing to supporting and encouraging our supervisees as they take this work forward into the changing world and the changing landscape of MBPs, including the shift in nature of curricula-based work to a much broader application of the MB approach within their work.

We see this assimilation learning within the MBS framework itself. The changing landscapes have influenced changes within the framework, and it is likely that, in time, there will be further changes to the framework. We demonstrate ways of applying the framework, illustrating that it has the capacity to flex and grow as needed while still holding the essential elements that support supervisees' work to be clearly mindfulness-based.

---

5   Crane et al., 2023, p. 8
6   Carroll, 2024

The process of writing the book

How did it come about?

For many years, I (Alison) have been developing MBS through my supervision, supervising others, training others to be MBS supervisors, and studying and writing about MBS. The idea of a book was lurking in the back of my mind. It seemed a ridiculous idea on some levels – I'm busy, don't perceive myself to be a natural writer, and suffer from not feeling good enough in relation to writing. However, the idea of a book wouldn't go away, like an itch that keeps coming back. Pamela and I worked on MBS training with a solid creative partnership for four years. When we met over a cup of tea in Bangor to discuss revisions of the MBS framework, I muted the 'crazy' idea. She didn't baulk and seemed interested. The idea came to fruition quickly after that, and as they say, the rest is history.

From my (Pamela) perspective, I had little experience writing; I, too, would consider myself not a natural writer, and I still work almost full-time, so where would I find time to write a book? However, I did recognise that Alison and I found a creative flow when we trained together. I had an immense trust in Alison's knowledge, experience and passion for MBS.

Our process

The way we have worked together as authors has been an important process. We began with clear, shared intentions about wanting to enjoy the writing process, knowing there would be challenging moments along the way. Our working relationship was critical to this. We spoke honestly with each other about co-authoring and how we intended to do it. This included a conversation about our potential strengths and edges in writing, bearing in mind that neither of us had written a book before, so it was all a bit unknown. What we did know from our already close working relationship is that when we come together in dialogue, there is creativity in our conversation; we are able to question, consider, wonder together, comment on each other's ideas, and springboard off each other. There is a fruitful co-creation. As you move through the book, you might see many parallels between this process and what happens within MBS, such as having a structure, lots of potential content, a relationship at the heart of it, and turning towards creativity and emergence.

Involving others

Continuing the collaborative nature of this work, we interviewed five people with lived experience within diverse cultures, contexts and settings of bringing an MB approach into their lives and their work and who are familiar with the MBS framework. Their generosity in sharing their experiences using the MBS framework has informed and influenced our approach to writing and the content. In Part

Three of the book, as we move closer to exploring the use of the framework within different contexts, the experience of our conversations with Uz, Debbie, Jem and Martin and the knowledge they shared with us helped shape these chapters. We introduce them at the beginning of Part Three.

Ted offered us invaluable insights into our framing of the book and MBS to reach the audience we hope to connect with. We introduce him here:

Ted Meissner (he/him) has been teaching since the late 1990s in academic, corporate, and traditional contemplative practice settings. He is a Certified MBSR Teacher from UMass Medical School (USA), training and supervising new teachers in the US and internationally. Ted is an advocate for continuing education for teachers and increasing global representation for more diverse mindfulness communities of practice.[7]

An invitation on how to approach and engage with this book

MBS is all about experiential learning and discovery through inquiry; the phrase Pamela often uses in training is 'I wonder'. So, we encourage you to 'wonder' as you read the book. Take your time, stop and reflect, talk to others, disagree, and link with your own experience. You might take frequent mindful pauses: noticing what is arising for you, feeling into the body, thoughts, feelings, memories and examples.

Give space for self-reflection, taking your time, engaging with the reflective questions at the end of each chapter and having a journal for your supervision reflections if you don't already have one. You may wish to highlight areas for further study and investigation and follow up on points of interest, perhaps using the references provided and the materials in the Appendices.

As MBS is a relational process, we also invite you to dialogue with others as you engage with the material, for instance:

- In your MBS.
- Through meeting with peer supervisors to either randomly pick up threads or more systematically read chapters, do reflective questions and dialogue.

Keep on pausing, keep on learning, keep on wondering.

---

7   For more information visit, https://mindfulness.voyage/

Pausing for self-reflection

Intention

Before you go any further, we invite you to take a moment to reflect on your intentions in purchasing and reading this book.

Take a moment to pause, feel your feet on the ground, your seat on the chair if you are sitting, your hands wherever they are resting, and your breath breathing. After taking some moments settling, we invite a reflection on your intentions – you may drop in questions such as:

- What is my interest in MBS?
- What are my intentions in purchasing this book?
- How do I want to approach reading and engaging with the material?

Allowing each question time to drop into your reflective practice, not having to find an answer as such, but seeing what arises. This may come in the form of thoughts, feelings or body sensations.

Staying with this reflection as long as you wish. And feel free to journal if you wish.

References

Evans, A., Griffith, G. M., & Smithson, J. (2024). What do supervisors' and supervisees' think about mindfulness-based supervision? A grounded theory study. *Mindfulness*, 15, 63–79. https://doi.org/10.1007/s12671-023-02280-8

Crane, R., Brewer, J., Feldman, C., Kabat-Zinn, J., Santorelli, S., Williams, J., & Kuyken, W. (2017). What defines mindfulness-based programs? The warp and the weft. *Psychological Medicine*, 47(6), 990-999. https://doi.org/10.1017/S0033291716003317

Crane, R. S., Callen-Davies, R., Francis, A., Francis, D., Gibbs, P., Mulligan, B., O'Neill, B., Williams, N. K. P., Waupoose, M., & Vallejo, Z. (2023). Mindfulness-based stress reduction for our time: A curriculum that is up to the task. *Global Advances in Integrative Medicine and Health*, 12. https://doi.org/10.1177/27536130231162604

Carroll, M. (2014). *Effective supervision for the helping professions*. Sage Publications.

Part One:
Introduction to Mindfulness-Based Supervision

Part One introduces you to the MBS framework. Chapter 1 starts with a brief description of its development and then an overview of the whole framework. Chapter 2 explores the theory and research that underpins MBS.

Chapter 1
Overview of the Mindfulness-Based Supervision Framework

MBS is a regular space that is contracted between supervisor and supervisee, which enables reflection on the supervisee's mindfulness teaching practice, or other mindfulness-based work, and how this interfaces with their personal mindfulness practice and their life. The process is dedicated to developing and deepening the growth, understanding, integrity, safety and effectiveness of the supervisee's application of mindfulness, both personally and in their working life.[8]

Development of the framework

The MBS framework has a long history of being created through collaborative relationships. In describing its creation and ongoing development, we wish to honour those who have played key roles.

---

8   Cindy Cooper and Jody Mardula developed this definition, which they refined in 2016 as part of supervision training delivered through the Centre for Mindfulness Research and Practice at Bangor University (non-italics added by us to illustrate the shift to a widening scope of MB work and, therefore, the scope of MBS).

The first version

It was an incredibly steep learning curve when I (Alison) began teaching MBCT in 2004. There were few training options then; a research trial was starting imminently, and I had to be 'ready'. So I had what you might call a 'fast track' beginning. MBS formed a vital part of my early learning; I had a range of talented and experienced mindfulness teachers offer me supervision. I was left with no doubt about the value of MBS as a vehicle for learning and support and as a place where I could take all my vulnerabilities around teaching. When I moved into training others, I took this with me and wanted to give them similar experiences of supervision. As I came towards studying for my MSc, it was natural for me to choose this topic, almost a sense of what else would I choose – it was so clear. I could see that people thought supervision was necessary; it was happening in significant ways, but not many people were talking or writing about it. Could I offer this as a contribution to the field? This passion for MBS and my wish to help articulate what it is, how we engage with it, and share the enthusiasm has remained alive, so here I am writing this book.

Alison's initial work involved collaborative interviews with supervisors from the UK, Australia, Netherlands, and the USA, exploring the nature of MBS from their direct experience, dialoguing around intentions, content, structure, and processes of MBS, and drawing out generic themes to create a framework. The initial framework was then refined (Figure 1.1) by further collaboration with co-authors drawing on their experiences as supervisors within different contexts and communicated through a peer-reviewed paper published in 2015.[9]

Figure 1.1 The MBS framework version one

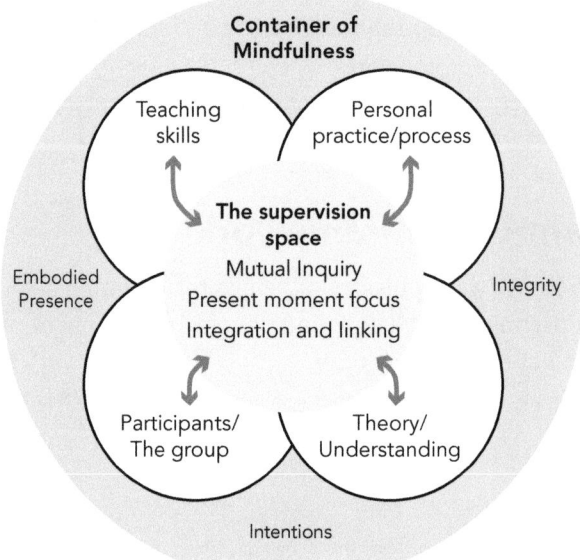

---

9   Evans et al., 2015

The second version

The second iteration (Figure 1.2) was soon afterwards, in 2015, when Alison, still at Exeter University, and Cindy Cooper from Bangor University, came together to discuss and share ideas and learnings. Jody Mardula was also instrumental in the MBS training at Bangor. The intention was to create an updated framework based on the work within the two centres and their experience supervising and training supervisors. This second version[10] has been used extensively in training MB supervisors.[11] There were also in-person gatherings in the UK of MB supervisors,[12] who freely gave their time, passion, and commitment to contribute to conversations and the development of MBS – all of their voices have influenced the development of the MBS framework, with a number of them more closely involved in helping to shape this 2015 version.

Figure 1.2 The MBS framework version two

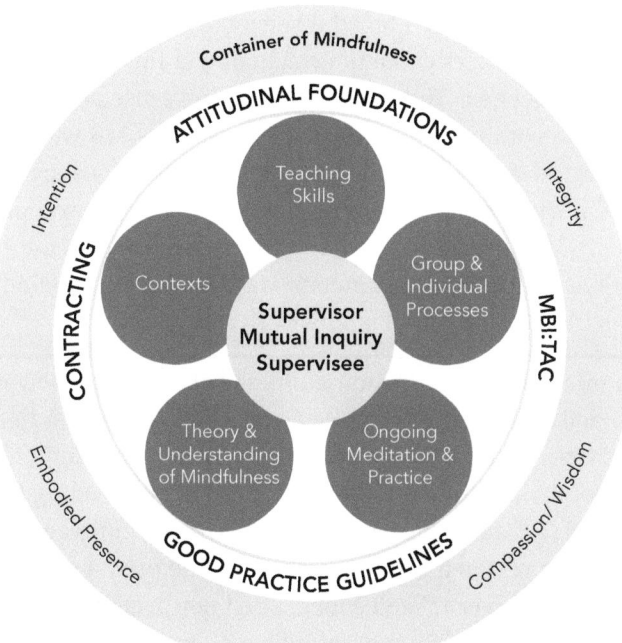

As Alison and Cindy began to train others to supervise, they discovered their shared passion for MBS. I (Alison) was able to collaborate with Cindy for four years until she died in 2017. It felt like a more extended period, and we shared so many stories and endeavours in putting MBS on the map. Cindy joined me at the Mindfulness Network as co-supervision lead. I learned much from Cindy, from her vast

---

10 Evans, 2021
11 These trainings have been delivered through the Mindfulness Network (MN) charity and the Centre for Mindfulness Research and Practice (CMRP) at Bangor University.
12 These supervisors had an affiliation with the MN and/or CMRP.

supervision experience, generosity, and enthusiasm. We had fun in our co-creative relationship developing this iteration of the framework along with Jody, refining the MBS training and sharing our vision to sing, dance and shout about MBS. She remains an inspiring force for me, and I think of her often and look at her picture on the wall behind my computer. I think she'd be delighted with this book.

The third and current version

Alison and Pamela updated the third version of the framework (Figure 1.3) in 2023, and it is this version that we will explore in detail in this book. Several factors influenced this latest version, and we noticed important threads that needed to be specifically named or emphasized sufficiently in the framework.

We started facilitating MBS training together in 2019, and a significant positive impact on our understanding and learning was the shift to offering the training online, which opened it up to an international audience. As we engaged in collaborative conversations with a broad diversity of supervisors and through our work as supervisors, our experiential understanding of the importance of culture and context began to deepen. There was also a strong sense of the MBS framework as a helpful structure within the ever-broadening scope of MB work. We began to see a shift in the work of supervisees, from teaching curricula such as MBSR and MBCT through to a wider range of programmes and different ways of conveying mindfulness. Many MB supervisees working within healthcare, education, and third-sector organizations were exploring different ways of bringing a mindfulness-based approach into their work and bringing this work to MBS.

Shifts have also influenced us in the mindfulness field itself, namely equality, equity, diversity and inclusion, creating safety (including safeguarding processes and trauma-sensitive mindfulness), naming the ethical dimension of supervision, the development of the Mindfulness-Based Interventions: Teaching Learning Companion (MBI:TLC)[13] and its use in supervision. This third version has also been influenced by Alison's research for her doctorate.[14] She used a grounded theory approach to explore supervisors' and supervisees' perspectives of the helpful and unhelpful processes within MBS. Another influence has been the work that Alison and colleagues Julia Wallond and Sarah Millband[15] have done in developing retreats specifically for MB supervisors; exploring core elements of the framework through mindfulness and compassion practices.

---

13 Griffith et al., 2021
14 Evans, 2019; Evans et al., 2024
15 We thank Julia Wallond for her work in developing the first MBS supervisors retreat with Alison. And to Sarah Millband for continuing to develop and cultivate retreats for supervisors, joining us as an MBS trainer and all her thoughtful work on safeguarding within supervision.

Figure 1.3 The MBS framework version three

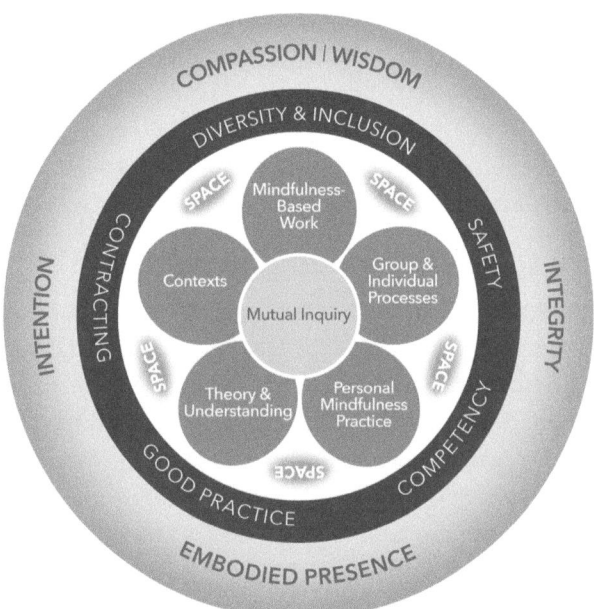

An overview of the framework

The MBS framework (Figure 1.3) has four concentric circles. The outer circle represents the concepts and practice of mindfulness as a Container for supervision; this includes mindful awareness and being grounded in the body, as well as attitudes of friendliness and compassion, so both the supervisor and supervisee thus embody a present moment awareness. The next circle represents the different frameworks that support safety, inclusion and integrity that we might draw upon from the mindfulness field and wider; we call this the Belt. The next circle represents the content that supervisees bring to supervision. This includes their MB work, personal mindfulness practice, an understanding of underpinning theory, skills in managing individuals and the group process, etc.; we call these the Petals. Around the Petals, there is Space, a crucial element of the framework, highlighting that between the content of MBS, there is a need for spaciousness and less content. The inner circle represents the process in MBS based on Mutual Inquiry. A safe space is created for supervisees to explore their MB work and personal practice issues through an embodied dialogue with the supervisor to enable integration back into work, practice, and life.

Here, we offer a brief overview of the framework, and then each element is explored in depth in Part Two.

The outer circle: the Container of mindfulness

The outer circle represents the Container of mindfulness which holds the entire supervision process, imbuing it with the characteristics of mindfulness. The four elements are Intention, Embodied Presence, Integrity and Compassion/Wisdom. These elements which overlap and connect with each other, point toward critical essential aspects of the mindfulness-based approach. These elements are called upon in all MB work and MBS.

The inner ring: the Belt – holding integrity

The inner ring represents guiding elements that hold the integrity of MB work and the supervision process, namely Good Practice, Safety, Diversity and Inclusion, Competency, and Contracting for MBS. Each element will have structures and frameworks that support the holding of this element, depending on the context within which the supervisor and supervisee are living and working. The Belt links strongly with the Integrity element in the Container and needs holding with a careful balance so these threads are not held too tight or too loose.

The inner Petals – the content of MBS

The Petals (Figure 1.4) can be summarized as the content of MBS and the learning of the *what, how,* and *why* of MB teaching and MB work. These are the subject matter of supervision. This is what the supervisor needs to know from their experience, what is brought into supervision by the supervisor and/or supervisee, and what the supervisee hopes to learn.

Figure 1.4 The Petals in the MBS framework

Space

Finding space is essential in mindfulness, within personal practice, when teaching and conveying mindfulness, and in MBS. Pauses can support tuning in with inner experience, accessing more of a 'felt' sense and giving some space when feeling more reactive. Within MBS, there can be many different ways of pausing, connecting with inner experience, and connecting with anchor points, such as a short silent pause at the very beginning of the session, a breathing space or a pause whenever a difficulty or strong emotion arises in the session, taking moments in the conversation to pause, ground and breathe, and a short silent moment or two at the end of the session can give space for settling.

The centre circle: Mutual Inquiry – the heart of MBS

At the heart of MBS is mindful inquiry. The supervisor and supervisee bring their experience of inquiry into the supervision session. To open to the supervisee, the supervisor must first know their own inner experience and be steady and grounded. From that embodied presence, the supervisor can then open to and inquire into the supervisee's experience – what has happened, what is happening right now, and how the supervisee can relate to that experience in a way that promotes reflection, development and understanding. The supervisor is modelling and embodying the inquiry process that is central to the MB approach, and the same process the supervisee will use within their MB work, including directly with their participants if they are teaching.

Key to this process is the ongoing development and establishment of trust between supervisor and supervisee. This requires a strong yet gentle foundation in the supervisor of consistency, reliability, competence, positive intentionality, safety, and kindness. All of these qualities spring from the supervisor's mindfulness practice and experience, which in turn allows those same foundational qualities to grow in the supervisee.

Inquiry in supervision is a dialogue between supervisor and supervisee that encourages the supervisee to explore their experience further than is usually possible by themselves. It supports the supervisee's turning towards and being with their experience, learning to relate to their experience in new ways. Mindful inquiry involves making a genuine, moment-to-moment connection with each other and engaging in a collaborative relationship.

Sometimes, the supervisor will need to be directive and give specific information, particularly to supervisees new to teaching. But ultimately, inquiry is about empowering the supervisee to find their own wisdom and insights.

The warp and weft within MBS

Let's return to the concept of MBS's fabric and to the metaphor of the warp and the weft to understand the different elements of the framework, how they relate to each other, and how the framework can be applied in different contexts.

The Container, Mutual Inquiry and Space are the warp threads, the essential elements that make the framework mindfulness-based. These essential elements convey the mindfulness-based theoretical and pedagogical background. These are the threads that are always present.

The Petals and the Belt are the weft threads and illustrate how the MBS framework can be applied in different ways, such as within different contexts and settings, to various ways of teaching or conveying mindfulness and engaging in MB work, and to the specific needs of each supervisee.

The pictures in Figures 1.5 and 1.6 illustrate how the same warp (the vertical threads) integrated with a different weft (the horizontal threads) creates very different looks. We suggest the weft can be varied in two main ways – with the supervisee in mind, and with the contexts in mind.

With the supervisee in mind

The weft is adjusted to meet the uniqueness of each supervisee, such as their culture, the content of what they bring, their supervision needs, and their learning style. For example, Figure 1.5 shows the adaptation of the weft according to the different stages of the supervisee's development.

Figure 1.5 Integrating differences in the weft according to developmental level

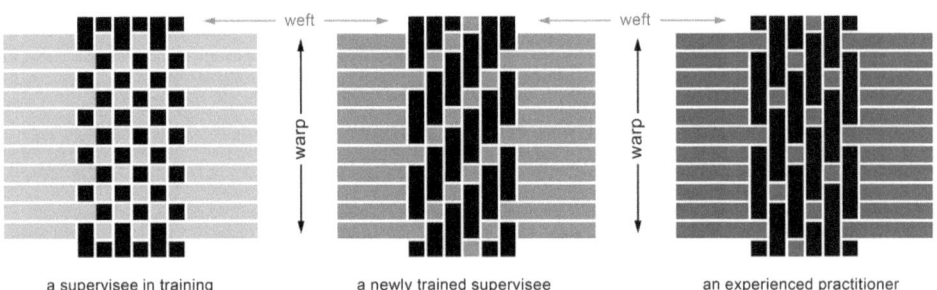

a supervisee in training   a newly trained supervisee   an experienced practitioner

With contexts in mind

The weft is adjusted to meet the uniqueness of the different supervisory contexts and settings, such as the appropriate curricula or form, the population and their needs, cultural factors, and geographical location. For example, Figure 1.6 shows the adaptation of the weft in relation to the geographical location and the form of MBA.

Figure 1.6 Integrating differences in the weft according to location and form

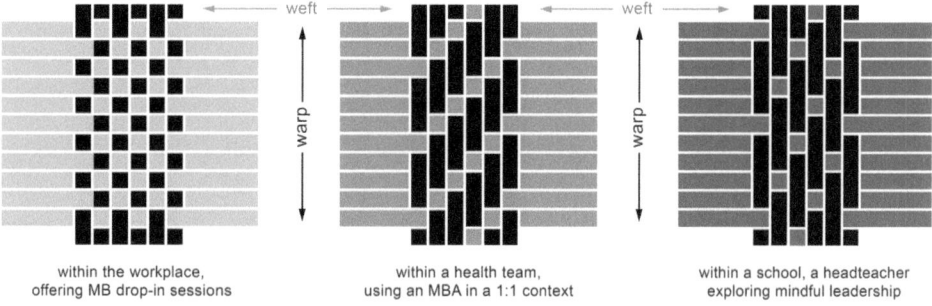

within the workplace, offering MB drop-in sessions

within a health team, using an MBA in a 1:1 context

within a school, a headteacher exploring mindful leadership

So, this metaphor helps us to see that the fabric of supervision is this interplay between the strong, consistent foundation of the lengthwise threads of the warp, the Container, Mutual Inquiry, and Space, and the weft, the Belt and the Petals, which allows for the flexibility and fluidity that is required to meet each unique supervisee, the context, and the emergent flow within each supervision session.

For MB supervisors bringing the MBS framework into their other supervisory or mentoring roles, the warp as described in this book is available as consistent threads to be drawn upon. Whereas, the weft will be particular to that way of working, which may be different from the weft we describe. For example, within clinical supervision, the supervisor might draw on Embodied Presence (warp), while the weft will be underpinned by the specific modality of the therapy.

We would also like to introduce another metaphor that we find helpful.

Mindfulness-based supervision as a dance

In our dialogue with supervisors during training, the metaphor of dance frequently arises as trainees begin to understand the intricacies of the practice of MBS more fully; this metaphor seems to capture both the emergent aliveness of the process that is taking place within the relationship between supervisee and supervisor and also, as one recent trainee stated, one needs to know *how* to dance – that it is to have the necessary skills and knowledge that underpin the process.

The definition of dance below speaks to both of these elements:

> *Dance is a powerful impulse, but the art of dance is that impulse channeled by skillful performers into something that becomes intensely expressive ... These two concepts of the art of dance—dance as a powerful impulse and dance as a skillfully choreographed art practiced largely by a professional few—are the two most important connecting ideas running through any consideration of the subject. In dance, the connection between the two concepts is stronger than in some other arts, and neither can exist without the other.*[16]

Throughout the book, we will use the two metaphors of MBS's fabric, warp and weft, and dance to illustrate the dynamic processes of supervision.

Summary

1. The development of the MBS framework is a culmination of collaborative dialogue over 12 years with experienced MB supervisors, supervisees, and attendees of MBS training, our direct experiences of delivering MBS training to international audiences, and empirical research.
2. The distinctive aspect of the MBS framework is that it is steeped in a mindfulness-based approach, which includes:
   - Drawing upon mindfulness-based theory, pedagogy and research (including research conducted by Alison into MBS).
   - Using a mindfulness-based inquiry approach for the dialogue.
   - Mindfulness practice as a core foundation.
   - Embodying mindfulness and mindful attitudes also as a core foundation.
   - Utilising other frameworks developed within the mindfulness field.
3. The framework integrates essential aspects of supervision such as holding integrity and safety, which are important in a field with guidelines but – as yet – no formal accreditation body.

Reflective questions

What is your relationship to supervision, and what draws you to explore it further?

What's important to you that deepening your understanding and practice of MBS could support?

Reflecting on your own experience of being supervised, are any of the dimensions of this MBS framework present in your supervisor and yourself as a supervisee?

What are your intentions for your learning?

---

16 Judith R. Mackrell, updated October 21, 2024 – Britannica https://www.britannica.com/art/dance

References

Evans, A. (2019). *Supervisors' and supervisees' perspectives of mindfulness-based supervision: A grounded theory study* [Doctoral thesis, University of Exeter]. https://ore.exeter.ac.uk/repository/handle/10871/37542

Evans, A. (2021). Mindfulness-based supervision. In R. S. Crane, Karunavira, & G. M. Griffith (Eds.), *Essential resources for mindfulness teachers* (pp. 156-166). Routledge. https://doi.org/10.4324/9780429317880

Evans, A., Crane, R., Cooper, L., Mardula, J., Wilks, J., Surawy, C., Kenny, M., & Kuyken, W. (2015). A framework for supervision for mindfulness-based teachers: A space for embodied mutual inquiry. *Mindfulness, 6*, 572-581. https://doi.org/10.1007/s12671-014-0292-4

Evans, A., Griffith, G. M., & Smithson, J. (2024). What do supervisors' and supervisees' think about mindfulness-based supervision? A grounded theory study. *Mindfulness, 15*, 63–79. https://doi.org/10.1007/s12671-023-02280-8

Griffith G. M., Crane, R. S., Karunavira, & Koerbel, L. (2021). The Mindfulness-Based Interventions: Teaching and Learning Companion (MBI:TLC). In R. S. Crane, Karunavira, & G. M. Griffith (Eds.), *Essential resources for mindfulness teachers* (pp. 125-148). Routledge. https://doi.org/10.4324/9780429317880

Chapter 2
The Theory Informing Mindfulness-Based Supervision

Know all the theories, master all the techniques, but as you touch a human soul be just another human soul.[17]

In this chapter, we provide an overview of the theory, pedagogy, and research that underpin the fabric of the MBS framework. This is the current picture which will evolve. When we consider our readers, we see that different people will know and not know different parts of this underpinning theory, depending on their context and experience. We invite you to bring a spirit of curiosity as you continue. We have chosen to organise this body of influence into five areas (Figure 2.1).

---

17 Jung, quoted in Adamson & Brendgen, 2021, p30

Figure 2.1 The theory, research and practice that informs MBS, drawing from a wide range of traditions

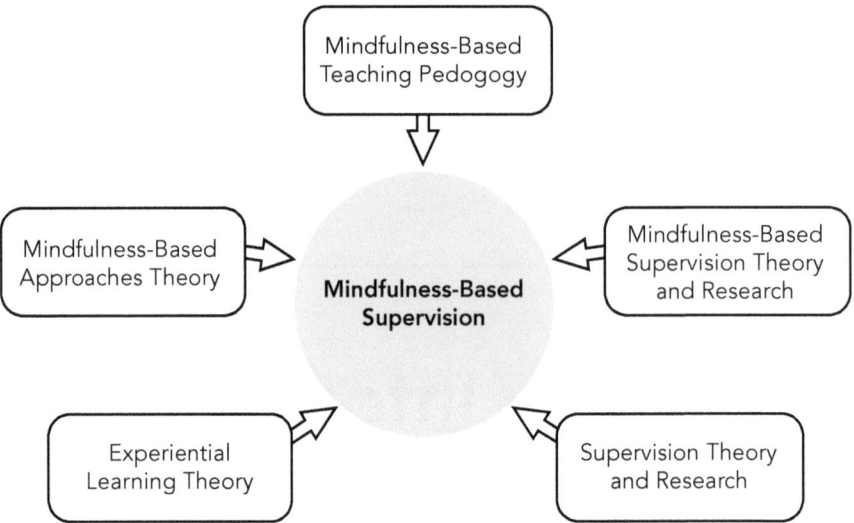

Often this theory is not obvious within a supervision session, but if we use our metaphor from Chapter 1 about the feel of MBS being like dancing, this theory forms part of this 'knowing how to dance'. When we first began this work, we drew mainly on the theory and practice within MBAs alongside the theory from other modalities around supervision and education. In more recent years, there has been an increasing articulation and clarity of the pedagogies used within MBAs, which also fit well with MBS, and we have been building a body of theory and research around MBS itself.

We focus mainly on theory which informs the processes within MBS. Subsequent chapters will expand aspects of the theory with examples, case studies, and practicalities to bring the theory to life.

Mindfulness-based approaches theory

In this section, we look at mindfulness from a mainstream MBA perspective, covering:

- The dimensions which link with the warp of MBS, namely:
    - awareness of experience
    - intentionality
    - attitudes of mindfulness
    - discerning and making choices
- Theory from contemplative traditions which inform MBAs.
- Social models.
- Relational mindfulness.

What is mindfulness from a mainstream MBA perspective?

Let's start by defining what we mean when discussing mindfulness or mindfulness-based. This is a challenging task; it is hard to define, and there are endless debates about what it is, perhaps due to the multifaceted nature of mindfulness. We lay out some of these dimensions within the mainstream MBA field that have a particular link with MBS.

Jon Kabat-Zinn gave an operational definition in 1994: *"Mindfulness is the awareness that emerges through paying attention on purpose, in the present moment, and non-judgmentally to things as they are."*[18] Shauna Shapiro, Linda Carlson and Broderick Sawyer define the construct of mindfulness as *"the awareness that arises through intentionally paying attention with kindness and curiosity."*[19] Baer summarizes how several contemporary definitions of mindfulness use two different elements: *what* one does when practising mindfulness (e.g. paying attention) and *how* one does it (the nature of the attention).[20]

These definitions point to different dimensions of mindfulness, with some commonalities, such as present moment attention, intention, awareness, openness, acceptance, compassion, non-reactivity, non-judging, decentring, reperceiving and metacognition. Christina Feldman and Willem Kuyken speak about mindfulness being *"like a diamond with many facets."*[21] Different combinations of these dimensions are helpful at various times.

The definitions used within MBAs have tended to favour silent practice with an internal focus on developing awareness and understanding of how the mind constructs experience, perceptions, and a sense of self. Donald McCown[22] takes a more social constructivist viewpoint within an MBA group, with a discourse of relational being. Some processes that occur in the group are core to the pedagogy of teaching MBAs, namely inquiry and group learning based on participation and co-creation. As McCown states, *"… mindfulness cannot be seen as a mind state in an individual; rather, it is the product of the practice of the pedagogy by the gathering."*[23] MBS is also a co-creation process, as two people, triad or group, come together to explore through this relational mutual dialogue and see what emerges. As one supervisee said, *"I never know what will happen in supervision."*

---

18 Kabat-Zinn, 1994. Updated version in Segal et al., 2013, p. 132
19 Shapiro et al., 2024, p. 11
20 Baer, 2015
21 Feldman & Kuyken, 2019, p. 15
22 McCown, 2013
23 McCown, 2013, p. 200

Dimensions of mindfulness which link with the warp of MBS
Awareness of experience

Awareness is both simple and complex. On a simple level, awareness is knowing, e.g. knowing you are breathing. Mindful practice is one way that awareness is cultivated. Shapiro et al. developed a model of mindfulness composed of three elements, namely, Intention, Attention, and Attitude (IAA model).[24] So, when you pay attention, you develop awareness of the object. Attention can be placed internally and/or externally on a single object with a narrow or broader focus. This awareness leads to *"an intellectual and conceptual knowing, and also a felt sense, a knowing with your whole being."*[25] On a more complex level, mindful awareness is a way of being, knowing the experience of life as it arises and passes, clearly seeing one's patterns and developing the quality of discernment that supports change where needed.

This placing and moving of attention is used within MBS. A supervisor might begin the session by gathering attention and regathering at different moments. The attention can be directed to the body, thoughts, and feelings, widening the awareness to take in various aspects of experience, such as the tone, the shifting nature, and the arising of wiser/more insightful thoughts.

Building external awareness, such as cultivating pro-social awareness and behaviours and awareness of bias and prejudice, is another way to use awareness within MBS. This is an essential shift in the MBA field to widen awareness and consider how to support greater diversity and inclusivity. Evans et al.[26] found in their research that supervisors and supervisees were beginning to have some awareness of the issues and impact of the lack of diversity among MB teachers and those accessing MBAs.

So, within MBS, the supervisor and supervisee shine a light on experience, opening deep, rich and multi-dimensional awareness and understanding, helping keep things fresh and alive. This includes awareness of internal experience, e.g. body sensation, awareness of individuals/groups and what is/has happened, and awareness of contextual situations, e.g. cultural factors affecting perceptions and possible bias. There is another person to dialogue with to support these investigations and shine light in places the supervisee might not have considered.

Intentionality

Intention, another element of the IAA model, can be on many levels, including overarching intentions about the motivations to practise mindfulness, teach/share mindfulness, and bring mindfulness into work. This could be seen as bringing in

---

24   Shapiro et al., 2006; 2024
25   Shapiro & Carlson, 2009, p. 4
26   Evans et al., 2024

your personal vision and values to shape practice, teaching, mindfulness work and how one lives one's life. Mindful practice can help bring values into awareness, helping discern what is important to pursue.

Intention is dynamic and evolving. Mindfulness practice may begin with an intention around a personal perspective, such as wanting less stress or how to work with pain. Or it may have started from a more professional perspective, such as wanting to teach mindfulness or bringing it into work in some way. Over time, intentions shift and change. In MBS, there are opportunities to reconnect with these deeper overarching and specific intentions. You may be familiar with the phrase, *"everything rests on the tip of intention."*[27] Indicating how bringing awareness, exploration, and discernment to intention is important in setting the course of the direction of travel in a way that supports wise, compassionate, and ethical action. This reconnection with intention can be especially useful in challenging moments. Intention feels such an important aspect of mindfulness that it forms a core element in our MBS framework. Intention can help in making choices about where to shine the light of attention – narrow, broad, internal or external. Intention can also shape ways of relating to all aspects of experience.

Attitudes of mindfulness

The way mindfulness is practised and the attitudes cultivated is the final element of the IAA model. Kabat-Zinn describes seven attitudinal factors that constitute the significant pillars of mindfulness practice.[28] The attitudes are *non-judging* – being with whatever arises that requires gentleness and kindness; *patience* – being completely in each moment, accepting it in its fullness; *beginner's mind* – approaching each practice as if it were your first time; *trust* – learning to trust one's own experience, feelings and intuition, loosening oneself from the tyranny of authority and inner harsh judgement; *non-striving* – almost everything we do, we do for a purpose, to get something or somewhere, so the attitude of non-striving is best understood as not straining or forcing for a result; *acceptance* – attending to one's experience with clarity and kindness, and *letting go* – of the tendency to want to hold on to what is pleasant in our experience and to reject what is unpleasant. Other necessary attitudes include curiosity, gentleness, kindness, compassion, generosity, and non-reactivity.

These attitudes modulate what we pay attention to during practice, during moments of teaching or MB work, during life, and during MBS. Attending without these qualities can lead to harsher, more judgemental, goal-driven practices and actions. Repeatedly returning to intention helps to make these qualities explicit, and these attitudes shape intentions. Within MBS, these attitudes are present in the supervisor

---

27 Feldman & Kuyken, 2009, p. 209
28 Kabat-Zinn, 2013

– they are bringing these attitudes and qualities into the way they relate to the supervisee. At times, the supervisor leans more into some attitudes rather than others. The supervisor supports the supervisee in cultivating these attitudes.

The attitudes of kindness and compassion are attitudes found both implicitly and explicitly within MBAs. In Buddhist teaching and contemporary mindfulness-based programmes (MBPs), specific practices develop kindness and compassionate attributes and behaviours. In Buddhist teachings, these qualities of heart are known in the Pali language as the *Brahma-viharas*. They are seen as foundations for all practice and have the potential to cultivate and train these qualities of friendliness, compassion, joy and equanimity.[29] One contemporary programme, Mindfulness-based Compassionate Living (MBCL),[30] has renamed these qualities, practices, and behaviours as the Four Friends for Life and points to how we can lean into them depending on the current internal and/or external 'weather'. Within the MBS framework, we have explicitly named the quality of compassion, with the other qualities present more implicitly. These concepts underlie the implicit expression of compassion conveyed through the supervisor and form part of the fabric of MBS's relational and embodied aspects.

Discerning and making choices

The capacity to be discerning and make skilful choices is developed through mindful awareness. Shapiro et al. discuss how intention, attention, and attitude lead to what is referred to as reperceiving.[31] Others have referred to decentring and metacognition. All these terms point towards a more expansive, open awareness that allows for more opportunity to respond as opposed to reacting. Responding refers to being more deliberate, intentional, pausing, taking in the wider context, and considering the implications of actions. Whereas, reacting describes a more automatic, impulsive, immediate way of behaving in emotional situations.

From this more open receptive awareness, it is possible to discern which aspects of the mind lead to the well-being of self and others and which do not, and skilful ways of responding and acting. In MBS, there is an opportunity to inquire into experience and discern the most helpful and ethical ways of responding. Supervisees are using MBS to make skilful choices about their MB work and what they take forward from supervision back into life. This is part of the learning process within MBS. Discernment includes making choices based on a holistic way of knowing, tuning into the intuitive as well as a more cognitive approach. It also includes taking time to reflect on the outcomes of actions. It taps into a wise heart/mind based on mindful attitudes, ethics and compassion. Discernment acts

---

29 Feldman & Kuyken, 2019
30 van den Brink et al., 2018
31 Shapiro & Carlson, 2006; Shapiro et al., 2024

as a forerunner to ethics and integrity through knowing intentions, considering the impact of any actions, knowing the underlying attitudes, and taking care to bring skilful actions into being. In the MBS framework, we name the quality of wisdom to capture these aspects of the process.

Ways of establishing mindfulness from a Buddhist perspective

We have already named Buddhist perspectives as part of the underpinning theory of MBAs, such as the practice of kindness and friendliness. Another teaching we would like to point to is a guide to how mindfulness can be established called the *Satipaṭṭhāna* discourse – the Four Foundations of Mindfulness.[32] The first foundation is mindfulness of the body, typically beginning with the breath and then including all bodily sensations. The second foundation is mindfulness of feelings, bringing attention to the feeling tones of all experience as pleasant, unpleasant and neither pleasant nor unpleasant, and noticing the habitual reactions. The third foundation is mindfulness of the mind/mental states and emotions and their accompanying thought patterns. The fourth foundation is mindfulness of our experience of the world, including what supports well-being and freedom and what hinders it.

These teachings are especially relevant within MBAs and contribute to the structure and curricula of the foundational eight-week programmes, MBSR and MBCT. Within MBS, they provide a foundation for the mutual inquiry process. They contribute to the form for the inquiry of a supervisee's own experience and how they inquire into others, especially inquiry into body, thoughts, and emotions.

Social models

There is an increasing interest and imperative to use a range of social models within MBAs to understand the world we are living in and its impact. This growing interest and imperative has, in part, been driven by critique.[33] Rebecca Crane and Bethan Roberts discuss the overarching heart of MBAs as a commitment to engage with the realities of suffering and how these sufferings *"might emanate from inner habit patterns, whilst some emanate from external context and systems."*[34] An increasing body of theory, programmes and teachings situate mindfulness within an organizational and societal level.[35]

A paper from 2023, 'MBSR for our time: A curriculum that is up to the task',[36] invites teaching in more inclusive ways that come from the lived, embodied

---

32   We point to two of the many places you can read about these four foundations of mindfulness. Goldstein, 2016; Feldman & Kuyken, 2019
33   E.g. Karlese, 2023; Kucinakas, 2018
34   Roberts & Crane, 2021, p. 191
35   E.g. Rhonda Magee, https://rhondavmagee.com/; the Urban Mindfulness Foundation, https://www.urbanmindfulnessfoundation.co.uk/
36   Crane et al., 2023

experience of the teacher. The group of authors writing this paper found that the diversity within the group supported understandings to emerge and highlighted the tangible benefits of bringing a greater breadth of wisdom through diverse lived experiences. Their accompanying resource pack includes social models developed and utilized by the Urban Mindfulness Foundation in their MBA programme. This resource pack aims to support MBA teachers and trainers in their personal practice, inquiry, and embodiment of socially aware mindfulness practice.[37]

In the latest revision of our MBS framework, through the lens of diversity and inclusion, we encourage the exploration of social models. Within MBS, this could involve using MBS as a place for the necessary ongoing personal work, such as increasing awareness of bias, prejudice and assumptions, expanding awareness of other frameworks and models that widen understanding for both the supervisor and the supervisee, understanding theories that support justice, equality, diversity and inclusion, and learnings drawn from ancient traditions. In terms of teaching MBAs, supervisees may be teaching specific programmes designed to support social justice or other creative ways of working with societal issues. If working with existing programmes such as MBSR, MBS will be encouraging increased contextual awareness, working actively to be inclusive and being explicit about anti-discriminatory practice. In MBS, we use these theories to support learning, inquire, ask searching questions, raise personal awareness, resource new learning and explicitly make changes in MBA delivery. As worded by Roberts and Crane, *"We are learners in this space"*,[38] so MBS offers a space to explore and learn. We can also see that the role of MBS is to support supervisees in taking a broad perspective and keeping abreast of current thinking and directions of travel. Hence, supervisors also need to keep up to date.

Relational mindfulness

Rebecca Crane, Karunavira and Gemma Griffith[39] speak about how mindfulness is a relationship practice in terms of relationship to inner experience, which then forms the ground for connecting and relating with others. Humans are social beings, so speaking and listening is part of life. Bringing mindfulness into the midst of communication is not always easy; attention can move elsewhere, it's not always easy to keep listening, there may be rehearsing of what to say, wanting to move into action, make decisions, fill the space, and lose touch with feelings and the body. Relational mindfulness can support steadiness, slowing down and embodying mindful attitudes, including befriending. Frits Koster, Jetty Heynekamp and Victoria Norton have edited a book dedicated to mindful communication,[40]

---

37   Resources for socially engaged MBPs https://home.mindfulness-network.org/mbsr-for-our-time-resources/
38   Roberts & Crane, 2021, p. 189
39   Crane, Karunavira & Griffith, 2021
40   Koster et al., 2023

introducing different mindful communication programmes of practice. In their introduction, they remind the reader of the place of the Four Friends for Life (kindness, compassion, joy and equanimity) in supporting wise and compassionate communication. MBS is a form of wise, embodied, compassionate communication and draws very much on the principles and practice of mindful communication. Further practice in mindful communication can help the supervisor and supervisee bring these qualities into dialogue.

When engaging in mindful communication, the focus can shift from the 'self' to the 'we' and the interconnection between the supervisor and supervisee. Several theories and bodies of research explore what happens when two beings come into connection with each other.[41] Whilst these theories vary in their descriptions of the mechanisms, there are some common threads about how one person impacts the other and how there becomes cooperation between them. Signals are sent and received, messages are given and received, which can support a co-regulation leading to feelings of safety or the opposite. They enter into a reciprocal relationship.

In MBS, there is an opportunity to support co-regulation through projecting positive cues, such as voice, facial expressions, gestures of welcome and accessibility, and calmness. When humans feel safe, they can connect and engage interpersonally with qualities such as curiosity, empathy and openness. This process supports both supervisor and supervisee to feel safe and connected.

Mindfulness-based teaching pedagogy

In this section, we outline the pedagogies (pedagogy is the method and practice of teaching) that are particularly relevant to the warp of MBS:

- embodying
- inquiry
- turning towards
- the Mindfulness-Based Interventions: Teaching Assessment Criteria (MBI:TAC)[42]

Embodying

Great emphasis is placed on mindfulness being implicitly embodied when teaching or conveying mindfulness through other formats. This helps participants move towards experiential rather than conceptual knowing. The term *embodying* can have several meanings and is hard to put into words. Trish Bartley and Gemma Griffith have embodying at the centre of their Inside Out Group model.[43] They emphasise

---

41 E.g. Barret, 2020 (co-regulation of body budgets); Porges, 2022 (co-regulation); Siegel, 2007 (attunement)
42 Crane et al., 2021
43 Bartley & Griffith, 2022; Griffith et al., 2019

that embodying is a process rather than a state, so it is an ongoing practice that is alive and dynamic. This process of embodying involves bringing mindfulness into the body, with an underlying understanding that the body and its sensory experience are in alignment.

The MBI:TAC describes how the MBA teacher embodies mindfulness whilst teaching through present moment focus (expressed through behaviour and verbal and non-verbal communication), present moment responsiveness (working with the emerging moment), calmness and vitality (steadiness, ease, non-reactivity and alertness), allowing (the teacher's behaviour is non-judging, patient, trusting, accepting and non-striving), and the natural presence of the teacher (the teacher is authentic to their intrinsic mode of operating).

This same process occurs within MBS, with the supervisor and, over time, the supervisee embodying the different dimensions and attitudes of mindfulness. Embodying comes out of mindfulness practice over the years through regular personal mindfulness practice, including formal longer practices and informal practices woven into everyday life, as well as more extended practice periods such as retreats.

Inquiry

An inquiry process is at the heart of MBS and is part of the pedagogy of teaching MBAs. Inquiry is a conversational way of exploring experience with particular features and several layers, and yet it also takes a non-structured and fluid approach to help people develop understandings. Rebecca Crane[44] outlines three elements of this participatory process: to draw out whatever was noticed, to encourage reflection and exploration of experience and work together through dialogue to find out what is being discovered, and to link these observations and discoveries to the aims of the programme and the person's life. These elements are often represented visually as circles to show how the dialogue may pass through these three concentric layers and is not a linear process.[45]

Inquiry is not a normal conversation. Instead, inquiry invites a deep curiosity into experience. The 'inquirer' listens deeply to the person talking, noticing their non-verbal communication and content. The 'inquirer' also pays some attention to their own experience as they speak and listen, especially what is happening in their body. The whole process and co-creation are central features of the relational construction that occurs within MBS.

---

44 Crane, 2017
45 Crane et al., 2021

Approach/turning towards

MBAs utilise an approach mode as opposed to an avoidant mode. There can be a common misconception that being an embodied mindfulness teacher is about perfection; however, it is more about how the teacher responds to so-called imperfections. The word vulnerability is often used and having a willingness to turn towards more challenging aspects of experience. Brené Brown[46] has explored vulnerability over many years through her qualitative social research in the home, relationships, work, and parenting. She defines vulnerability as uncertainty, risk and emotional exposure. For many, showing vulnerability is seen culturally as a sign of weakness. Brown suggests otherwise, stating that it takes courage to show and be with vulnerability and that it can, in fact, be a strength. Within MBS, supervisees are invited to let their vulnerability in, to turn towards it, and to allow and warmly befriend it during the mutual inquiry process. This approach helps to allow more acceptance and less striving to make things different from the way they are.

The MBI:TAC

We are naming the MBI:TAC[47] as a pedagogical tool because it articulates processes, skills, and observable behaviours linked to teaching and conveying mindfulness to others. It stresses a developmental way of learning (see Chapter 10). It was originally developed as an assessment tool but has evolved to be used as part of training and ongoing development, offering a framework for reflection and skill building. The tool outlines six domains of teaching: coverage and pacing, relational skills, embodying mindfulness, guiding mindfulness practices, conveying course themes, and holding the group learning environment. These are further divided into key features which provide a helpful way of focusing on different aspects of teaching. The Mindfulness-Based Interventions: Teaching Learning Companion (MBI:TLC),[48] based on the MBI:TAC and utilising the six domains, is designed more as a reflective tool. It offers new ways for self-reflection for MBP teachers and opens up reflective dialogue in supervision. The MBI:TAC and MBI:TLC are being used more within MBS, especially within MBP training contexts. Alison and colleagues wrote a peer-reviewed paper laying out principles for integrating the MBI:TAC into MBS.[49] Both of these tools continue to evolve and change as the field grows.[50]

---

46 Brown, 2012
47 Crane et al., 2021
48 Griffith et al., 2021
49 Evans et al., 2021
50 The Bangor University website is a good place to find the latest versions, translations and addendums https://mbitac.bangor.ac.uk/mbitac-tool.php.en

MBS research and theory

MBS research and theory has the MBA theory and pedagogies as underpinnings, which we have already outlined. In this section, we delve more into the MBS literature, theory and research for additional underpinnings of the warp of MBS, covering:

- MBS research
- relational inquiry within MBS

MBS research

As far as we know, there is just one published research study about MBS.[51] This research was a doctoral study entitled *Supervisors' and Supervisees' Perspectives of Mindfulness-Based Supervision: A Grounded Theory Study*.[52] As the title suggests, it is a grounded theory study looking at the perspectives of MB supervisors and supervisees about MBS. The questions the study explores are: Does MBS support learning and development? What aspects of MBS do supervisors/ees think make a difference to the teaching of MBPs? What aspects of MBS, if any, need to change?

The full thesis and the peer-reviewed paper are available for reading in more detail, so we offer a summary of the conceptual framework and a brief discussion of the key findings related to the warp. The conceptual framework, the Relational Inquiry within Mindfulness-Based Supervision model (RIMBS), was developed through the research analyses and represents the different categories, subcategories and the relationship between them (Figure 2.2).

The first category is *Valuing MBS*; this represents both the intention and desired outcome of supervisees who come to supervision to learn and find their own authenticity and embodiment as MBP teachers. The second category is *Learning within MBS*, which represents how learning is a crucial function of MBS and why it is an integral part of training and ongoing good practice. This category encompasses the different aspects of learning, namely, the *what*, *how*, and *why* of teaching. The third category is *Supervision interventions*, which represent the variety of interventions used within MBS, e.g. feedback, self-reflection, embodying mindfulness, and mindfulness practice. The fourth category is *Relational inquiry within MBS*, which represents the embodied conversation that occurs within MBS. The fifth and final category, *Balancing professional and ethical issues and practice*, is represented at the bottom of the figure and shows how MBA teaching is held within this broader context of professional and ethical issues.

---

51 Evans et al., 2024
52 Evans, 2019

Figure 2.2 The Relational Inquiry within Mindfulness-Based Supervision model (RIMBS)

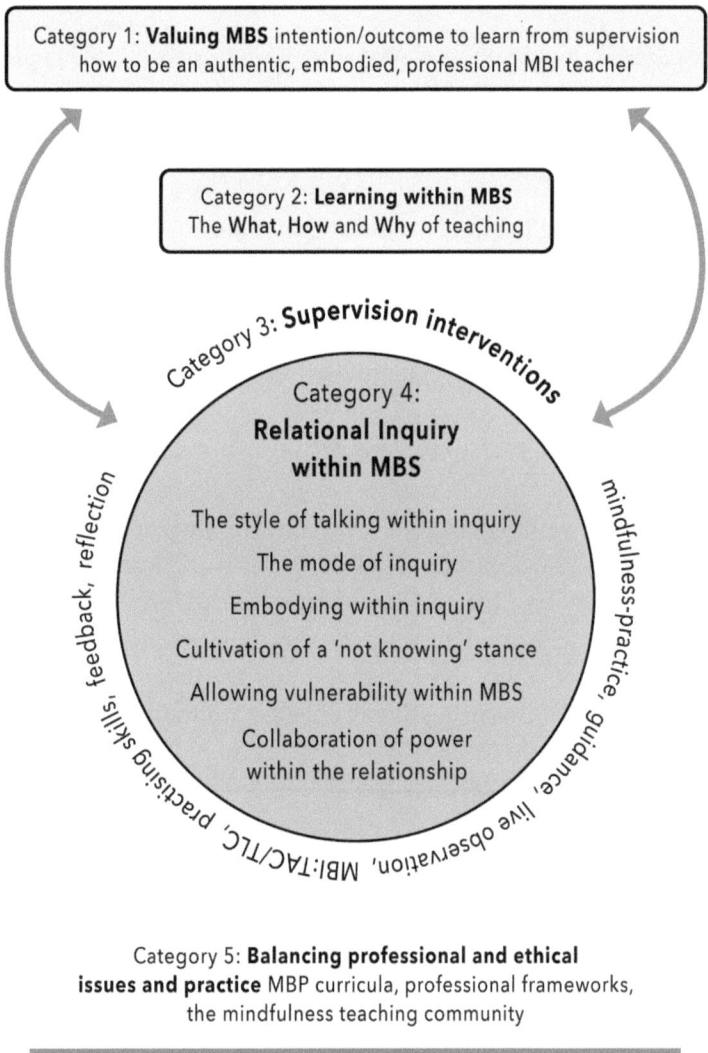

Learning is an essential aspect of MBS. Supervisees want to learn in various ways, and that learning continues and evolves. There are different aspects of what there is to be learned, which were named in this research as *what*: all the practical details about teaching, the curricula, the different exercises, and the practices; *how*: more linked with the way mindfulness is taught and conveyed, the embodying of mindfulness and a mindful way of being, and the ways of relating to experience, and *why*: a deeper understanding of the underlying theory and research, understanding intentions of curricula, practices and pedagogies used. All these ways of learning and developing ways of knowing are important and have their place in MBS.

Chapter 2 The Theory Informing Mindfulness-Based Supervision

The primary process by which each aspect of learning is explored in MBS is through relational inquiry. The relational inquiry was the most extensive and detailed category in the research. They define relational inquiry as:

> ... *an embodied conversation grounded in open curiosity and the practice of mindfulness (e.g., connected to body sensations, slowed down with time for pausing). This relational inquiry is the primary process of what is happening within MBS (and is arguably what makes it mindful).*[53]

Six subcategories describe the dimensions of this somewhat nuanced inquiry process. The style of talking is very similar to that within other MBAs, but more collegial and more naming of what might be taken forward from the supervision session. The mode supports an intuitive, 'felt' sense of knowing. Coming to this non-conceptual mode is supported by bringing awareness to direct experience, especially the body, to find new ways of knowing and understanding. Embodying has already been described earlier in this chapter. MBS offers a place for supervisees to explore embodying the qualities of mindfulness whilst in a relationship with another, as well as seeing and feeling the embodying modelled by the supervisor. MBS creates a space for exploration, favouring spaces and pauses so that new discoveries might be made. There tends to be a leaning towards a stance of 'not knowing' and giving space for a more organic form of emergence. This does not mean there are no times for guidance and explicit advice to be shared, but often there is a slowing down, inquiry, or pause before this sharing. Being able to turn towards vulnerability in all its forms was felt to be an essential part of MBS, so building a safe and trusting relationship is vital before supervisees feel able to open and turn towards more challenging aspects of experience.

The supervisory relationship aims to build a sense of trust and collaboration, and there are inevitably power imbalances that can be recognized and worked with. This research noticed a lack of critique and a tendency to be positive. We might view this as part of how, through mindfulness practice, we develop ways of holding an equanimous and steady stance, being non-judgemental, and appreciating the good – and we might bear in mind how to keep including a critique within MBS, having challenging and searching questions and being able to hold different viewpoints.

Relational inquiry within MBS

The relational aspect of this embodied dialogue is necessary for the inquiry. The stronger the relationship, the more there is a sense of safety and trust so that the supervision can be more transformational. Fiona Adamson and Jane Brendgen centre their book around a case study of the evolution of their supervisory

---

53   Evans et al., 2024, p. 70

relationship.[54] They reflect on key moments that brought about transformation, enhancing their personal and professional development. In their words, *"A relational mindfulness approach can establish an emotional climate that is conducive to the emergence of a compassionate dialogical process, and it is this mutual process that creates the freedom to learn."*[55]

They found that mindfulness is the cornerstone of the relationship, both the capacity to be attentive with another and the qualities of mindfulness that create a certain atmosphere that allows being with what is here and turning towards all aspects of experience.

Supervision theory and research

In our work, we have found drawing upon other modalities that link with the MBS framework helpful. One is the supervision theory and research from a broad range of helping professions, where giving and receiving supervision has been part of professional practice for many years. Some of these maps and models that have been developed are applicable across different forms of supervision. The ones that we draw more closely upon cover:

- developmental approaches to supervision
- the functions of supervision
- cultural responsivity

Developmental approaches to supervision

Cal Stoltenberg and Brian McNeill[56] have developed a model around the developmental stages of learning for counsellors and therapists from their training and beyond. Stoltenberg[57] recognizes that supervision is a complex process that can be viewed through stages of development whilst also understanding the many nuances rather than this being a purely linear journey. Supervisees are going to develop differently in different domains at any one time. However, based on their experience and research, they have found some patterns in supervisees' needs at various stages of learning, which require a different emphasis in supervision and the supervisor's behaviour. In MBS, we can usefully bear the developmental approach in mind to support supervisors in meeting supervisees where they are and patiently being alongside them. Supervisors are also passing through stages of development. We explore developmental models further in Chapters 10 and 14.

---

54 Adamson & Brendgen, 2021
55 Adamson & Brendgen, 2021, p. 6
56 Stoltenberg & McNeill, 2010
57 Stoltenberg, 1997

The functions of supervision

As we draw upon supervision within the different helping professions, many use a framework around the various functions to describe the different roles a supervisor might take and categorise the varied functions of supervision. Francesca Inskipp and Brigid Proctor[58] are the most widely known. They talk about three key functional aspects of supervision: *formative* – with a focus on learning and development; *restorative* – with a focus on the emotional and personal side of the work; and *normative* – with a focus on the ethical side of the work. Along with colleagues, Alison used this framework in relation to MBS and identified key intentions for each function.[59] Within MBS, the supervisor can be aware of these different aspects of supervision and their roles and intentionally lean into them as and when needed. We explore this further in Chapter 3 when we look at intention.

Cultural responsivity in supervision

We draw upon literature and research within the clinical supervision field about bringing cultural sensitivity and responsiveness into supervision. We want to unpack some of these terms and describe them here. Vekaria et al.[60] describe how, in culturally responsive supervision, there is an assumption that the supervisee's cultural background and experiences permeate all aspects of clinical practice and supervision. Cultural responsiveness within supervision promotes cultural competence in three ways: responsivity, reflective discussion and the supervisor modelling their own cultural competence. Cultural competence is defined as the supervisor's and supervisee's development of cultural awareness, knowledge, and skills to provide an effective and responsive service for people across all cultural groups. Culture is a construct conceptualized by numerous contextual variables, such as race, gender, class and age. Vekaria et al.[61] focused their research on cultural responsivity around race/ethnicity from the perspective of supervisees. They found five themes: integrating race/ethnicity into the profession, attending to the supervisory relationship, increasing cultural competence, addressing the power dynamic, and promoting cultural humility. There is a proposed emphasis that the supervisor takes the initiative to bring these conversations into supervision safely and sensitively. In future chapters, we return to cultural responsivity to highlight how working intentionally and sensitively with cultural awareness needs to be woven into many aspects of MBS.

---

58 Inskipp & Proctor, 1993; 1995
59 Evans et al., 2015
60 Vekaria et al., 2023b
61 Vekaria et al., 2023a

Experiential learning theory

Both supervision and learning are social and relational processes steeped in experiential and participatory processes. In this section, we have drawn on two theories from the educational field that fit closely with MBS:

- experiential learning cycles
- learning with the support of a guide

Experiential learning cycles

David Kolb is well known for his work on experiential learning. He builds on the origins of other work in the field of learning, such as William James, John Dewey, Kurt Lewin, Jean Piaget, and Lev Vygotsky.[62] Experiential learning is drawn upon within the MBA literature in relation to inquiry.[63] We also draw upon this concept of learning from experience as a practical framework to support the process of inquiry within MBS as an ongoing cycle (Figure 2.3).

Figure 2.3 The inquiry process in MBS as an ongoing cycle

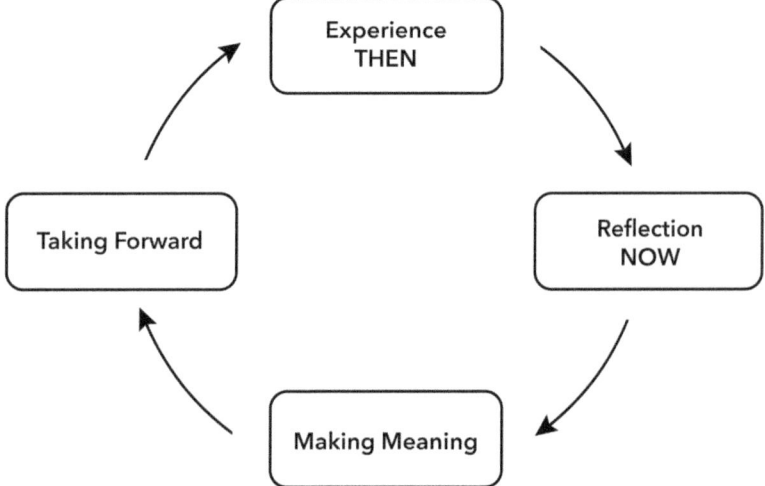

In MBS, the supervisee brings the experience of 'there and then' into the 'here and now' and looks ahead to future applications. When the supervisee brings to mind a past experience, it becomes present within them, to some degree or other, in that moment – complete with its physical sensations, emotions and thoughts. The mutual inquiry process within MBS uses this to bring a supervisee's past experience into the present, where it can be fully explored and worked with before making choices about how to take this learning forward.

---

[62] Kolb, 2015. We recommend this book for a detailed dive into experiential learning and Kolb's work.
[63] Segal et al., 2013, p. 251

Learning with the support of a guide

We hear supervisors and supervisees say that the word 'supervisor' can conjure up the wrong image of someone standing over you and checking up on you. In contrast, the relationship is much more about having someone alongside you. We see a link with Vygotsky's work about having an experienced mentor to guide. Vygotsky[64] saw learning as a social process where individual learning is shaped through mentoring from more 'knowledgeable' community members. This experienced mentor is essential in aiding supervisees in reaching new zones of proximal development. Evans[65] found examples scattered through their research data about the supervisor being in this more 'knowledgeable' role, e.g. supervisees perceiving that embodiment is reflected in the supervisor, being able to have affirmation from the supervisor about actions to take, for the supervisor to be able to guide what will happen if you do not teach in certain ways, simple conversations to sort things out, being able to check things out with a more experienced practitioner, and the supervisor sharing their experience, ideas and wisdom.

Mindfulness-based theory informing supervision in other modalities

We have noticed that professionals working in other modalities are drawing on some of the practices of mindfulness and embodiment into the practice of supervision, so in the same way we are seeing supervision theory influencing MBS, we also see how mindfulness theory and practice are influencing other supervision modalities.[66]

Summary

We have outlined five bodies of theory that inform the practice of MBS.

1. Mindfulness-based approaches theory and practice
    - Awareness, intentionality, attitudes of mindfulness, and the ability to discern are important dimensions that underpin MBS.
    - Cultivating mindfulness through personal mindfulness practice is essential.
    - MBS draws upon Buddhist teachings, e.g. the four ways of establishing mindfulness and the compassion-based teachings.
    - Social models can support widening perspectives. In MBS, explorations include personal awareness of bias, prejudice, and assumptions and working explicitly in ways that support non-discrimination and inclusivity.

---

64 Vygotsky, 1978
65 Evans, 2019
66 In education – Haberlin, 2024; homeopathy and other helping professions – Ryan, 2008; systemic therapists – Levitt, 2017; integrative therapists – Žvelc & Žvelc, 2023

- Mindfulness and compassion can be explicitly explored in relationships and communication to support embodied conversations. This includes drawing on the bodies of theory around co-regulation and attunement.

2. Mindfulness-based pedagogy
   - Core pedagogies utilized in MBS include embodying, inquiry, turning towards.
   - We introduce the MBI:TAC and MBI:TLC as pedagogical tools.

3. MBS theory and research
   - We introduced the research-based Relational Inquiry in Mindfulness-Based Supervision model (RIMBS).
   - Learning the *what*, *how* and *why* is an essential aspect of MBS.
   - Mindful inquiry is the heart of the process within MBS.
   - Critique and asking challenging questions needs to be part of MBS.

4. Supervision theory and research
   - The supervisor adjusts supervision to meet the changing developmental needs of supervisees.
   - There are three main functions of supervision – formative, restorative, and normative – that inform intentions.
   - Cultural responsiveness within supervision promotes cultural competence through responsivity, reflective discussion, and the supervisor's modelling of their own cultural competence.

5. Experiential learning theory
   - The supervisory session and inquiry process draws upon experiential learning theories, bringing the experience THEN into reflection NOW, Making Meaning and Taking Forward.
   - An MBS supervisor is like an experienced mentor alongside you to support growth in ways that are not always possible on your own.

Reflective questions

What is **your** sense of the underlying foundations and theoretical underpinnings of MBS?

Which aspects of theory/research are most relevant for you now?

Which of those named resonate with you? Have interested you?

Which ones overwhelmed you? Seemed a bit dry? Bit complicated? Did you disagree with it?

Is there anything you want to follow up further? Find out more about? Explore in more depth?

Are there any other theories/frameworks not named that you draw upon in MBS?

Do any questions come up for you? (You might take these questions into your reading, personal reflections, into dialogue with your supervisor or peers.)

If there is one thing you could take forward into your subsequent supervision (either as a supervisee or supervisor), what would it be?

References

Adamson, F., & Brendgen, J. (2021). *Mindfulness-based relational supervision: Mutual learning and transformation.* Routledge. https://doi.org/10.4324/9781315161280

Baer, R. (2015). Ethics, values, virtues, and character strengths in mindfulness-based interventions: A psychological science perspective. *Mindfulness, 6,* 956-969. https://doi.org/10.1007/s12671-015-0419-2

Barret, L. F. (2020). *Seven and a half lessons about the brain.* Picador. (Chapter 5 – Your brain secretly works with other brains)

Bartley, T., & Griffith, G. (2022). *Teaching mindfulness-based groups: The inside out group model.* Pavilion Publishing.

Brown, B. (2012). *Daring greatly: How the courage to be vulnerable transforms the way we live, love, parent, and lead.* Penguin.

Crane, R. (2017). *Mindfulness-based cognitive therapy: Distinctive features* (2nd ed.). Routledge. https://doi.org/10.4324/9781315627229

Crane, R. S., Karunavira, & Griffith, G. M. (Eds.). (2021). *Essential resources for mindfulness teachers.* Routledge. https://doi.org/10.4324/9780429317880

Crane, R. S., Soulsby, J.G., Kuyken, W., Williams, J. M. G., & Eames, C. (2021). Mindfulness-Based Interventions: Teaching Assessment Criteria (MBI:TAC) (3rd version). https://mbitac.bangor.ac.uk/mbitac-tool.php.en

Crane, R. S., Callen-Davies, R., Francis, A., Francis, D., Gibbs, P., Mulligan, B., O'Neill, B., Williams, N. K. P., Waupoose, M., & Vallejo, Z. (2023). Mindfulness-based stress reduction for our time: A curriculum that is up to the task. *Global Advances in Integrative Medicine and Health, 12.* https://doi.org/10.1177/27536130231162604

Evans, A. (2019). *Supervisors' and supervisees' perspectives of mindfulness-based supervision: A grounded theory study* [Doctoral thesis, University of Exeter]. https://ore.exeter.ac.uk/repository/handle/10871/37542

Evans, A., Crane, R., Cooper, L., Mardula, J., Wilks, J., Surawy, C., Kenny, M., & Kuyken, W. (2015). A framework for supervision for mindfulness-based teachers: A space for embodied mutual inquiry. *Mindfulness, 6,* 572-581. https://doi.org/10.1007/s12671-014-0292-4

Evans, A., Griffith, G. M., Crane, R. S., & Sansom, S. A. (2021). Using the mindfulness-based interventions: teaching assessment criteria (MBI:TAC) in supervision. *Global Advances in Health and Medicine, 10,* 1-6. https://doi.org/10.1177/2164956121989949

Evans, A., Griffith, G. M., & Smithson, J. (2024). What do supervisors' and supervisees' think about mindfulness-based supervision? A grounded theory study. *Mindfulness, 15,* 63–79. https://doi.org/10.1007/s12671-023-02280-8

Feldman, C., & Kuyken, W. (2019). *Mindfulness: Ancient wisdom meets modern psychology.* Guilford Publications.

Goldstein, J. (2016). *Mindfulness: A practical guide to awakening.* Sounds True.

Griffith, G. M., Bartley, T., & Crane, R. S. (2019). The inside out group model: Teaching groups in mindfulness-based programs. *Mindfulness, 10,* 1315–1327. https://doi.org/10.1007/s12671-019-1093-6

Griffith G. M., Crane, R. S., Karunavira, & Koerbel, L. (2021). The Mindfulness-Based Interventions: Teaching and Learning Companion (MBI:TLC). In R. S. Crane, Karunavira, & G. M. Griffith (Eds.), *Essential resources for mindfulness teachers* (pp. 125-148). Routledge. https://doi.org/10.4324/9780429317880

Haberlin, S. (2024). *Awakening to educational supervision: A mindfulness-based approach to coaching and supporting teachers.* Rowan & Littlefield.

Inskipp, F., & Proctor, B. (1993). *The art, craft and tasks of counselling supervision: Making the most of supervision* (Part 1). Cascade Publications.

Inskipp, F., & Proctor, B. (1995). *The art, craft and tasks of counselling supervision: Becoming a supervisor* (Part 2). Cascade Publications.

Kabat-Zinn, J. (1994). *Wherever you go, there you are: Mindfulness meditation for everyday life.* Piatkus.

Kabat-Zinn, J. (2013). *Full catastrophe living, how to cope with stress, pain and illness using mindfulness meditation* (Revised edition). Piatkus.

Karelse, C. M. (2023). *Disrupting white mindfulness: Race and racism in the wellbeing industry.* Manchester University Press.

Kucinskas, J. (2018). *The mindful elite: Mobilizing from the inside out.* Oxford University Press.

Kolb, D. (2015). *Experiential learning: Experience as the source of learning and development* (2nd ed.). Pearson Education.

Koster, F., Heynekamp, J., & Norton, V. (Eds.). (2023). *Mindful communication: Speaking and listening with wisdom and compassion.* Routledge.

Levitt, O. (2017). Mindfulness: Bringing body and breath to supervision. In J. Bownas, & G. Fredman (Eds.), *Working with embodiment in supervision* (pp. 131-146). Routledge. https://doi.org/10.4324/9781315762456

Magee, R. V. (2021). *The inner work of racial justice: Healing ourselves and transforming our communities through mindfulness.* Penguin.

McCown, D. (2013). *The ethical space of mindfulness in clinical practice: An exploratory essay.* Jessica Kingsley Publishers.

McCown, D., Reibel, D., & Micozzi, M. S. (2010). *Teaching mindfulness: A practical guide for clinicians and educators.* Springer.

Porges, S. W. (2022). Polyvagal theory: A science of safety. *Frontiers in Integrative Neuroscience*, 16, 871227. https://doi.org/10.3389/fnint.2022.871227

Roberts, B., & Crane, R. (2021). Societal themes. In R. S. Crane, Karunavira, & G. M. Griffith (Eds.), *Essential resources for mindfulness teachers* (pp. 189-199). Routledge. https://doi.org/10.4324/9780429317880

Ryan, S. (2008). Mindful supervision. In R. Shohet (Ed.). *Passionate supervision* (pp. 70-85). Jessica Kingsley Publishers.

Segal, Z. V., Williams, J. M. G., & Teasdale, J. D. (2013). *Mindfulness-based cognitive therapy for depression* (2nd ed.). Guilford Press.

Shapiro, S. L., Carlson, L. E., Astin, J. A., & Freedman, B. (2006). Mechanisms of mindfulness. *Journal of Clinical Psychology*, 62(3), 373-386. https://doi.org/10.1002/jclp.20237

Shapiro, S. L., & Carlson, L. E. (2009). *The art and science of mindfulness: Integrating mindfulness into psychology and the helping professions.* American Psychological Association.

Shapiro, S. L., Carlson, L. E., & Sawyer, B. A. (2024). *The art and science of mindfulness: Integrating mindfulness into the helping professions.* (3rd ed.). American Psychological Association.

Siegel, D. J. (2007). Reflections on the mindful brain: A brief overview. Adapted from Siegel, D. J., *The mindful brain: Reflection and attunement in the cultivation of well-being.* W. W. Norton. Retrieved January 10, 2025, from https://www.openground.com.au/assets/Documents-Openground/Articles/0e39aa6bc0/reflections-on-the-mindful-brain-siegel.pdf

Stoltenberg, C. D. (1997). The integrated developmental model of supervision: Supervision across levels. *Psychotherapy in Private Practice,* 16(2), 59-69. https://doi.org/10.1300/J294v16n02_07

Stoltenberg, C. D., & McNeill, B. W. (2010). *IDM supervision: An integrative developmental model for supervising counselors and therapists* (3rd ed.). Routledge.

van den Brink, E., Koster, F., & Norton, V. (2018). *A practical guide to mindfulness-based compassionate living: Living with heart.* Routledge. https://doi.org/10.4324/9781315268491

Vekaria, B., Harrydwar, L., Thomas, T., & Ononaiye, M. (2023a). Supervisee perspectives on improving cultural responsivity in clinical supervision. *Clinical Psychology Forum,* 1(371), 66-76. https://doi.org/10.53841/bpscpf.2023.1.371.66

Vekaria, B., Thomas, T., Phiri, P., & Ononaiye, M. (2023b). Exploring the supervisory relationship in the context of culturally responsive supervision: a supervisee's perspective. *The Cognitive Behaviour Therapist*, 16, e22. https://doi.org/10.1017/S1754470X23000168

Vygotsky, L. S. (1978). *Mind in society: The development of higher psychological processes* (Vol. 86). Harvard University Press.

Žvelc, M., & Žvelc, G. (2023). *Mindfulness and compassion in integrative supervision.* Routledge.

Part Two:
The Mindfulness-Based Supervision Framework

In Part Two, we unpack the different aspects of the MBS framework in detail, taking a chapter for each.

Chapter 3
The Container

These [the warp] threads need to be strong because they form the backbone of the fabric.[67]

The Container of mindfulness is one of the three warp threads, strong enough to hold the entire supervision process. The Container comprises four elements that describe the fundamental essence of a mindfulness-based approach and are present within all mindfulness-based practice and work: Intention, Integrity, Compassion/Wisdom, and Embodied Presence. Different words might have been chosen, but we feel that these encompass all we see as fundamental foundations of a mindfulness-based Container. These elements are interrelated and complement each other.

The concept of 'container' conveys that there are necessary preparations and ongoing attention by the supervisor to establish and maintain conditions that support the cultivation of a mindfulness-based approach within supervision and the supervisory relationship. A significant foundation in creating and maintaining this Container will undoubtedly be the MB supervisor's personal practice, both on and off the cushion. In a documentary with Bill Moyers, Jon Kabat-Zinn spoke about one's personal practice as like weaving a parachute, which is woven every day so that when it's needed, it can hold us.[68] This is the same concept with the Container of mindfulness in that its existence and stability depend on the supervisor's commitment to cultivating mindfulness within their practice and lives. This helps

---
67 Luisa, July 12, 2023, *Warp and weft – Meaning & differences* https://blog.treasurie.com/warp-and-weft/
68 Moyers, 1993, *Healing from within* (episode from the Healing and the Mind series https://billmoyers.com/content/healing-from-within/)

distinguish this approach from other supervision models where there may be elements of mindfulness added in, such as mindfulness techniques and practices, but the mindfulness-based approach is not part of the fundamental fabric as it is within the MBS framework.

As well as informing the way the supervisor is and how they hold the space, these elements will also be discussed explicitly within MBS, as part of the content, the Petals.

We examine each of the four elements in turn and explore how they contribute to the Container's essential nature and stability.

Intention

The concept of intention is so central to mindfulness practices because it shapes our body, mind, and world of the moment.[69]

As outlined in Chapter 2, intention is part of the definition of mindfulness, "… *on purpose.*"[70] Intentions support the purposeful cultivation and embodiment of mindfulness within both the inner world (body, emotions and thoughts) and the outer world (speech and actions). Whereas a goal suggests a specific endpoint, an intention points to a direction of travel with a focus on the journey rather than just the destination. An intention includes an expression of the foundational mindful attitudes and could be seen as a heart wish, whereas a goal has more to do with the mind and the domain of thinking. Intention guides where to place attention, helps to remind why one is practising mindfulness in the first place,[71] and helps shape outcomes.[72] So, this intentionality has a broader aspect of connecting/reconnecting with values and aspirations and a more specific element of considering the intentions of a particular task or course of action. Intentions change over time, have flow and movement; aspirations, when first beginning on a particular path, may evolve as one becomes more familiar with the nature of the work and one's own heart.

Intention has an implicit as well as an explicit role within MBS: it guides how the supervisor is within the moments of supervision (implicit) and will also be a topic itself within supervision, helping inform the content of supervision (explicit). There will be times out of habit when thoughts, speech or actions are not in keeping with intentions. However, in setting an intention, there is also a commitment to notice when choices are not aligned with aspirations, bringing patience and openness to oneself and a willingness to return to intention whenever needed. MBS can be a place to support supervisees to reflect and reconnect with intention, and supra-

---

69   Feldman & Kuyken, 2019, p. 190
70   Segal et al., 2013, p. 132
71   Kabat-Zinn, 2013
72   Shapiro, 1992

vision is a place for supervisors to do the same. In this way, as part of reflective practice, intention is linked to integrity through the exploration of actions and adherence to good practice and the upholding of ethical and professional standards.

Connecting with intention for engaging in the work of MBS

There may be many factors behind the decision to become an MB supervisor. For example, a sense of having enough experience within a particular field and having something to offer others or as part of ongoing personal development. Some practitioners can feel pressured into taking on the role of supervisor, perhaps finding themselves as the most 'senior' or experienced practitioner within their context and more 'junior' practitioners in need of supervision. For others, there may be a sense that it is a natural part of career progression. Most likely, there is also a deeper motivation, a calling, we might say – a heart wish.

Let's pause to reflect on your intentions for engaging in the work of MBS.

Pausing for self-reflection
Connecting and reconnecting with intentions

Taking time now to put down the book and establish a steady posture. Maybe spending a few moments with awareness of the body resting and the breath moving within.

When you are ready, dropping in the question, *What brings me here to this work as a supervisor?*

Perhaps, like the initial splash of a pebble dropping into a body of water, there is an initial response.

Then, the invitation to allow the question to drop deeper, like the pebble dropping deeper into the water, *What really brings me here?*

And staying in silent, open inquiry. Seeing what arises. Perhaps words, maybe wordless – a sense in the body or the heart.

What brings me to this work?

Nothing to be forced. There may be a lot arising or nothing much at all. Just listening.

Perhaps there is a connection with a deeper longing, a deeper calling, as you continue to be curious.

Sitting with this inquiry for a few more moments and then when you are ready, returning attention to the breathing body.

Offering yourself time to sit quietly with this inquiry from time to time can strengthen your connection with heart intentions and motivation for engaging in this work.

As well as reconnecting with the broader intentions for offering supervision, it is also helpful to connect/reconnect with your intentions with your supervisee before a supervision session. In this way, the supervisor's choices and actions within a supervision session link to both broad and specific intentions. Let's look at how intentions might explicitly and specifically shape a supervision session.

The roles of the supervisor

The widely known work of Francesca Inskipp and Brigid Proctor[73] describes three key functions within supervision: Formative, Restorative and Normative. We see these functions more as roles for the supervisor to inhabit, discerning when each is needed, and covering all of them over a period of supervision. It is important that the supervisee also comes with an intention to explore the different aspects that supervision can offer. Based on interviews with experienced MB supervisors[74] and from research,[75] we use the Inskipp and Proctor framework to draw out the specific intentions of each role within MBS (Table 3.1). We encourage supervisors to familiarise themselves with these three roles and the specific intentions within each one, to be aware of their habits regarding which roles they tend to inhabit more and which less so, and to be curious about choice points to move around the different roles.

Table 3.1 Examples of intentions for MBS

Overarching roles	Examples of key intentions within MBS for each role
Formative To focus on learning and development	To stimulate curiosity, reflection and understanding about the individuals, group, broader context and 'self', keeping a sense of inquiry to the whole process. To develop and enhance understanding and skills in core competencies, e.g. within MB teaching work, using the MBI:TLC across the six domains.

---

73 Inskipp & Proctor, 1993; 1995
74 Evans et al., 2015
75 Evans et al., 2024

		To deepen the supervisee's knowledge and understanding of concepts and theory and link this with their MB work so the supervisee learns the *what, how, and why.*
		To explore and offer feedback on strengths and learning edges, which can be incorporated into the supervisee's MB work.
		To promote reflective practice and tuning into intention for learning to take place, allowing for choice points/different options.
	Restorative To acknowledge the emotional and personal side of the work	To establish a trusting, safe, supportive, and nourishing working relationship—a place to unpack the impact of the work, overcome obstacles to learning, be creative, and receive guidance in times of need.
		To support a compassionate relationship with the vulnerabilities that come with being human.
		To be culturally responsive, understanding, appreciating, and appropriately including and responding to the cultural variables that inform and influence us as supervisors, our supervisees, and the interaction between us.
		To cultivate a brave space that acknowledges the vulnerability and challenge in discussing sensitive topics such as race and power.
		To offer an embodied, present-moment space that imbues a mindfulness-based approach.
		Within MB work, to support developing and deepening ongoing personal mindfulness practice and its interface with teaching and everyday life.
	Normative To connect to professional and ethical issues	To promote ethical and safe practice and maintain standards and duty of care.
		To have safe contracting and reviewing processes within MBS.
		To ensure that what is being taught/conveyed balances adhering to core curriculums with insightful innovations to enable mindfulness to benefit a diverse group of people.
		To ensure strong connections to underlying theories and ethical and professional frameworks.
		To engender a sense of responsibility for the supervisee and the people they are teaching/working with.
		To do no harm.
		To challenge misunderstandings, poor practice, and blind spots.
		To provide formal evaluation or reports where they are required.
		To bring in the wider context of the mindfulness field and its approach to ethical and professional practice.

The supervisory relationship

Looking more closely at intentions in relation to the supervisory relationship, as part of the restorative role, what factors are likely to support aspirations in building a trusting working relationship? Entering into this relationship with another fellow human being requires a willingness to fully meet oneself and the other just as we are, accepting all that we are, recognising what each brings into the shared space and an openness to learn. Since we are all cultural beings, this includes understanding how our values, beliefs and behaviours are shaped by one's past and present culture, a willingness to be curious and learn about the supervisee's cultural practices and being aware of differences and how these might impact the relationship and interactions within supervision.[76]

Given the inherent power difference within a supervisory relationship, it is important that supervisors initiate these discussions, starting at the contracting stage and keeping them alive throughout supervision. Vekaria et al. describe this commitment to cultural responsiveness as "... *both supervisees and supervisors must take personal responsibility for self-examination, cultural humility, keeping cultural issues on supervision agendas and continued learning with supervisors taking the lead."*[77] These explorations and discussions around culture and cross-cultural themes can be tender and challenging, however, they contribute to the Container's stability, which can then hold other tender and challenging conversations that will naturally be a part of supervision. To support these dialogues around themes of diversity and social justice, there is a call that alongside the creation of safe spaces, there is a need to create brave spaces.[78] Brave spaces encourage individuals to have courageous conversations, where they feel able to share their experiences, opinions and ideas, knowing that they will be taken care of. Setting an intention to create and maintain a safe space and a brave space within supervision will be part of the learning and ongoing development of the supervisor, seeking out training, engaging in personal reflections, and discussing within their own supervision and supra-vision.

Intentions are also a helpful place to return to when there are moments of tension or difficulty within supervision, the supervisory relationship or when the supervisee's actions in some way could compromise the integrity of their work. In returning to intentions within moments of misunderstanding, the supervisor may notice there is not a shared intention around the issue being explored, the broader intentions of supervision or the supervisory relationship. Before inviting discussion around issues linked to integrity, it can be supportive to revisit with the supervisee the supervisor's intentions and make connections with all three of the functions of supervision: the normative aspect of upholding standards and integrity, the formative function in

---

76 Hardy & Bobes, 2016; Vekaria et al., 2023
77 Vekaria et al., 2023a, p. 74
78 Arao & Clemens, 2013; Ali, 2017

terms of supporting the supervisee to learn and grow from experiences especially those that are tender, and the restorative function in terms of allowing space for the supervisee to experience and express painful emotions within a supportive relationship.

Intention within supervision

Supervisors and supervisees can directly shine a light on intention in various ways during supervision itself, such as:

- Part of contracting and re-contracting includes exploring the supervisee's goals for supervision, what they are looking for from supervision, why they are coming, and what will keep them coming back. Encouraging the supervisee to connect with their aspirations and motivations for undertaking their work can support them in identifying goals that are connected more deeply to their intentions. This could include an invitation to engage in a reflection on intentions.
- It can be especially helpful when a supervisee is faced with challenges in their MB work to encourage them to reconnect with their broader intentions and why they chose to engage with the work that they do. This can be particularly important for supervisees who are moving into new areas of conveying an MBA or working as a sole MB practitioner when there can be a sense of overwhelm or uncertainty.
- Intentions will be explored within supervision as they link to the content of supervision, the Petals. For example, exploring the intentions for a particular part of the curriculum or a particular exercise/technique/approach and how it links with the underlying theory.

Integrity

Without integrity, mindfulness is morally meaningless.[79]

According to the Oxford Dictionary, integrity is aligning the mind and actions with ethical and moral principles.[80] It is a state of being whole, unified, and consistent, where one's choices are in keeping with foundational ethical principles such as honesty, authenticity, fairness, trustworthiness, beneficence (promoting the well-being of others), nonmaleficence (doing no harm), justice, and autonomy (informed decision making). In Inskipp and Proctor's model, integrity is linked to the normative role.[81] In the MBS framework it links directly with the Belt

---

[79] Yang, 2017, p. 215
[80] Oxford Dictionary. Retrieved January 11, 2025, https://web.archive.org/web/20170823041543/https://en.oxforddictionaries.com/definition/integrity
[81] Inskipp & Proctor, 1993; 1995

which articulates key structures and frameworks that hold integrity and support professional practice, such as good practice guidelines and policies to support equality, equity, diversity and inclusion. The Belt is part of 'outer' integrity.

We use three headings to explore integrity in further detail:

- ethics
- fidelity
- the supervisory relationship

Ethics

Ethics are an inherent and inseparable aspect of most professions and connect to 'inner' integrity. The supervisor and/or supervisee may have a core profession and will be guided by those ethical principles, often articulated in a professional code of ethics, part of the 'outer' integrity. The International Mindfulness Integrity Network offers an articulation of personal integrity:

> *The teacher/trainer demonstrates integrity in their profession, ensuring safety, to the best of one's ability, and offering reliability, honesty, equality, inclusion, and openness in their actions, and acting with confidence, but with a modest attitude as appropriate to the culture in which they are teaching. This includes honesty regarding one's level of training and transparency in stating one's experience within these guidelines.*[82]

Although written from the perspective of teaching MB curriculum/programmes, the elements named above are equally relevant to the widening range of contexts and ways that supervisees may be engaging in MB work. Susan Woods, Patricia Rockman and Evan Collins[83] encourage MB practitioners to also reflect on a personal code of ethics, making this an explicit and intentional process that will arise out of their personal practice, which concurs with Kabat-Zinn's original view that integrity within MB teaching is held by the teacher themselves.[84] This combination of personal values and professional ethics work together to uphold integrity and safety within MB work.[85]

The supervisor commits to keeping the recipient of the MBA at the centre. In MB teaching, this will be the participant, in health and helping professions, the client/patient/service user, in education, the student, and in business, the client and/or the workforce. MBS supports the supervisee in practising safely, effectively, and in non-discriminatory ways.

---

82 International Mindfulness Integrity Network, 2024, p. 5
83 Woods et al., 2019
84 Kabat-Zinn, 2011
85 Baer & Nagy, 2017

As trust and safety are cultivated within MBS, supervisees will feel safe enough to bring ethical moments or dilemmas from their mindfulness work, hopefully with an openness to change. It's not always easy to face ethical issues; integrity can act as an anchor to return to, reminding the supervisee and supervisor that this is a practice. It's often through the exploration of these ethical moments that supervisees find their own inner integrity, as well as having outer structures to support them.

Example – ethical practice

A supervisee has a clear intention to follow good practice and an inner wish to do this 'well'. Over the past few supervision sessions, they have been sharing brief video-recorded excerpts of their MB teaching, and the supervisor has been encouraging an exploration of both their strengths and learning edges. On this occasion the supervisee deliberately chooses to bring a clip from their most recent class that shows an unskilful response during inquiry that resulted in distress for a participant. They state that although it is difficult to acknowledge their unskilful actions and to see their impact, they also know the supervisor will be honest in the service of helping them grow; they know it is in everyone's best interests to take a look at 'mistakes'. They explore the supervisee's painful emotions together and acknowledge their desire to ease suffering rather than cause it. From this honest and compassionate place, the supervisee is able to hold this piece of teaching in perspective, learning from it while not exaggerating its impact and letting go of feelings of shame. They clearly decide together on approaches and actions that are needed going forward and for this to be different if this situation arises again and agree to check in again with each other.

In this example, as well as demonstrating the inner integrity of the supervisee, it also highlights their trust in the integrity of the supervisor, trust in the integrity of the supervisory relationship whilst holding aspects of the Belt, outer integrity, in the background; from this foundation, the supervisee is willing to move into a place of vulnerability and trusts that the supervisor will support and guide them as they develop insight and wisdom around ethical practice.

Within MBS, the supervisor nurtures the supervisee's development in practising with integrity and challenges the supervisee's practice when necessary. When the supervisor becomes aware of acts of omission or commission, either intentionally or out of awareness, that compromise the integrity of the supervisee's work in some way, they bring these issues to supervision. Integrity links with Compassion/Wisdom as the supervisor explores how to find the right balance of care and honesty. The supervisor themselves may take these issues to supra-vision to support themselves in acting with integrity.

Fidelity

Fidelity, meaning being faithful or loyal, as it relates to supervision, is about adherence to the underlying philosophy and theory of the supervisee's work. Here, the supervisor is the upholder of standards, ensuring the supervisee's work stays true to the particular theoretical approach while also staying open to thoughtful adaptations/adjustments as needed, as their work meets the context and world within which they practise. As discussed in Chapter 1, there is a need for a broadening and opening of how MBAs are offered,[86] and supervisors can draw on the work of researchers and pioneers with lived experience to help guide them and their supervisees in bringing an MB approach into their particular context. Having leaders in the field with collective visions and consensus around what constitutes good practice supports MB practitioners in practising with professionalism and integrity.[87]

Coming back to the work of the International Mindfulness Integrity Network, they describe the integrity of the programmes taught:

> *Strong effort is expected to align and respect the integrity of the curricula of MBSR, MBCT or whatever particular course or program is offered (as published by the founders or institutions involved in curriculum development). While using those program names teachers will adhere to the published curricula without adding elements from other programs or subtracting elements to suit other objectives.*[88]

We encourage supervisors and supervisees to draw on research within the MBA field which supports in navigating this balance between fidelity and adaptation. Increasingly, supervisees are coming to MBS with clear intentions around bringing an MB approach into their context in new and innovative ways. Supervisors have a valuable role in encouraging and supporting supervisees to be a part of the next generation of practitioners, teachers and conveyers of mindfulness while promoting a strong sense of connection to the fundamental theory and principles of the MBA.

The supervisory relationship

Finally, integrity shapes the supervisory relationship itself. Establishing a professional relationship begins at the contracting stage, clarifying expectations and boundaries through conversation and a written document. In this way, the supervisor and supervisee are making a commitment to each other and to the process. The supervisor conveys integrity by honouring this commitment and establishing conditions of mutual respect within the relationship. Recognising and working wisely with the inherent power imbalance within the supervisory relationship is an important part of the ethical framework of supervision. In order for the supervisee to learn they need to feel

---

[86] Crane et al., 2023
[87] Crane, 2017
[88] International Mindfulness Integrity Network, 2024, p. 5

psychologically safe enough to take what are called interpersonal risks without fear of negative consequences.[89] These interpersonal risks include things such as speaking up, disagreeing, sharing ideas, giving and receiving feedback, opening to vulnerability, acknowledging mistakes and pointing out mistakes made by others, especially those in positions of power, which, of course, is the position of the supervisor. These are all part of the mutual inquiry process within MBS. To support integrity, the MB supervisor conveys humility, actively encourages different perspectives, and conveys a sense that they, too, are a learner.

Compassion/Wisdom

The human heart is basically very compassionate, but without wisdom, compassion will not work. Wisdom is the openness that lets us see what is essential and most effective.[90]

The whole process of MBS is suffused with these heart qualities of compassion and wisdom. Strauss et al.[91] consider compassion to have five aspects (listed first), which can be linked to the elements of our mindful Container (listed second):

- Recognising suffering: Embodied Presence.
- Understanding the universality of suffering in human experience: Wisdom.
- Feeling empathy for the person suffering and connecting with the distress: Embodied Presence, Compassion.
- Tolerating uncomfortable feelings aroused in response to the suffering person so remaining open to and accepting of the person suffering: Embodied Presence.
- Motivation to act to alleviate suffering: Intention, Integrity and Wisdom.

Compassion is part of human evolution, part of a hard-wired caregiving system that enables care for others who are vulnerable.[92] Compassion is considered essential for well-being and survival, stimulating the soothing systems that help humans feel safe, connected and calm. Wisdom is defined in the Cambridge Dictionary as the ability to use knowledge and experience to make good decisions and judgements.[93] According to Buddhist tradition, genuine compassion includes wisdom and loving kindness.[94] We need to feel empathy and kindness toward the other *and* understand the nature of the suffering (wisdom) that we wish to alleviate.

---

89   Edmondson, 1999
90   Venerable Khandro Rinpoche, October 25, 2021, *Compassion and wisdom* https://www.lionsroar.com/compassion-and-wisdom/
91   Strauss et al., 2016
92   Gilbert, 2010; Goetz et al., 2010
93   Cambridge Dictionary, Retrieved January 16, 2025, https://dictionary.cambridge.org/dictionary/english/wisdom
94   Dalai Lama, 2005

So, the MB supervisor has the intention to balance both aspects; if the supervisor has compassion without wisdom, they may be overwhelmed and find it difficult to support the supervisee to find skilful ways of responding to the challenges of their work; if the supervisor has wisdom without compassion, they won't make a genuine heart connection with the supervisee and as such, may lose the sense of understanding and mutuality within the relationship.

The cultivation of these heart qualities

In order to know something of these qualities of compassion and wisdom, they are intentionally cultivated through personal mindfulness practice. Wisdom is cultivated as one explores the nature of one's heart and mind and begins to see things more clearly, discovering the true nature of reality, and the heart opens to the inevitable suffering of oneself and others as part of the human condition. Christina Feldman and Willem Kuyken state, *"In the face of suffering, the shift from aversion to welcoming, befriending and accepting is the most radical emotional and psychological shift a person can make."*[95] This links with Embodied Presence, the experiential understanding that comes from one's own practice. As well as cultivating compassion and wisdom within the regular practice, having opportunities for extended periods of practice is essential and, as such, is, a part of good practice.

Alongside regular mindfulness practices, compassion may be explicitly cultivated through specific compassion practices. Known as the *Brahma-viharas* within Buddhist teachings and the Four Friends for Life in the MBCL programme, we can choose to intentionally cultivate qualities of kindness, sympathetic joy, compassion, and equanimity.[96] These qualities are seen as supporting wisdom and compassion in our relationships with ourselves and with others. The authors of MBCL use the metaphor of a barometer, an instrument used to check changes in the weather, encouraging a tuning into an 'inner barometer' to discern the emotional weather conditions and then choosing which heart qualities to practise within different conditions. They describe kindness as an all-weather friend that is always helpful to practise. In the face of challenge or distress, when the weather is bleak, the quality of compassion is needed. When things are going well, sunny and fair conditions, we may cultivate sympathetic joy. At times of extreme weather and unpredictability, the quality of equanimity can help in staying steady in the midst of turbulence.

So, through this experiential cultivation of wisdom and compassion within the laboratory of one's own body, mind and heart, it becomes clear that compassion and wisdom cannot exist without the other. In the Tibetan Buddhist tradition, compassion and wisdom are often compared to the two wings of a bird, in that both are necessary in order to take flight.

---

95 Feldman & Kuyken, 2011, p. 151
96 van den Brink et al., 2018

Compassion/Wisdom in MBS

In MBS, the supervisor draws on this experiential foundation as they move into relationship and dialogue with the supervisee. This balancing of compassion and wisdom is part of the dance within the MBS space; this moment-to-moment discernment of what is needed as the supervisor and supervisee engage in mutual inquiry. Wisdom derived from experiential learning cultivated through practice, trial and error, and combined with knowledge of theories, provides a broad overview of the terrain. At the same time, compassion supports a direct connection with this supervisee's unique experience and the willingness to engage and act.

Here are some ways that Compassion/Wisdom and the Four Friends might infuse MBS:

Tuning into shared experience. As well as awareness in the broader perspective of the sense of shared humanity, having direct experience in the same type of work/ profession as the supervisee, the supervisor will likely also find a more specific sense of shared experience having encountered the same or similar difficulties; they know something of the challenges within this context and understand its part of the territory. This wisdom naturally gives rise to compassion towards the supervisee. Here is where self-disclosure can be supportive, saying something like *"I can remember having those feelings. And I still do!"* or even *"I have heard others express this too."* The supervisor is conveying *"You are not alone."*

Attending to the restorative function of supervision. The supervisor is interested in how the supervisee is and how their work impacts them. The supervisor embodies the heart-mind qualities as they recognise and are moved by the supervisee's difficulty/distress. They meet their uncertainty, anxiety, fear, frustration, and self-doubt with attitudes of care and kindness and a willingness to turn towards and be with it. They are communicating through embodiment and words that supervision is just the place to bring the difficult, explore it, and learn about and from it. Supervision may start with a simple question, *"How are you?"* and begin with a brief practice that invites a tuning-in to the present-moment experience.

Celebrating the supervisee and their work. The supervisor takes care to highlight areas of growth and development, no matter how small; through the cultivation of sympathetic joy, we encourage recognition and celebration of insights, development, and the skilful work of our supervisees.

Opening to the difficult. When a supervisee brings a problem to supervision, the supervisor allows space to explore rather than rushing to fix it. They encourage the supervisee to turn towards and explore the difficulty with a sense of friendliness and care, inviting an inquiry into their direct experience of the difficulty and their relationship to it, noticing conditioned patterns of judging/blaming/shaming, trying to get rid of and trying to fix. Within an MB approach, it is not that there is not a focus on problem-solving, but rather it is about encouraging a different understanding of what we mean by problem-solving. Feldman and Kuyken articulate this difference: *"Although there is not always a solution to suffering, there is always a possible response."*[97]

Opening to vulnerability. In creating a compassionate space, the supervisor communicates that it is okay for the supervisee to be open and honest about the realities of their work rather than having to filter anything out. It is often through the most painful experiences, such as when mistakes are made or actions are unskilful, that there is the most potential for growth – this opportunity to open to vulnerability. Through mutual inquiry, the supervisee can begin to recognise their reactive habit patterns in the face of difficulty and discover new ways of responding. Encouraging the supervisee to bring self-compassion towards mistakes rather than harsh and critical judgement of themselves opens the space for potential learning, including how to make amends and prevent similar mistakes in the future. It is through this process that they develop their own wisdom. In this way, we can see how Compassion/Wisdom links to Intention and Integrity.

Discerning the right response. In making choices about how best to respond, the supervisor will be drawing on their Wisdom, which in turn will be influenced by many factors, such as the duration and stability of the supervisory relationship, developmental frameworks, zone of proximal development,[98] the supervisee's goals and agenda for the session. The Supervisor may be exploring 'soft' and 'hard' edges, deciding when it is helpful to challenge gently, when they determine that development is within the supervisee's reach, and times when there are issues of safety when there is a need to lean more towards a hard edge. The THINK acronym[99] brings a modern perspective to the ancient words of the Buddha and can be a useful guide:

T	Is it Timely? Is it True?
H	Is it Honest? Is it Helpful?
I	Is it Insightful? Is it Inspiring?
N	Is it Necessary?
K	Is it Kind?

Navigating ruptures. The supervisor's commitment to compassionate and wise responsiveness is especially called upon when there are tensions, a disagreement or a rupture within the supervisory relationship, such as miscommunication, different expectations, cultural conflict, avoidant or aversive habit patterns of the supervisor or supervisee, difficulties linked with the power imbalance within the relationship.

---

97   Feldman & Kuyken, 2011, p. 157
98   Vygotsky, 1978
99   Koster et al., 2023

This is where the fourth friend, equanimity, can be most supportive, helping the supervisor to stay steady in the midst of difficulty. The quality of equanimity is often described as cool.[100] This does not mean cold or indifferent; it is still steeped in warmth and care for others. Equanimity supports an acceptance of what we could call the 'Both/And' nature of experience, staying steady and calm in the presence of pleasure *and* pain, liking *and* disliking, being attuned with our supervisee *and* times when there is miscommunication or disagreement. Through personal practice, there are many opportunities to open to the changing nature and constant flux of experience, and to practise staying steady rather than wanting things to be different than they are. Bringing this quality of equanimity into relationships supports the acceptance that tensions and challenges within the relationship are part of the natural process of being in a relationship with another. Nothing has gone wrong; no one has made a mistake, but rather, it is an opportunity to bring this cool and steadying attitude right into the moments of interpersonal tension, trusting that together supervisor and supervisee can connect to their collective wisdom to support them in navigating this unsteady terrain.

Outside of a supervision session. The supervisor may intentionally cultivate these heart-mind qualities towards a supervisee, either in preparation for a supervision session or after a session as part of the post-session reflection. This may be a brief pause, bringing the supervisee to mind, sensing what heart quality feels most nourishing and needed, and at other times, bringing the supervisee into a longer befriending practice.

We offer an invitation to pause here for practice.

Friendliness practice

Taking some moments to arrive into a stable and steady posture, and sensing into present moment experience. Noticing sensations of breath breathing or an alternative anchor point.

When you are ready, bringing to mind your supervisor or supra-visor, someone you recognise as a mentor and benefactor. Connecting in with a felt sense of this person, noticing how this feels in the body and in the heart. And an opportunity to offer friendliness to this person, in some way sending them well-wishing, perhaps appreciation or gratitude for their presence in your life and their support. Not needing to force anything or feel a certain way – just inclining the heart towards friendliness and seeing what you notice. You may use a phrase(s) that capture the sentiment of your well-wishing.

---

100 Feldman & Kuyken, 2019; Goldstein, 2016

Then choosing to expand the practice towards your supervisee, bringing them to mind and sensing into how this feels in body and heart. You might like to use the MBCL idea of tuning into your inner barometer, feeling into the particular 'weather pattern' that is arising as you hold the supervisee in mind and heart, and sensing into what particular heart quality would be most supportive within these weather conditions. You may feel into these qualities, using the breath as a support, and/or choose to bring some particular phrases to mind that support the cultivation of friendliness:

- Kindness is like an all-weather friend and is always helpful to practise – maybe offering a phrase around well-wishing, or a sense of your belief in them.
- In the presence of the supervisee struggling or suffering in some way, where the weather is rather bleak or cold, then perhaps cultivating Compassion would feel most needed. Offering a recognition that they are suffering and perhaps wishing them freedom from this suffering.
- If the supervisee is feeling good about their teaching or had a recent success such as an insight or a piece of skilful teaching, sunny and warm weather conditions, perhaps choosing to cultivate Sympathetic joy. Savouring and celebrating their success, offering appreciation of their presence and your gratitude around knowing them.
- At times of more extreme or stormy weather, when the supervisee is in the midst of instability or unpredictability, the quality of Equanimity may be most supportive. Phrases that acknowledge the presence of impermanence or imbalance, and offering a wish for regaining moments of balance and steadiness in the midst of the uncertainty.

Continuing to practise as long as feels helpful, in a way that feels right for you, using phrases or inclining the heart-mind towards friendliness.

When you are ready to bring the practice towards an end, returning awareness to a sense of the body and breath. Then broadening awareness out to your surroundings as you end the practice.

Embodied Presence

The essence of working with another person is to be present as a living being. And that is lucky, because if we had to be smart, or good, or mature, or wise, then we would probably be in trouble. What matters is to be a human being with another human being ...[101]

Embodied presence is the present moment awareness of both inner and outer experience. It is an intentional process cultivated through practice and is imbued with a number of attitudinal qualities.[102] The development of these qualities within the supervisor's practice and life establishes them as a strong foundation, part of their way of being, and this supports their ability to draw upon them within moments of supervision. In essence, the supervisor is making a commitment to living life in an authentic and connected way, and this is at the heart of how they are in the supervisory relationship. A closer look at some of the attitudinal qualities highlights how embodied presence is part of the fabric and stability of the Container:

- **Acceptance.** The supervisor brings an intention to be receptive to all that arises in supervision, both the delights and the difficulties. Embodied presence includes the supervisor being aware of their own reactivity and that of the supervisee, with their practice supporting a steadiness even in the midst of the difficult, opening to and allowing moments of vulnerability and uncertainty. It is bringing a kindly presence towards themselves and the supervisee just as they are.
- **Patience.** Susan Woods speaks of a *"gentle and compassionate attentiveness and steadiness"*[103] that supports staying open to not knowing and not needing to rush to find answers or move into fixing.
- **Beginner's mind.** The supervisor brings a sense of wonder and freshness into the explorations within supervision, encouraging themselves and the supervisee to approach each experience as if for the first time.
- **Non-striving.** While acknowledging the intention around supporting the growth and development of the supervisee, the supervisor lets go of needing to force anything and instead trusts that by cultivating supportive conditions, growth will happen.
- **Gratitude.** Cultivating a sense of appreciation for the supervisee and the work they are doing.

---

101 Gendlin, 1990, p. 205
102 Kabat-Zinn, 2013
103 Woods, 2009, p. 467

Embodied conversations

The supervisor is really 'showing up' for themselves and the supervisee, aware of and tuning into their own physical and emotional experience while also tuning into the supervisee, their posture, breathing, facial expression, words, *and* tuning into how they are relating to and with each other. Figure 3.1 illustrates the three axes that the supervisor is attending to within these embodied conversations.

Figure 3.1 The three axes of Embodied Presence during inquiry

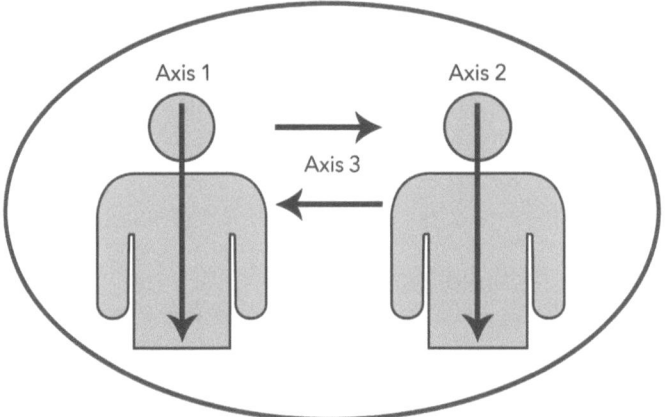

- **Connecting with self (Axis 1):** Embodied presence begins with anchoring awareness in present moment inner experience, including the whole body from the head right down into the feet and seat, tuning into and tracking the changing nature of body, thoughts and emotions, and finding a sense of steadiness within. This felt sense is an internal body awareness that is more than emotion and body sensation; it requires space and attention to tune into, and communicates a deeper wisdom held within the body, a holistic intuitive knowing.[104] Stephen Porges places great significance on this felt sense, so much so that he encourages a move from Descartes's statement, *"I think, therefore I am"*, to *"I feel myself. Therefore I am."*[105]
- **Encouraging the supervisee to bring internal awareness (Axis 2):** From this grounded place, the supervisor opens to the supervisee and their experience – what has happened, what is happening right now, and supports the supervisee to also connect with their experience, promoting reflection, development and understanding. With practice and experience the supervisee is likely to be engaging in this process without so many prompts from the supervisor.

---

104 Gendlin,1996; Teasdale, 2022
105 Porges, 2022, p. 5

- **The relational piece (Axis 3):** As the supervisor begins to resonate with the supervisee's inner experience, there is a sense of attunement, which gives the supervisee a sense of 'feeling felt'. Dan Siegel states this is crucial *"to feel vibrant and alive, to feel understood and to feel at peace."*[106] This links with the concept of neuroception,[107] whereby this feeling of alignment influences the other person's nervous system, tapping into their social engagement system so they feel a sense of safety.

Bringing it all together, the supervisor's awareness is anchored within their own body while sensing the unfolding and emerging experience, both inner and outer, including sensing what is unfolding within the interpersonal space itself. So embodied presence is a relational process. This fine-tuned awareness then supports present-moment responsiveness as the supervisor discerns what is needed moment by moment within the mutual inquiry.

Developing, cultivating and sustaining Embodied Presence

The supervisor brings an intentionality to the cultivation of embodied presence before, during and after each supervision session, for example:

Before: The supervisor 'clears the decks' so they can be truly present, saying to themselves, *"This is what I am doing right now"*. They take time to prepare through practice, to tune into the supervisee, the themes of their supervision and intentions for this session. The supervisory relationship is held in high regard, with the supervisor establishing conditions that enable them to give their full attention to the upcoming supervision session.

During: The supervisor is modelling and encouraging this way of being present during the mutual inquiry within the supervision session. This supports the supervisee in cultivating this way of being within the supervision space and in their work and life. We explore Mutual Inquiry in depth in Chapter 4.

After: The supervisor takes a few moments after supervision to pause and reflect, tuning into their felt sense now, noticing any resonance from the discussions, perhaps deliberately cultivating a particular attitudinal quality, and considering what, if anything, they want to bring forward to the next contact with this supervisee. The supervisor also encourages the supervisee to engage in embodied post-supervision reflections.

---

106 Siegel, 2007, p. 1
107 Porges, 2022

Summary

1. As part of the warp, the Container is an essential aspect of what makes MBS mindfulness-based. It is the interconnectedness of all four of the elements that contribute to the stability and robustness of the Container.
2. The elements are cultivated through the supervisor's personal practice as they attend to their intrapersonal experience, and they bring this same mindful awareness into the interpersonal realm as they engage in mutual inquiry with the supervisee.
3. We explored each of the four elements in turn:
   - Intention
     - Intentionality shapes present moment choices, and aligning with intentions means actions are purposeful, directed and true to values.
     - Intention shows up in supervision implicitly as it guides and informs the supervisor's decisions and actions. It is also explicitly brought into the content of supervision as it relates to the supervisee and their MB work.
   - Integrity
     - Integrity within MBS has three main elements: safeguarding the recipient through the development of ethical practice, staying true to the underlying philosophical and theoretical principles of the supervisee's work, and as a key component of the supervisory relationship itself.
     - Integrity links to the normative function of supervision and is upheld by the content of the Belt.
     - Cultivation of a safe, professional and boundaried supervision space is crucial in supporting integrity. This includes a recognition of the inherent power imbalance between the supervisee and supervisor.
   - Compassion/Wisdom
     - Compassion/Wisdom points to important attitudinal qualities that infuse MBS.
     - Compassion arises as the supervisor connects with the vulnerability of the supervisee, and they draw on their wisdom to discern the most skilful action to support the supervisee's growth and development.
     - Both qualities of compassion and wisdom are essential and finding the balance between them is part of the dance of MBS.
   - Embodied Presence
     - Embodied Presence is the present moment awareness of inner experience, awareness of the supervisee and their experience, and the felt sense moment by moment of the relationship between supervisor and supervisee.
     - Embodied Presence is a relational process imbued with particular attitudinal qualities and is the heart of mutual inquiry.

- It helps build a sense of safety and trust within the relationship. It supports the supervisee to cultivate this way of being within supervision and within their work and their lives.

Reflective questions

Reflect upon a time in supervision **as a supervisee** when you experienced one of the elements of the container. What was that experience like, and what was the impact? You might like to repeat this for each of the elements: Intention, Integrity, Compassion/Wisdom and Embodied Presence.

As a supervisor, how are you cultivating these elements in your mindfulness practice, work and life?

If you are already supervising or when you do, reflect upon a moment where you brought one of the elements into the supervision space. What was the experience like? What was the impact?

Where are your areas for growth and development in the context of creating a mindful Container? When did you last take this to your supervision or supra-vision?

Moving forward, how could you continue to cultivate the elements of the Container outside of supervision? In your practice? Pre- and post-supervision? Perhaps you have a specific intention?

References

Ali, D. (2017). Safe spaces and brave spaces: Historical context and recommendations for student affairs professionals. *NASPA Research and Policy Institute*, 2, 1-13.

Arao, B., & Clemens, K. (2013). From safe spaces to brave spaces: A new way to frame dialogue around diversity and social justice. In L. M. Landreman (Ed.), *The art of effective facilitation* (pp. 135-150). Routledge.

Baer, R., & Nagy, L. M. (2017). Professional ethics and personal values in mindfulness-based programs: A secular psychological perspective. In L. M. Monteiro, J. F. Compson, & F. M. Musten (Eds.), *Practitioner's Guide to Ethics and Mindfulness-Based Interventions* (pp. 87-111). Springer.

Crane, R. S. (2017). Implementing mindfulness in the mainstream: Making the path by walking it. *Mindfulness*, 8, 585-594. https://doi.org/10.1007/s12671-016-0632-7

Crane, R. S., Callen-Davies, R., Francis, A., Francis, D., Gibbs, P., Mulligan, B., O'Neill, B., Williams, N. K. P., Waupoose, M., & Vallejo, Z. (2023). Mindfulness-based stress reduction for our time: A curriculum that is up to the task. *Global Advances in Integrative Medicine and Health*, 12. https://doi.org/10.1177/27536130231162604

Dalai Lama. (2005). *Essence of the heart sutra: The Dalai Lama's heart of wisdom teachings*. Wisdom Publications.

Edmondson, A. (1999). Psychological safety and learning behavior in work teams. *Administrative Science Quarterly*, 44(2), 350-383. https://doi.org/10.2307/2666999

Evans, A., Crane, R., Cooper, L., Mardula, J., Wilks, J., Surawy, C., Kenny, M., & Kuyken, W. (2015). A framework for supervision for mindfulness-based teachers: A space for embodied mutual inquiry. *Mindfulness*, 6, 572-581. https://doi.org/10.1007/s12671-014-0292-4

Evans, A., Griffith, G. M., & Smithson, J. (2024). What do supervisors' and supervisees' think about mindfulness-based supervision? A grounded theory study. *Mindfulness*, 15, 63–79. https://doi.org/10.1007/s12671-023-02280-8

Feldman, C., & Kuyken, W. (2019). *Mindfulness: Ancient wisdom meets modern psychology*. Guilford Publications.

Feldman, C., & Kuyken, W. (2011). Compassion in the landscape of suffering. *Contemporary Buddhism*, 12(1), 143-155. https://doi.org/10.1080/14639947.2011.564831

Gendlin, E. T. (1990). The small steps of the therapy process: How they come and how to help them come. In G. Lietaer, J. Rombauts, & R. Van Balen (Eds.), *Client-centered and experiential psychotherapy in the nineties* (pp. 205-224). Leuven University Press.

Gendlin, E. T. (1996). *Focusing-oriented psychotherapy: A manual of the experiential method*. Guilford Press.

Gilbert, P. (2010). *The compassionate mind: A new approach to life challenges*. New Harbinger Publications.

Goetz, J. L., Keltner, D., & Simon-Thomas, E. (2010). Compassion: An evolutionary analysis and empirical review. *Psychological Bulletin, 136*(3), 351-374. https://psycnet.apa.org/doi/10.1037/a0018807

Goldstein, J. (2016). *Mindfulness: A practical guide to awakening*. Sounds True.

Hardy, K. V., & Bobes, T. (Eds.). (2016). *Culturally sensitive supervision and training: Diverse perspectives and practical applications*. Routledge.

Inskipp, F., & Proctor, B. (1993). *The art, craft and tasks of counselling supervision: Making the most of supervision* (Part 1). Cascade Publications.

Inskipp, F., & Proctor, B. (1995). *The art, craft and tasks of counselling supervision: Becoming a supervisor* (Part 2). Cascade Publications.

International Mindfulness Integrity Network. (2024). Ethics and standards document. *A framework for the integrity of mindfulness-based programs. A living document* (3rd ed.). https://iminetwork.org/

Kabat-Zinn, J. (2013). *Full catastrophe living, how to cope with stress, pain and illness using mindfulness meditation* (Revised edition). Piatkus.

Kabat-Zinn, J. (2011). Some reflections on the origins of MBSR, skillful means, and the trouble with maps. *Contemporary Buddhism, 12*(1), 281–306. https://doi.org/10.1080/14639947.2011.564844

Koster, F., Heynekamp, J., & Norton, V. (Eds.). (2023). *Mindful communication: Speaking and listening with wisdom and compassion*. Routledge.

Porges, S. W. (2022). Polyvagal theory: A science of safety. *Frontiers in Integrative Neuroscience, 16,* 871227. https://doi.org/10.3389/fnint.2022.871227

Segal, Z. V., Williams, J. M. G., & Teasdale, J. D. (2013). *Mindfulness-based cognitive therapy for depression* (2nd ed.). Guilford Press.

Shapiro, D. H. (1992). A preliminary study of long-term meditators: Goals, effects, religious orientation, cognitions. *Journal of Transpersonal Psychology, 24*(1), 23–39.

Siegel, D. J. (2007). Reflections on the mindful brain: A brief overview. Adapted from Siegel, D. J, *The mindful brain: Reflection and attunement in the cultivation of well-being*. W. W. Norton. Retrieved January 10, 2025, from https://www.openground.com.au/assets/Documents-Openground/Articles/0e39aa6bc0/reflections-on-the-mindful-brain-siegel.pdf

Strauss, C., Taylor, B. L., Gu, J., Kuyken, W., Baer, R., Jones, F., & Cavanagh, K. (2016). What is compassion and how can we measure it? A review of definitions and measures. *Clinical Psychology Review, 47,* 15-27. https://doi.org/10.1016/j.cpr.2016.05.004

Teasdale, J. (2022). *What happens in mindfulness: Inner awakening and embodied cognition*. Guilford Press.

Van den Brink, E., Koster, F., & Norton, V. (2018). *A practical guide to mindfulness-based compassionate living: Living with heart*. Routledge. https://doi.org/10.4324/9781315268491

Vekaria, B., Harrydwar, L., Thomas, T., & Ononaiye, M. (2023a). Supervisee perspectives on improving cultural responsivity in clinical supervision. *Clinical Psychology Forum, 1*(371), 66-76. https://doi.org/10.53841/bpscpf.2023.1.371.66

Venerable Khandro Rinpoche, October 25, 2021, *Compassion and wisdom* https://www.lionsroar.com/compassion-and-wisdom/

Vygotsky, L. S. (1978). *Mind in society: The development of higher psychological processes* (Vol. 86). Harvard University Press.

Woods, S. L. (2009). Training professionals in mindfulness: The heart of teaching. In F. Didonna (Ed.), *Clinical handbook of mindfulness* (pp. 463-475). Springer.

Woods, S. L., Rockman, P., & Collins, E. (2019). *Mindfulness-based cognitive therapy: embodied presence & inquiry in practice*. New Harbinger Publications.

Yang, L. (2017). *Awakening together: The spiritual practice of inclusivity and community*. Wisdom Publications.

Chapter 4
Mutual Inquiry

Mutual Inquiry is one of the three warp threads within the MBS framework. Along with the other warp threads of the Container and Space, it is what makes it mindfulness-based. Inquiry is a pedagogy at the heart of MBAs and MBS. In their research, Alison and colleagues write about relational inquiry as "... *an embodied conversation grounded in open curiosity and the practice of mindfulness (e.g. connected to body sensations, slowed down with time for pausing)*."[108] It is both structured and fluid.

In this chapter, we will examine inquiry more closely, as if we are placing Mutual Inquiry and the different aspects of the process under the microscope. We will organise the chapter around the RIMBS model, discussed in Chapter 2 (Figure 4.1). We will build upon these different dimensions of inquiry, drawing upon our knowledge and experience of MBS.

---

108 Evans et al., 2024, p. 70

Figure 4.1 The RIMBS model

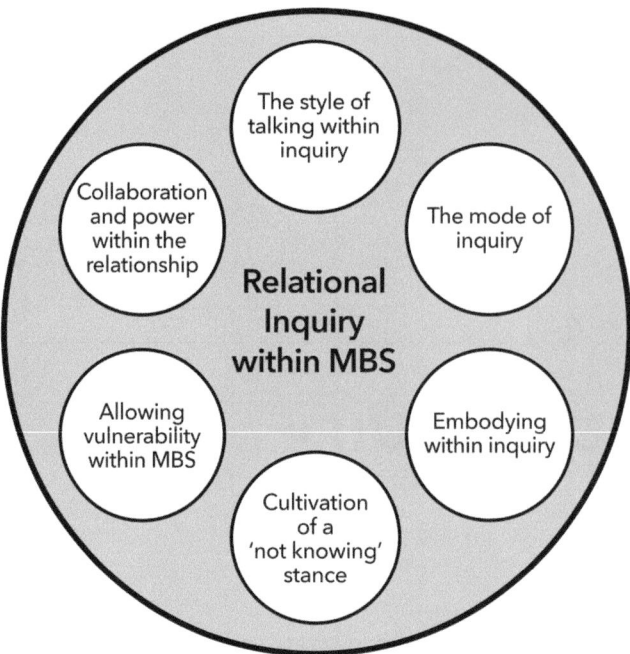

As we move through the chapter, we will give examples to bring a practical and tangible understanding of the inquiry process. Woods et al. view inquiry as *"a process-orientated contemplative dialogue"*[109] and stress that it does not rely solely upon specific methodology. So, we do not offer a step-by-step guide, as the process is alive, dynamic, and focused on the present moment, but we provide pointers and structures. If we return to our dance metaphor, we offer some choreography and encourage freer expression within the aliveness of that moment and that relationship.

The style of talking within inquiry

In her MBS research, Alison found particular speaking styles apparent in MBS, including pauses, unfinished sentences, taking time to reflect and think aloud, and frequent open-ended questions. We build upon this research and offer in this section some of the different styles of talk that we have observed and experienced within MBS, beginning with a summary of key styles of talk:

- Asking questions – the supervisor uses questions to invite exploration and respond to what supervisees bring.
- Paraphrasing – the supervisor uses paraphrasing to show they are listening, clarifying their understanding, and mirroring the supervisee's words back to them.

---

109 Woods et al., 2016, p. 3

- Normalising of experiences – not simply to reassure but also to widen perspective so it is more than just the supervisee's experience.
- Reframing – offering a different perspective and seeing how it lands, a kind of floating possibility.
- Emphasising and summarising, using phrases such as, *"I think what I hear ..." "It sounds like ..."*

These styles have an investigative quality, offering a moment to reflect and consider. They support exploration, revealing, and going deeper, and help shine a light on places the supervisee may not immediately see, e.g. strengths and bias. Our adapted version of an experiential learning process,[110] outlined in Chapter 2, can be a helpful way of seeing the stages of what is loosely a cyclical process, with much back and forth, during a supervision session. We use this framework here to examine how a supervisor might use questions during an MBS session (Figure 4.2).

Figure 4.2 The flow of the inquiry process within an MBS session

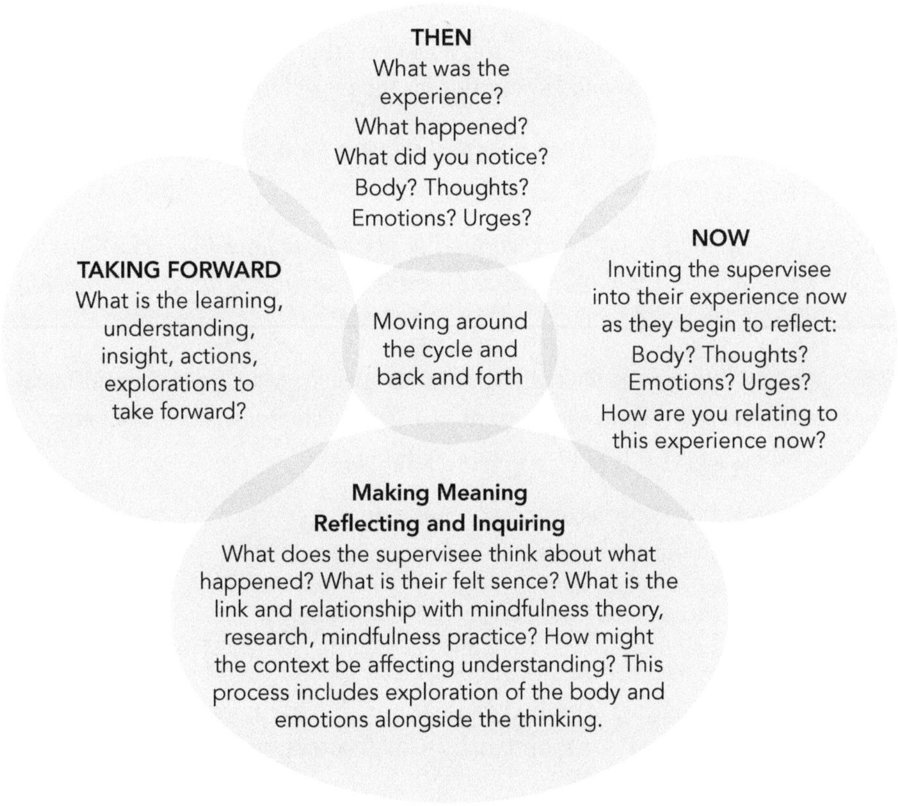

THEN
What was the experience?
What happened?
What did you notice?
Body? Thoughts?
Emotions? Urges?

NOW
Inviting the supervisee into their experience now as they begin to reflect:
Body? Thoughts?
Emotions? Urges?
How are you relating to this experience now?

Making Meaning Reflecting and Inquiring
What does the supervisee think about what happened? What is their felt sense? What is the link and relationship with mindfulness theory, research, mindfulness practice? How might the context be affecting understanding? This process includes exploration of the body and emotions alongside the thinking.

TAKING FORWARD
What is the learning, understanding, insight, actions, explorations to take forward?

Moving around the cycle and back and forth

---

110 Which draws on the work of Kolb, 2015 and Segal et al., 2013, p. 251

The use of questions within the inquiry process

We offer an example from MBA teaching to illustrate the use of questions within the inquiry process at these different stages. In this example, the THEN and NOW are intertwined, so we have merged them. The process follows the cycle but also loops back to different stages. We have not included all the interactions and speech but have chosen to highlight the questions used by the supervisor.

Issue the supervisee is bringing to MBS

This is a moment of teaching from session five of MBCT. A participant in the group became upset after the working with difficulty practice.

Experience THEN and NOW

The supervisee begins by describing the situation and context. They also highlighted what they were finding difficult, namely that, as well as being upset, the participant was angry with the supervisee for inviting this working with difficulty. The supervisee named their concern for the individual and what was happening in the group.

In this partial transcript, we focus on the questions that the supervisor was asking, intending to bring curiosity and exploration to the experience:

> Supervisor – *"Are you OK if we slow that down a bit and unravel some of those aspects?"*

> Supervisor – *"The first bit I was wondering about was how you picked up the anger, that first point you made. What were they saying? What was happening in their body?"*

> The supervisee responds with the content of speech, tone, posture, and facial expression and takes time to reflect on the event. They also speak of being aware of the group waiting to see what will happen.

> The supervisor gives a brief summary, and compassion is conveyed through tone of voice and facial expression.

> Supervisor – *"And at that time, what was happening for you? And it may be being evoked now as we speak?"* (pointing towards the NOW inquiry)

> The supervisee responds with body sensations that are noticed then, and *"so I have that now too"* – rubbing belly – their attention focusing more on body sensations.

> *"But I know what I had at the time as well"*, *"Fuzzy in the head"*, *"Thinking, oh gosh, I don't know where to go with this?"*

Supervisor – *"And any emotion?"*

After a bit of pausing, the supervisee identified some emotions and thoughts.

Supervisor – *"And any urges to act?"*

Immediately, the supervisee responds by remembering the urge to want to make it right.

The supervisor picks up on body language, bringing in humour and compassion and says to the supervisee, *"I don't know if you realise you did a little puff of air when speaking"*, and the supervisor does one too – coming alongside the supervisee.

Supervisor – *"And if you take a moment to breathe now – feeling your feet on the ground ..."* (little pause)

Supervisor – *"So where did you go next?"*

The supervisee responded that as they were reflecting together now, *"my response was okay, but I went into explaining."*

Making Meaning

They start unravelling this experience that the supervisee has identified as slipping into explaining.

The supervisor offers another way of phrasing this: *"Like you were offering a sort of supportive rationale?"*

The supervisee agrees and thinks they did too much of this.

Supervisor – *"What makes you feel it was too much?"*

On reflection, the supervisee felt they were avoiding staying with the participant. They also include some ways they responded that they felt were okay. But overall, they feel they could have stayed more with the NOW experience.

Supervisor offers – *"So maybe the rationale came a little bit too quickly?"*

The supervisee agrees and can see their underlying wish to make it right.

Supervisor – *"What might have been other intentions for bringing in a rationale?"* (The supervisee is being a bit critical of their intervention, and the supervisor is helping them to widen their perspective)

The supervisee speaks about wanting to acknowledge to the participants that this is a strange practice.

The supervisor agrees (coming alongside the supervisee).

The supervisee recognizes wanting to respond to the whole group. As they reflect aloud, the supervisee sees, *"Oh, I might have done this by asking the whole group – I can see this when I think about it now."*

The supervisor draws out the intention to help people gain a framework and understanding while recognising there may be different ways to do that. The supervisor also draws attention to the supervisee's own questioning of whether the choice came from a more reactive mode on this occasion.

The supervisee comes to NOW: *"I remember this group has coped with difficulty, and I can see I lost some trust in myself at that moment. I forgot this in the heat of the moment."*

The supervisor affirms – *"Yes, and this happens."*

TAKING FORWARD

Supervisor – *"And I wonder what might support you in future times, to feel resourced in those moments, especially in session 5."*

The supervisee reflects on how they can prepare—connecting with the themes again, reminding, trusting in the practice, reminding themselves where the group is, and trusting them; *"I don't have to fix it this session."*

The supervisor – summarizes and emphasizes the embodied sense of being with difficulty that comes from mindfulness practice.

THEN

The supervisor—then goes back to THEN to ask about participant's experience of the practice and whether that was inquired into. There is a little exploration about this, and the supervisee identifies another action to take forward, e.g. spend plenty of time in the home practice inquiry in the next session on working with difficulty practice.

NOW

Supervisor – *"So inviting you now to take a little pause ... Coming into your body ... noticing body ... thoughts ... emotions ... Breathing ... What's around now?"*

Supervisee – *"It was all okay".*

Supervisor – *"And the body?"*

The supervisee also noticed some excitement about the next session. *"Letting myself off the hook, it wasn't so bad."*

Supervisor – *"Yes, a little bit of friendliness towards yourself".*

TAKING FORWARD

Supervisor – *"And just before we finish, if there were some things to take forward from this exploration, some learnings. Is there anything you take forward from our dialogue today?"*

The supervisee pulls out several things, noticing reactivity in the moment, which they may play within the next session, spotting their urge to fix and staying open to inquiring more.

Supervisor – *"And in relation to that urge, I wonder if there is anywhere in your body that helps you to see that coming up?"*

The supervisee recognizes belly and head.

Supervisor – *"You mentioned these two places earlier."*

There is a bit more reflection from the supervisee.

The supervisor puts a hand on the belly and head and says, *"So here are your cues, going in remembering belly and head".*

Joint laughter.

Supervisor – *"Does that feel OK to finish here?"*

This example shows how the supervisor steers the inquiry back and forth and around the cycle. We have emphasized the talk here, but more is happening in these other warp threads of inquiry. In our MBS training, we often get questions about what is meant by the making meaning and taking forward part of the cycle.

This meaning-making process can be misunderstood as a more conceptual analytical process. In our use of this cycle within MBS, we are very much speaking about making meaning as an exploratory process with all the different warp threads of inquiry. This process encourages exploring the body experience and the emotions alongside thinking. It uses all the ways of talking described in this section: open questions, deep listening, paraphrasing, clarifying, reframing, and summarising. Sometimes, the supervisor is floating possibilities, lightly offering interpretations and observations, often to give a kinder possibility to the meaning-making. At times, the supervisor brings in more challenging questions that stretch the supervisee's view to widen and open alternative perspectives. They may draw upon theory in this process too. All of this is in the spirit of both the supervisee and the supervisor receiving these words, reflecting, pausing, seeing what resonates for them and coming to ways of understanding the experience.

The taking forward aspect may come out at any point in the supervision session, as well as towards the end of the session. It supports the supervisee in reflecting upon what learning, understanding, insight, actions, or explorations to take forward into their work, practice, and life. There are numerous ways to do this, from practical actions to further reflection. We offer some examples to give a sense of the scope of what might be taken forward: how the MBP session fits together, how to lead a particular practice or exercise, resources to read/listen to, personal mindfulness practice pointers, aspects of inquiry to play with in MB work, a feeling of confidence, ways of staying connected with the body when speaking and listening, the intentions for MB work – broad and specific, mindful ways of being in relationship with another, bringing the attitudinal foundations into life, safeguarding actions, actions from feedback and continued reflection on discoveries within MBS.

The supervisor might move to this stage by inviting a pause with a reflective question such as: What do you take forward from today? What is the most important thing for you to remember? What will you do differently as a result? What are you taking away from this supervision? The supervisee takes time to reflect on what is important for them; the supervisor may also point out something that they have witnessed in the supervision and wonder if this might also be something the supervisee carries forward, such as naming the strengths that have been identified. This process encourages any impact and learning from MBS to seep into their work, practice, and life – it may be one of those moments in supervision when the supervisee writes a few words as a reminder, which they can then reflect on later and expand upon in their own way.

The mode of inquiry

The inquiry is a conversation that comes from a different mode than many other life conversations. There is a deliberate stance of moving into a mode that invites tuning into what is happening within the body, taking a decentred perspective of emotion and thinking, and noting urges and impulses without needing to react. Whilst conceptual knowing is very useful in life, within MBS there is also foregrounding of a 'felt sense' way of knowing.

John Teasdale has written in detail about these different ways of knowing.[111] In brief, conceptual knowing tends to be the default mode. It has the characteristics of goal-seeking and is helpful for task completion, so we can see how we might draw upon this way of attending to experience as we move through life. Whereas a holistic intuitive knowing is associated with experiential and embodied qualities where experiences are 'felt' and 'sensed'. This 'felt' sense way of knowing can open up new perspectives, providing a different lens on experience, leading to

---

[111] Teasdale, 2022

new understandings and possibilities. In the previous section, we discussed using questions within MBS. These questions can support this way of knowing; they are not designed to have a conceptual answer but to invite more attention to the body, a more spacious awareness, and access to this felt sense.

When supervisors and supervisees move into this mode of exploration, they often find something different to just staying on a more conceptual level. There is a more mindful mode, and this inquiry in MBS is another form of practising mindfulness within a relational dialogue. This mode links strongly with the embodying aspect of MBS, which we will discuss in the next section. It is often hard to find words to articulate what is meant by this more intuitive way of being with experience, so we offer an example to illustrate.

Imagine a supervisee coming to supervision and being asked a question such as, *"What do you think was happening when ..."*

Then imagine a slightly different scenario where the supervisee is invited to pause for a moment, dropping into body and taking a moment to feel into their sense of what was happening in that moment. What comes up? What do they notice?

So, in the first example, the supervisee may take a moment to think, reflect, and ponder, and some fruitful explorations may follow, which might go in all sorts of directions. This is great and likely to be a useful conversation that could well support the supervisee's learning.

In the second example, there is another option. The supervisor is inviting a more deliberate shift into another mode, slowing down and accessing a more holistic way of exploring the experience that connects with the body and emotions, often connecting more with the present moment, and potentially giving access to this embodied way of knowing. As they move below the radar of thought, the supervisee can discover things that were not available to them in the more conceptual mode.

We are not suggesting that conceptual knowing doesn't have a place, but accessing this other mode can be enormously helpful. It can also help to 'bed in' conceptual understandings. For example, as people begin to practise mindfulness, they come across the concept of curiosity. An understanding develops about what curiosity might mean and what it looks like in experience. And over time, as this curious attitude is repeatedly practised, it becomes known less as an idea and more as part of how one is. It becomes more embedded into the fabric of being; it is known bodily, is available, and doesn't require thinking. Within MBS these repeated explorations support embedding knowledge more deeply than an initial conceptual knowing.

So, how is this mode accessed within MBS? The supervisor encourages a non-verbal space within MBS. There are challenges in finding words to describe a more somatic experience, so the supervisor will likely use bodily gestures, expressions, and tone of voice to convey and invite more of this felt sense. The supervisor can intentionally invite the supervisee into an exploration mode which is part of how they make meaning.

Let's give an example from an MBS session to illustrate:

Example – moving into a different mode

This example is taken from a supervisor's perspective of working with a supervisee who brought mindfulness into their work with a client.

A supervisee was talking about a so-called 'challenging client'.

When the supervisor asked what was it about the client's behaviour that had bothered them and that they had found challenging, the supervisee said they didn't know but felt a lot of strong emotions.

The supervisor asked how it felt in the body, and the supervisee could locate a tightness and holding in the throat and chest, with tears arriving quickly. The supervisee recognized that it linked to old patterns, a theme they often had difficulty with (they didn't share the story as this wasn't necessary).

The supervisee then acknowledged shame about this, shame that they were judging the client when, indeed, it was more about them, not the client. The supervisor invited them to return to the body, to the tightness and holding, and just notice. Together, they tracked the sensations for a few moments and noticed they started to subside.

The supervisee recognized how powerful this was, and they moved on with much more compassion to dialogue about how best to respond to the client.

This example illustrates how coming to the body as a place to explore opened up new understanding. The body gave the supervisee some crucial insights into what was happening to them underneath this experience. By spending time in this mode, they could not only recognise but also allow these feelings and sensations to be there and then see them move on. There was no need to go into the narrative and understand why they felt like this; there was enough known to consider a different response to the client. This mode of inquiry supports an inner inquiry, which we continue to build upon in the next section around embodying within inquiry.

There may be times within the supervision session where the supervisor points out what they are observing to the supervisee, for example, particular body postures, movements within the body, facial expressions, and the speed, tone, and volume of speech. The intention here is to give the supervisee access to their body, any messages, and any underlying knowledge that may become available. It might go something along the lines of *"I don't know if you are aware, but your body is moving between an open stance to having your head down with more of a frown as you speak about ..."* taking a little pause for the supervisee to bring their attention to the body and reflect. So then, the inquiry can continue in whatever direction it might go.

Similarly, the supervisor may sometimes offer their bodily reaction/felt sense to what is being discussed. This needs some care, as it may just be the supervisor's response, but it can support in several ways. Firstly, it invites the supervisee to stop and see what is happening in their body/felt sense. Secondly, the two often resonate, with the supervisor picking up on the underlying emotional or felt sense. It is important that the intention here, on the part of the supervisor, is to open up possibilities for the supervisee and give space to see if there is any resonance or not. The supervisor has their own supra-vision to work in more detail with their reactions and responses.

At times in supervision, metaphors and images can support different ways of knowing. The supervisor or supervisee might bring in a metaphor or image during the exploration. This is usually a spontaneous arising during the inquiry that aids an understanding or insight into something often words cannot express in quite the same way. If it's the supervisor offering an image or metaphor, they then pause to see if it resonates with the supervisee or not and discern if they want to use it to go a little deeper into the inquiry. If the supervisee brings in a metaphor, the supervisor helps them expand if they wish to.

Embodying within inquiry

As we named in Chapter 3, the Embodied Presence element of the Container provides the foundation for embodying within inquiry. Here, we look specifically at some aspects of embodying within inquiry, which are often linked to the mode during MBS. We bring more of a microscopic view of the actual MBS session in three areas: what embodying looks like in the body, the attitudes, and the embodying of mindfulness's underpinnings. These qualities, behaviours and actions would be what the supervisor is aspiring to bring into the session and encouraging the supervisee to do so as well. This would be conveyed explicitly through active guidance and implicitly through modelling on the supervisor's part, hoping that this supports the supervisee in moving into this way of being.

Firstly, a reminder about what we are speaking about when we use the term *embodying*. Embodying within inquiry includes being aware of one's own inner experience, steadiness and responsiveness, acting in ways aligned with attitudes, e.g. patience, non-striving, trust, and being authentic to one's way of being in the world.[112] Zindel Segal, Mark Williams and John Teasdale speak about the embodied qualities that the teacher uses when they lead the inquiry, which *"… constitute the essential foundation on which the process of effective inquiry rests."*[113] These qualities include being genuine, warm, curious, interested and not knowing. Woods et al. talk about embodying mindfulness as being *"a pragmatic attitude to living life fully"*[114] which comes from one's mindfulness practice and life.

Suppose we imagine what we would observe in the supervisor's body if a supervision session was being viewed. It would be likely that steadiness in the body would be seen throughout the session, even during more challenging or stimulating moments. Even if only the top half of the supervisor were visible, there would be a sense that their feet were on the ground. The top half of the body would be open and upright. This does not mean an enforced stillness; the body would still be making natural movements and gestures using the body and facial expressions, so it's not a motionless or expressionless stance. The supervisor would display engagement and presence, looking at the supervisee, and not distracted by external events or demands from other electronic devices. It would be clear that they were listening closely as they repeated back to the supervisee, a mirroring of active expressions, nods, and gestures in relation to the supervisee's sharing – a calm and measured listening. The steadiness and holding of pace would also be seen through the spaces for the supervisee to pause, think, speak, and take their time without the supervisor jumping in and filling the space.

The next area of embodying is the embodying of attitudes, often felt and sensed but also conveyed through the supervisor's behaviour and actions. We focus here on two attitudes, curiosity (interest and willingness to investigate experience) and compassion (care and kindness), which are particularly pertinent for inquiry. Susan Woods, Patricia Rockman and Evan Collins also highlight these two attitudes as essential to the embodied mindful presence within inquiry.[115] We might see curiosity being embodied through this use of questions that we have previously outlined. The supervisor conveys a genuine interest through these questions and their responses to the supervisee. The supervisee is not rushed onto something else, and there is a willingness to stay with explorations and let them unfold with a sense of wonder. The tone of voice and body posture convey wanting to know more with an aliveness and vitality. Compassion is embodied in what is said, as well as in non-verbal

---

112 Evans et al., 2024
113 Segal et al., 2013, p. 256
114 Woods et al., 2016, p. 6
115 Woods et al., 2019

communication and behaviour. For example, in a session, the supervisor will show warmth and kindness with smiles, sometimes use sounds to express empathy and be alongside (a sigh, an argh, ooh, hmm, ouch), ask about well-being, and between sessions, the way exchanges such as email are conducted. The supervisor is showing an understanding of what is happening for the supervisee in their context.

The embodying of the underpinnings of mindfulness is happening much of the time. The supervisor is embodying living a life with awareness. They bring this into the session in terms of paying attention, both focused and widening out, recognising what is happening for themselves and the supervisee, and between them, having awareness and insight into their own behaviour. They also consider that they may be unaware of things and have blind spots, so they remain open. The supervisor is also embodying the next layer of awareness – one's relationship with experience. With awareness of the relationship with experience, the supervisor can begin to have choices and bring the discerning dimension of mindfulness to support the making of skilful choices. Two other mindfulness underpinnings are embodied within MBS, which we discuss in subsequent sections of this chapter, turning towards (vulnerability section) and non-fixing/letting be (not-knowing section).

We set out an example here of a situation that occurs quite frequently in MBS: a supervisee arrives in a reactive mode due to events prior to the session.

Example – embodying

In this example, a supervisee arrives for supervision a few minutes late, having had problems finding the Zoom link. They look hot and flustered, and when asked how they are, they move into a rapid and detailed description of the events preceding supervision. The supervisor is finding ways not to get scooped up into the supervisee's story and emotions, but equally not shutting them down and making them feel they have got something wrong, meeting them where they are with compassion. The supervisor offers a steady presence, calm and spacious. After a short period of listening, the supervisor comes in quite firmly to suggest a pause. They choose to guide a pause to help support the supervisee, rather than a silent moment. They then invite a brief inquiry before checking in on the agenda for the session. The supervisee has a moment to consider if they want to bring the situation they arrived with to the session. The possibility of turning towards this experience is still there, but the supervisor is embodying how this might happen within MBS from a more spacious place of actively choosing. The supervisor is attuning to where and how to place awareness. This differs from how a friend, peer or colleague might meet this experience. Something different is embodied – holding a space that can meet what is here from a wider, more grounded perspective.

In this example, there were ways that the supervisor had set things up before the supervision session to support embodying to be more possible in the moment:

- setting up their physical space: putting other things down, clearing the desk and screen, and checking that they had a good view and sound
- setting up comfort: the chair was positioned well, feet were on the ground, they visited the toilet, had a drink, stretched, and were warm enough, all helping them to be present
- checking the supervisee's notes, bringing them to mind, and checking in with intention
- taking a mini practice to connect with an anchor point and body and bring friendliness towards the supervisee

Looking back at the diagram from Chapter 3 (Figure 3.1), we are reminded of the three axes of Embodied Presence within the inquiry process (Figure 4.3).

Figure 4.3 The three axes of Embodied Presence during inquiry

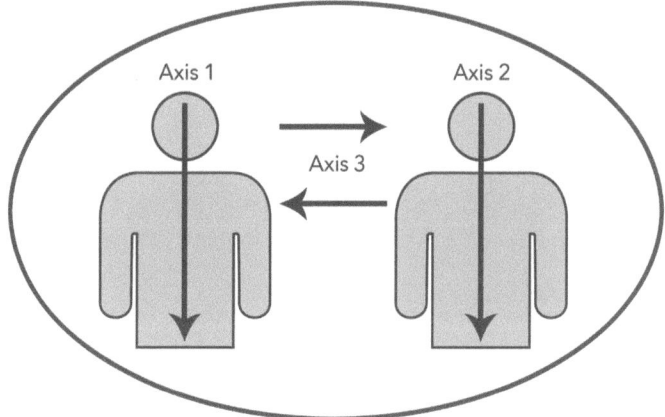

The supervisor is aware of inside experience and brings a steadiness and willingness to explore inner and outer experience. To open to the supervisee, the supervisor must first know their own inner experience and be steady and grounded with that, accessing their own body, emotions and thoughts – the whole sphere of experience as they listen and process. From that embodied presence, the supervisor can then open to and inquire into the supervisee's experience – what has happened and what is happening right now.

This mutuality supports them both in staying in this embodying mode. The exchange between the two, embodies warmth, curiosity, and compassion. There may be times when the embodying is coming more from the supervisor to supervise, for example, if the supervisee is newer to mindfulness and this mode of being in conversation with another, but the encouragement is for both to be actively embodying. It is a mutual endeavour that supports mindful communication. Mindful inquiry involves making a genuine, moment-to-moment connection with each other and engaging in a collaborative relationship.

MBS is a place for supervisees to explore this embodying while in relationship with another. The supervisor is modelling embodying, and using the same inquiry process the supervisee may use with their participants/in their work. This embodying is cultivated within the supervisor and the supervisee and then transferred into MB work, as named by a supervisor in MBS research, *"It's that kind of cascade, if you like, if you have an embodied supervisor, you are more likely to have an embodied supervisee, which will then carry that into the group."*[116] MBS supports supervisees in finding an embodied way of knowing so they can stay open and curious in the midst of their mindfulness work.

Cultivation of a 'not knowing' stance

Earlier in this chapter, we showed that MBS utilizes asking questions that don't require an answer, which supports this dropping into a 'not knowing' space. As Segal et al. point to in their book, MBA teachers are engaged in a process of guiding discovery, which requires an openness without knowing how the inquiry will unfold, rather than steering it towards a particular outcome or agenda. They use words such as *"trust the process and trust emergence"* to describe this willingness to *"not know"* and *"patience and humility"* as allies for the teacher to develop.[117] Woods et al. speak about *"… not adopting an expert role …"*, *"… allowing each moment to reveal itself, being comfortable with not-knowing and being at ease with uncertainty and transience of all things."*[118]

Fiona Adamson and Jane Brendgen describe being open to emergence and not knowing as one of the meta-skills within mindfulness-based relational supervision. They speak of resting in not-knowing, and point to John Keats's 1817 concept of 'negative capability' to help describe this deliberate cultivation of being with uncertainty. They discuss how negative capability, *"the ability to let go of the need to control, the need to find resolution or answers and to sit in silence, opening to the uncertainty inherent in the present moment"*[119] supports the supervisor and supervisee to rest in more expansive awareness.

---

116   Evans et al., 2024, p. 72
117   Segal et al., 2013, p. 257
118   Woods et al., 2016, p. 6
119   Adamson & Brendgen, 2021, p. 81

So why might this deliberate cultivation of not knowing be an important aspect of the MBS inquiry?

- To offer an open and emergent space.
- The ability to be with uncertainty supports working in the present moment.
- For curiosity to emerge.
- To have other possibilities from our usual preferences and patterns of needing knowledge and certainty.
- To prepare us to be in co-created spaces, e.g. relationships and offering mindfulness in different contexts, where we don't know what people will say, how they will respond, or what their discoveries will be.
- To learn to be in this 'not knowing' stance, not just to tolerate that we don't know, but also to see that it has its own inherent wisdom.
- It requires cultivation, as in many cultures, reason and rational thought are highly valued; it isn't always our personal or culturally familiar stance.

There are several ways that this 'not knowing' stance gets cultivated in MBS, with strong links to giving space and the supervisor being receptive to receiving and cultivating an openness to whatever emerges. They are coming as a supervisor who is not all-knowing; they don't necessarily have ready answers to solve the situations the supervisee is bringing. Just to be clear, this does not mean that they do not offer advice and share knowledge; this is not about being mean-spirited and ungenerous in offers of guidance. But there is a deliberate pause at times, a stepping back from jumping in, to create a space for silence, inquiry, and for the supervisee to make their own discoveries. The following quote illustrates the surprise and unexpected aspects of supervision: *"Supervision should be a conversation you've not had before."*[120]

Very often, the supervisee does know more than the supervisor, for instance, about their context, and their participants/clients/students. Therefore, the attitudes of *beginner's mind* and *humility* can be supportive for the supervisor. Supervisors and supervisees have things they do not know and can be open to what is not known, including preferences and biases. In MBS, there is another person to dialogue with to support these investigations and shine a light on places which might not have been considered. There is a paradoxical nature here; supervisees do want an 'experienced' other to be guided and held by, and the supervisor does not want to come across as an all-knowing 'expert'. This is part of that dance that we have been referring to.

Having some structure, knowledge, clear understandings, experience, and confidence can help the supervisee to move into letting go of the need-to-know and come more to the moment-by-moment unfolding. When a supervisee is new

---

[120] Shohet & Shohet, 2020, p. 205

to practice and bringing mindfulness into their work, they may need structure to gently lean into this 'not knowing' stance. There may be personal and/or cultural backdrops that make this stance less familiar. Feeling safe and secure are good grounders for letting go and opening.

As is being named in this chapter, this is a relational process. We offer an example to illustrate what this might look like within an MBS session.

Example – being with not knowing

A schoolteacher arrives at supervision feeling pulled in different directions throughout their day and over recent weeks/months/years. The tension is strong around the dissonance between their values about what education is versus the curricula and structure they find imposed upon them. They arrive with thoughts and words such as, *"I don't know what to do"*, *"This dissonance is exhausting"*, and *"I don't know whether to leave, ditch my values and aspirations, fight for things to be different; it all goes round and round in my head"*. The supervisor gives space for this to be named, sees how the narratives are feeding distress, so chooses to bring in a pause.

In the words of Adamson and Brendgen about negative capability, the supervisor encourages *"letting go of the need to control (even if just for a moment), the need to find resolution or answers and to sit in silence, opening to the uncertainty inherent in the present moment"*. The supervisor lightly guides this quiet space, supporting grounding through attention to the feet and seat and opening to this uncertainty in the body and feelings. They continue to drop into these pause moments throughout the session, resting and inquiring with a more expansive awareness rather than steering it towards a particular outcome or agenda. The supervisee can listen more deeply to themselves (coming to the felt sense).

At the end of the session, the situation the supervisee is in is still far from ideal; it hasn't been resolved by magic in MBS. However, the supervisee has found more of their inner wisdom, allowing for the mismatch between their values and the need to work within the structures. Not being in a fight to fix it immediately gives some relief from the tension. They begin to feel more creative about resourcing themselves in their environment, which includes self-care at school and home. They discover that this way of reflecting is helpful for making future decisions, instead of searching for an answer, they can first open to the uncertainty, which gives some room for clearer seeing rather than frantically trying to figure it out. This process doesn't happen once in MBS, it gets revisited often and they take this way of reflecting and making discerning choices into life.

Allowing vulnerability within MBS

As the trust grows within the relationship, MBS becomes a place to allow for vulnerability. In Chapter 2, we referred to the work of Brené Brown,[121] who defines vulnerability as uncertainty, risk and emotional exposure. These are areas of experience that we might usually keep more within ourselves or not even approach at all. Within MBS we are bringing particular attitudes and orientations to vulnerability, namely, *Allowing, Turning Toward, Approaching* and *Befriending*. We give some examples of aspects of MBS that might have a tenderness and element of emotional risk:

- The process of coming into supervision in a 1:1 relationship can feel exposing, and many feel nervous at the beginning.
- Being able not to know, express doubts, lack of confidence, being with imperfections.
- Receiving feedback, particularly on more challenging aspects of mindfulness work.
- Viewing recordings of mindfulness work and being seen by another.
- Inquiry in general, especially as it moves deeper into the experience and what is underneath the surface layer.
- Uncovering one's own patterns and habits, becoming more personal.
- Inquiry around cultural awareness and responsiveness.
- Inquiry into blind spots and bias.
- Questioning and critiquing the norms within the field.

Example – bringing vulnerability into MBS

We offer an example from a supervisee in a leadership role within their business. We give a snapshot of some session sections, highlighting the supervisor's words and actions. The supervisee is bringing several challenges in their workplace that they feel fired up about and want to resolve. The supervisor picks up a hint that there is also a lot of stress in other areas of life that are adding to the mix. The supervisor brings this to the supervisee's attention.

"It sounds as if a lot is going on in other areas of your life too".

The supervisee nods

"Shall we take a brief pause moment?"

After the pause the supervisor invites the supervisee to share.

---

[121] Brown, 2012

"Often when a lot is happening in life it has all sorts of impact on us. (Allowing and normalising) *There is no need to share lots of the detail of the actual situation, but I wonder if you would like to spend a moment exploring what is around for you outside of work."* (Inviting turning towards personal vulnerability)

Supervisee agrees and mentions something of their situation, with the supervisor being alert to not needing to go into lengthy explanations.

"What comes up for you now as you speak?" (Approaching)

"Embarrassment" is mentioned, thoughts like *"I just need to get on with it and to stop making a big deal. I'm meant to be a leader for goodness sake. I feel a bit stupid telling you this."* There is less awareness of the body but tension is named.

The supervisor moves into befriending, which they know from previous sessions is not easy for this supervisee. They genuinely feel compassion for the supervisee which they express (Befriending) and explicitly name that they too have those thoughts and feelings at times (Befriending and normalising).

"I wonder what it might be like to allow this to be here at the moment? You don't have to like it but what might it be like to acknowledge that it is here." (Allowing and approaching)

"I may be going a bit far here, but what might it be like to befriend these thoughts, feelings and emotions that are here right now?" (Befriending)

The session continues, and gradually they move back to the original agenda of the work challenges. However, the supervisee now comes from this place of being more in touch with their own inner landscape and how that lens is affecting their perception of the work situation and the choices they can see. The need for inner practice and inquiry is linked with their outer world and actions.

One thing they take forward from supervision is some simple and practical ideas about bringing allowing and befriending into their day. The supervisor guides a brief practice and points them towards some recordings.

These orientations of *Allowing*, *Turning Toward*, *Approaching* and *Befriending* are important aspects of a mindfulness-based approach. As we can see in this example, turning towards in this way can help supervisees get a fuller picture of what is behind the scenes and how it is impacting them, and they can learn to shift orientation towards and lean more into attitudinal qualities such as allowing and befriending. In MBS, supervisors are inviting coming to an inner landscape with a view to that aiding how to meet the outer world. If experience is approached in this manner, there can be increased confidence for the supervisee to support those they meet in their MB work to do so too.

For some, showing vulnerability is seen personally and/or culturally as a sign of weakness. It takes courage to show and be with vulnerability, and it can, in fact, be a strength. There are conditions within MBS that can support, such as, psychological safety, skilful boundaries, and the ability of the supervisor to hold a space for more difficult experiences. MBS is supervision, and the explorations are inquiry-based, not therapy. The establishment of trust is developed through the supervisor's consistency, reliability, competence, positive intentionality, and the establishment of psychological safety and kindness, all of which spring from their mindfulness practice and experience and are part of the Container of mindfulness, which holds the whole process of MBS. The supervisee learns to approach through their own mindfulness practice, which may support them to find the courage to bring more challenging and tender experiences into MBS. There is a mutual vulnerability, implicitly and sometimes explicitly, within a supervision session. Careful timing is required with both the willingness and capacity of both parties to know when to turn towards.

Example – more on bringing vulnerability into MBS

We have mentioned cultural awareness as one place where vulnerability might show up in MBS. I (Alison) had an experience of this in peer triad supervision. I was speaking about the publication of my paper about MBS and how there was much joy but also some fear of stepping up publicly. In the pause moment, I also noticed something about feeling proud, which strongly links with my upbringing and family background. For me in my family, this is unusual, not the norm to engage in academic endeavours. It's a big deal, and my family are proud (and I can imagine my deceased grandparents would be too) – I could feel the tenderness as I put this experience within my cultural background/context. I shared this with my peers; I was tearful, felt sensitive, and took a risk in showing something more of myself, revealing something. It was met with such kindness and resonance, and I felt safe and held. Even though I have practised for years, supervised, and been supervised for years, and feel very safe with my two peers, I still needed to take a little pause and look round before making the choice. In that moment I saw the courage we need for this kind of work.

Collaboration and mutuality

If you want to go fast, go alone. If you want to go far, go together.[122]

On several occasions during MBS training, we have been asked why we call it 'mutual' inquiry. This is because we see the process of supervision as a mutual endeavour. Yes, the supervisor and supervisee have different roles during the process and may have slightly different intentions, but there is, when it's going well, cooperation between them, a co-creation of this learning space. Mindful inquiry involves making a genuine, moment-to-moment connection with each other and engaging in a collaborative relationship emphasising mindful speaking and listening. We begin by looking at what each might bring to the space in their different roles with varied responsibilities, which will depend on factors such as experience and context. We offer a broad-brush stroke view here:

The supervisor's responsibilities include:

- Setting out the contractual agreement and arrangements.
- Facilitating and steering the inquiry, with all the dimensions described in this chapter (the amount of steering will vary, and the supervisor is tuning into what is needed).
- Supporting the supervisee in a learning process which includes all the elements of inquiry as well as guidance, sharing from own experience, and sharing resources. At times needing to be directive and giving specific information, particularly to supervisees who are new to MB work, but ultimately empowering the supervisee to find their own wisdom and insights.
- Within this learning process, supporting and guiding the supervisee to be within their proximal zone of development.[123]
- Meeting supervisees where they are developmentally, contextually, and personally, and being able to adapt and refine the approach.
- Attuning to the supervisee to discern and make choices about direction, which question to invite and finding the appropriate response for the moment.

The supervisee's responsibilities include:

- Reading and asking questions about the contracting process as necessary before agreeing.
- Preparing for the session, considering themes and what they want to bring to the agenda.
- Taking responsibility for their learning.
- Being willing to enter into the mindfulness-based aspects of supervision.

---

122 Proverb – origin unknown
123 Vygotsky, 1978

- Presenting their MB work honestly and openly.
- Reflecting before and after each supervision session and applying the learning to their mindfulness work.
- Considering what they need from supervision and periodically checking that their current supervision meets their needs.

One aspect of sharing, that supervisors might consider carefully is sharing personal experience/self-disclosure. This can be enormously helpful in bringing in a shared sense of common experience and vulnerability. It's helpful to take a moment to pause, check intentions, and discern if this adds anything to the shared dialogue – is it in the service of supporting the supervisee and their learning? As a supervisor, you do not always make the right choice and have times when you find your sharing was not so helpful, so bringing awareness to how this is known, reflecting upon it and using the experience to support learning for the future.

The above supports the mutual inquiry to unfold with these shared qualities:

- Mutual trust and respect.
- Mutual intention to deliver MB work in the best and most ethical way that is possible, e.g. includes adhering to codes of conduct, awareness of cultural issues, and keeping up to date.
- To have agreement on ways of working with each other within MBS.
- To enter into a mutual exploration – neither knowing what might happen.
- To 'wonder' together in a way that both are learning.
- To bring curiosity to experience and ways of relating.
- To bring vulnerability into MBS in ways that feel safe and timely, with an acknowledgement of the diverse nature of the vulnerability, shaped by social context, cultural background and experience, so there is a shared vulnerability in the space, but many ways it might manifest.
- Mutual participation, commitment, and engagement.
- Mutual deep listening, non-verbal as well as verbal.
- An honouring of practical arrangements and each other's time.
- A mutual keeping of the participants, clients, and recipients of the supervisee's MB work in mind.

Working skilfully with power

Whilst collaboration and equity are key aspects of the relationship within MBS, it is important to have an awareness of the power that may be inherent in the nature of the roles, other positions held, cultural background and experience, and personal patterning. With that awareness and openness, the supervisor can move towards skilful action, which supports collaboration and mutuality. Supervisors can use the authority that the role brings with care, not ducking out of authority and not overusing it, being respectful and empowering supervisees. Remember that supervisees have their rights, needs and responsibilities within the MBS space. At times, the supervisor does need to lead the way, steer and be quite directive, e.g. encouraging the use of videotape if a supervisee needs to for their training, if the supervisor thinks they are ready and it would support their learning, edging towards the less comfortable. It can also be helpful to remember that the words used by a supervisor can carry a lot of weight and influence, so taking care of how to phrase things, such as, *"This is one way"* or *"This is how I do it, there are other ways."*

Example – speaking up

I (Alison) experienced discomfort with my supervisor's response to the issue I was bringing to MBS some years ago. Their words had landed strongly and felt like a dismissal of something I was very dedicated to. I felt hurt and undermined. My habit would have been letting it go; they were a very senior teacher, and I wanted to avoid conflict. With some reflection, I began to think there is another way; I, too, am responsible in this relationship and can speak to them. I did, and their response impressed me. They were very open, they listened to the detail and wanted to understand the impact of their words, before making apologies for any harm and then explaining their response. I left feeling heard and empowered to speak honestly, knowing it could be received well.

There are other aspects of power around societal themes, such as race, class, and gender, that might come into play within the relationship. In Chapter 2, we highlighted the need for cultural sensitivity and responsiveness within supervision. Supervisors can bring awareness and openness to how their cultural background and experiences might bring a certain power dynamic. An openness and sensitivity as to how the supervisee's cultural background and experience might set up certain patterns of how they feel and act within the relationship is also required. In their research, Vekaria et al. found that many racially/ethnically minoritized (REM) supervisees were aware of the inherent power dynamic.[124] They needed supervisors to create safety and address power dynamics by speaking openly about their own cultural identity and initiating cultural conversations with sensitivity to the impact. This requires not just being a compassionate supervisor within MBS; it is also about being able to hold different experiences, perceptions, and viewpoints. Supra-vision can be a place for supervisors to unpack and see more clearly what might be happening, bearing in mind that the supra-visor may also come from a similar cultural background and experience, so may not see either.

---

124 Vekaria et al., 2023a

There are some areas within MBS where working skilfully with power dynamics might be particularly relevant:

- Early stages of supervision when building trust within the relationship.
- Contracting, including bringing in cultural responsiveness.
- Negotiating money.
- Offering feedback – note the use of the word offering rather than giving, take care of how much to offer at any one time, check how it's landing, and sense when to challenge and when to hold back.
- Actively encouraging a review and checking out process, which might cover the relationship, power, feedback to each other, what helps, what hinders, balance of action and reflection, strengths and edges, safety and challenge, what and where next. Reviewing supervision each session and periodically.
- The completion of any reports/statements/references.
- Working transparently with any potential conflicts of interest.
- The ending of a supervisory relationship.

In this chapter, we have explored the varied aspects of Mutual Inquiry, and how it is a highly relational process. When our MBS training was in person, we used to bring in a walking practice. Trainees were invited to move around the room, walking with awareness in the feet and also a wider awareness of others in the room as they meandered in the space together. After a while, without any words, there was an invitation to find a partner to walk with. Once paired up, the dyads began to walk together. These two previously independent 'walkers' walked in synchronization. It was hard to tell who was leading whom; sometimes, it felt as if one was leading the direction or speed and the other following, and then it would seem to switch, and at times neither leading. The walking would tend to get more creative over time, with different steps – sidewards, backwards, diagonally, big steps, little steps, often with laughter and smiles emerging. Each one is in tune with the movements of the other and working together. Maybe you have walked in this way or could imagine this practice; perhaps you have a peer you could have a go with. We think it illustrates what happens in this mutual inquiry where two people come together openly and creatively. This links back to the dance metaphor we have been holding in mind.

Summary

We have discussed and given examples of the different dimensions of inquiry with MBS.

1. The style of talking within inquiry
   - Includes asking questions, paraphrasing, normalising experiences, reframing, emphasising and summarising.
   - Questions are a core part of the inquiry cycle, bringing the experience THEN into reflection NOW, Making Meaning through exploration and inquiry, and discerning what to Take Forward.
2. The mode of inquiry
   - MBS foregrounds an intuitive, 'felt sense' way of knowing and the more familiar conceptual ways of knowing.
   - Coming to the body is often encouraged as a place to open to new knowledge and understanding.
3. Embodying within inquiry
   - Embodying can be observed through the body, through posture and gestures, the quality of the speech and tone.
   - The supervisor is embodying attitudes, such as curiosity and compassion.
   - Embodying includes the underpinnings of mindfulness, such as awareness, the willingness to turn towards and being comfortable with a more fluid emergence.
4. Cultivation of a 'not knowing' stance
   - In MBS, there is a deliberate cultivation of a 'not knowing' stance.
   - This creates an open space for emergence.
   - There is a possibility within that space for new discoveries, wisdom and creativity.
5. Allowing vulnerability within MBS
   - Within MBS we are bringing particular attitudes and orientations to vulnerability, namely, *Allowing, Turning Toward, Approaching* and *Befriending*.
   - Certain conditions support safely turning towards, such as psychological safety, trust within the relationship, clear boundaries, and both parties having the willingness and capacity to turn towards.
6. Collaboration and mutuality
   - MBS supervisors are encouraging a collaborative relationship, with each having their role and associated responsibilities, with a high level of mutuality in the process of MBS.
   - Mindful communication for both the supervisor and supervisee supports this mutual inquiry.

7. Working skilfully with power
   - Bringing awareness and being open to the different ways that power might be alive in MBS gives the opportunity to work with it in skilful ways that minimise negative impacts.
   - Cultural awareness, responsiveness and developing competencies as a supervisor support working skilfully with the inherent power imbalance.

Reflective questions

What do you value about the inquiry approach as a supervisee?

As a supervisee, what is it about being asked questions in the inquiry process that you find useful? What questions specifically have you found supportive?

What kind of questions do you use as a supervisor? In what way do they support the supervisee, e.g. opening, encouraging exploration, revealing something unseen?

As a supervisor, how do you hold an inquiry approach and not slip back into your default mode?

How do you access a 'felt' sense? What does this experience bring to your own reflective process and dialogue in relationships?

Take some time to reflect on embodying within supervision, either from the perspective of being a supervisor or supervisee. What is happening in the body, attitudes, and underpinnings of mindfulness? How do you know embodying is taking place?

You may like to reflect on other attitudes, as well as curiosity and compassion, and consider how they are embodied within supervision. Are there any ways you could lean into embodying them even further or more frequently?

What is 'not knowing' like for you? What supports you to be in this place of allowing emergence?

What supports you to explore vulnerability, e.g. trust, safety, attitudes, your own practice? Reflect further upon the detail, for example, what allows you to feel safe?

How might you move closer to vulnerability within supervision, as a supervisor or supervisee?

Reflect upon a recent supervision session; in what ways was it mutual and collaborative? What supports you to enter a collaborative dialogue?

In what ways do you feel the position of being a supervisor inherently puts you into an influential/powerful role? (You might consider your role as a supervisor, your position/other roles, personal patterns, and cultural background.) How do you work skilfully with these factors within MBS?

References

Adamson, F., & Brendgen, J. (2021). *Mindfulness-based relational supervision: Mutual learning and transformation.* Routledge. https://doi.org/10.4324/9781315161280

Brown, B. (2012). *Daring greatly: How the courage to be vulnerable transforms the way we live, love, parent, and lead.* Penguin.

Evans, A., Griffith, G. M., & Smithson, J. (2024). What do supervisors' and supervisees' think about mindfulness-based supervision? A grounded theory study. *Mindfulness,* 15, 63–79. https://doi.org/10.1007/s12671-023-02280-8

Kolb, D. (2015). *Experiential learning: Experience as the source of learning and development* (2nd ed.). Pearson Education.

Koster, F., Heynekamp, J., & Norton, V. (Eds.). (2023). *Mindful Communication: Speaking and listening with wisdom and compassion.* Routledge.

Segal, Z. V., Williams, J. M. G., & Teasdale, J. D. (2013). *Mindfulness-based cognitive therapy for depression* (2nd ed.). Guilford Press.

Shohet, R., & Shohet, J. (2020). *In love with supervision: Creating transformative conversations.* PCCS Books.

Teasdale, J. (2022). *What happens in mindfulness: Inner awakening and embodied cognition.* Guilford Press.

Vekaria, B., Harrydwar, L., Thomas, T., & Ononaiye, M. (2023a). Supervisee perspectives on improving cultural responsivity in clinical supervision. *Clinical Psychology Forum,* 1(371), 66-76. https://doi.org/10.53841/bpscpf.2023.1.371.66

Woods, S. L., Rockman, P., & Collins, E. (2019). *Mindfulness-based cognitive therapy: embodied presence & inquiry in practice.* New Harbinger Publications.

Woods, S. L., Rockman, P., & Collins, E. (2016). A contemplative dialogue: The inquiry process in mindfulness-based interventions. Available online at: https://mbpti.org/wp-content/uploads/2016/04/Woods-S.-L.-Rockman-P.-Collins-E.-2016-A-Complentative-Dialogue.pdf.

Vygotsky, L. S. (1978). *Mind in society: The development of higher psychological processes* (Vol. 86). Harvard University Press.

Chapter 5
The Space

Fire
What makes a fire burn
is space between the logs,
a breathing space.
Too much of a good thing,
too many logs
packed in too tight
can douse the flames
almost as surely
as a pail of water would.
So building fires
requires attention
to the spaces in between,
as much as to the wood.
When we are able to build
open spaces
in the same way
we have learned
to pile on the logs,

> *then we can come to see how*
> *it is fuel, and absence of the fuel*
> *together, that make fire possible.*
> *We only need to lay a log*
> *lightly from time to time.*
> *A fire grows*
> *simply because the space is there,*
> *with openings*
> *in which the flame*
> *that knows just how it wants to burn*
> *can find its way.*
> Judy Brown[125]

In this chapter, we turn to the Space in our MBS framework, one of the three warp threads that make supervision mindfulness-based. In the MBS framework (Figure 1.3), we have placed the Space in between the Petals to convey that between all the content, there is also a need for times with less content. This is conveyed in the poem's lines at the beginning of this chapter, "*So building fires requires attention to the spaces in between, as much as to the wood.*" We know how easily space can be lost, not seen, and not valued, so we name it explicitly as a 'thing'. However, the visual 2D representation of the MBS framework has its limits, and we would like to stress how space permeates all aspects of MBS, including space between the warp threads themselves and what happens before and after a supervision session. In this chapter, we describe why it is essential to have space and offer different ways of creating it and its impact.

We begin with defining what we mean by space, as there are many definitions. It is a widely used word in many contexts and includes a physical space where certain activities can occur or more internal processes such as 'head space' – time to think or be free from mental pressures. In the online Cambridge Dictionary,[126] one of their definitions reads, "*empty place, an empty area that is available to be used*", with examples of the use of the word. We have used these examples and adapted them to relate to MBS:

- **Space for MBS** – giving space to reflect upon one's MB work with another person.
- **Make space** – the need to make space for MBS in the midst of work and life.

---

125 Copyright © Judy Brown, 2016, reproduced with kind permission from the author. https://www.judysorumbrown.com/

126 Cambridge Dictionary, Retrieved January 11, 2025, https://dictionary.cambridge.org/dictionary/english/space

- **Space between** – within MBS, there is space between words, both the supervisor's and the supervisee's, space between one thought, emotion, body sensation and the next, space between to be more aware of experience.
- **... Space** – (an area with a particular purpose) *"let's take a breathing space to give a moment to pause"*.

Similar words that fit with what we describe as the Space within MBS are roomy, capacity, opening, and expansion. It might not always feel this way in the midst of a supervision session, but the supervisor aspires to bring more spaciousness into MBS. Different words and synonyms include ample, generous, wide, extended, and boundless. Words describing the opposite include limited, confined, restricted, narrow, cramped, confined, and tight. We do not want to make this sound unachievable or too grand; sometimes a supervisor creates a 'good-enough space', a little shift, a tiny opening, and it's not always boundless. We are pointing to both the physical and metaphorical spaces of the supervision mode. We often talk about space as something that needs to be filled rather than having its own intrinsic value. As we said earlier, it is a thing and an important thing!

Pausing for self-reflection

How do I experience space?

You might like to take a moment to pause now. Feeling your feet on the ground, your seat on the chair if you are sitting, your hands wherever they are resting, and your breath breathing.

Taking some moments settling. And then inviting a reflection on how you experience space, dropping in questions such as:

In this moment, how do you experience space in your body, your mind, your environment?

How about your experience of space within relationships, in conversations within the contexts of life – with family, friends, and work colleagues?

How about your experience of space in the different activities of your day?

Allowing each question time to drop into your reflective practice, not having to find an answer as such, but seeing what arises. This may come in the form of thoughts, feelings or body sensations.

Staying with this reflection as long as you wish. And feeling free to journal.

You may wish to let this reflective inquiry into your experience of space ripple into the rest of your day.

The importance of having space

> *"... it is fuel, and absence of the fuel together, that make fire possible ..."*
> from the opening poem.

In Chapter 6, we explore the Petals, the content of supervision, which we might call 'the fuel'. And here we are considering why we need space, this absence of fuel. What is it that becomes possible in this space? We think space allows coming into closer contact with a mindfulness-based approach. This begins with the simple yet massive act of carving out space in the diary to have a contained and dedicated space for reflecting with another. If we return to Jon Kabat-Zinn's operational definition from Chapter 2,[127] we can see the linkage between the space within MBS and accessing awareness.

"awareness that emerges" – within MBS, a space is created to slow down and reflect, giving awareness a prominent place. The term *emerges* also implies that it needs space to happen.

"paying attention" – there is space to pay attention; both supervisor and supervisee are paying attention to the content of what is being shared, their internal responses – thoughts, feelings, body, the relationship between them, and mind wandering.

"on purpose" – there is an intention within MBS to keep the process grounded in mindful awareness, protecting and dedicating the space to this shared endeavour, which includes entering into a different way of being. The space allows the supervisor and supervisee time to check in with their intention and direction.

"in the present moment" – even though connecting with past and future, the supervisor brings in a present moment focus to the session, noticing what is happening in each moment is part of the dialogue. To be in the moment often requires a degree of spaciousness to come out of the busyness of everyday life.

"and non-judgmentally to things as they are" – MBS is imbued with attitudes of openness, allowing, friendliness, which enables a curiosity about what is present, including being able to turn towards difficulty. It provides a space to practise bringing in these attitudes and supporting and embodying them, which continues beyond supervision.

By creating and inhabiting a more spacious place, supervisors and supervisees can access awareness more easily, give time for reflection, time to connect with inner experience, and shift into a different mode of being – into a 'felt' sense. The impact of these shifts is experiencing another way of seeing, broader perspectives, perhaps with more clarity, and the possibility of stepping back (decentring), all of which

---
127 Kabat-Zinn, 1994; Segal et al., 2013, p. 132

support the discerning aspect of mindfulness. Within MBS, the supervisor can make choices about what is needed next to best support the supervisee, e.g. encouraging further exploration of the supervisee's internal experience, or moving out wider.

Relational aspects of space

Using pauses and space are critical aspects of mindful communication; when we take a moment to pause we become more aware, and the other way around we have a moment of awareness that gives us a pause. This quote conveys the importance of this space so clearly: *"There is a space between stimulus and response. In that space lies our freedom to choose a response. In that response lies our growth and freedom."*[128]

In their chapter about non-violent communication, Oren Jay Sofer and Sietske de Haan talk about how compassion and connection can be chosen in that moment and give a space for pausing within a relationship, and this impacts what comes next, as the worlds we live in get created.[129] In the same way, MBS brings mindfulness and compassion into the supervisory relationship, creating spaces and moments of pause, for learning and discovery between the supervisor and supervisee.

In the previous chapter about the inquiry process within MBS, we gave examples of this creation of space and pausing, illustrating its place and importance within MBS.

Ways of creating space

> *"… we are able to build open spaces in the same way we have learned to pile on the logs …"* from the opening poem.

Space is created before, within, after and between supervision sessions in various ways, which we give a flavour of here. Supervisors can actively learn to build and incorporate space into MBS.

Before MBS

There are ways that both supervisor and supervisee can create some space before the supervision session, some of which is continued into the supervisory space. So ideally, giving yourself 5-15 minutes before supervision to 'prepare' yourself.

- Clearing the physical space you are in from distractions and clutter so there is a feeling of space.
- Protecting the space in your diary and having a protected space where you won't be disturbed.

---

128 Quote often used in mindfulness-based teaching, attributed to Viktor Frankl
129 Sofer & de Haan, 2023

- Moving the body, which can just be taking a minute or two to stretch.
- Awareness of the space around you, not just in front of you, inhabiting all the space in your room, which might include moving around the room and looking out of the window.
- Taking a moment to reflect on the last session and tune into your intention for this session.
- Paying attention to your posture, and choosing one that supports your body, openness and the intention you are bringing to MBS.

Within MBS

- Paying attention to postures that support openness.
- Moving the body from time to time, attending to areas of tightness and tension, not getting stuck – opening physically.
- Awareness of the space around you, not just in front of you, especially if supervising via a screen, and the space around your supervisee.
- Slowing down speech, taking mini pauses as you find your words.
- Supporting reflection, through pauses and inquiry.
- Mindfulness practice within MBS, which might include:
  - Starting supervision with an intentional space, linking back to Embodied Presence. A short practice at the beginning of the session for grounding, noticing what is here, and being with it. This is particularly important for the supervisee, who may arrive at the session caught up in busyness, distraction or difficult emotions. Options include a silent period, a few breaths, a guided practice, or a reflection on what is alive for MBS.
  - A three-stage breathing space/STOP practice /mini grounding practice[130] whenever a difficulty or strong emotion arises in the session, perhaps when giving feedback or in challenging moments.
  - Movement practices – encouraging the supervisee to move the body, expressing through a movement, or guiding a short movement practice, e.g. shaking the body, rocking, tapping, massaging, rubbing the body in response to difficulty, stretching tighter areas, loosening.
  - Frequent mini pauses – which could be from either the supervisor or supervisee just taking a breath or two between words, through to inviting a moment to pause and see what is being experienced right now and beginning to speak again when ready.
  - Momentarily connecting with inner experience, especially at times of uncertainty or difficulty, e.g. through the breath, feet on the ground, hands

---

130 There are a range of mini practices within most MBAs to choose from, we offer a few examples.

in the lap, feeling emotional resonance, a soothing touch. This may be made explicit to the supervisee or not, but it is excellent modelling of mindfulness either way.

- A supervisor might guide the supervisee in a particular practice and do an inquiry around it – to demonstrate the practice or because that practice may be needed at that moment.
- A short, silent moment or two at the end of the session can give space for settling whatever has been happening.

After MBS

- Taking a moment, however brief, to pause and have an immediate sense of what has resonated and touched you within supervision.
- Giving time to reflect upon and make notes from the session. This may be immediately following the session or a little time afterwards, ideally not too long, so the felt sense isn't lost.
- There may be occasions when further space for reflection is needed, so setting this time aside. This could include taking things to supra-vision.

When considering becoming a supervisor or at any point, you may need to reflect upon whether you have the time in your life at the moment to become/be a supervisor. Is there enough space to give your supervisees time and attention before, within, after and between supervision?

Many of the attitudinal qualities we have named as part of the Container support creating space. The quality of patience might be essential, with many of us living fast-paced lives where we are moving quickly, needing to get things done, and moving on to the next thing. As Susan Woods, Patricia Rockman and Evan Collins put it, *"It takes patience to slow down and reset the busyness of the mind to allow things to reveal themselves in their own time."*[131]

Supervisors and supervisees learn to create space through their mindfulness practice, finding spaciousness within longer practices, pausing in the midst of the day, and practising mindful communication in regular conversations. We are not talking about having perfect conditions; learning to find spaciousness within the busy is possible. We are also recognising that different people will prefer some of these ways of creating space more than others, for example, stillness may not be the preferred option. So, within MBS, the supervisor is attuning to what supports each individual and the relationship.

---

[131] Woods et al., 2019, p. 99

The impact of creating space

> *It's a transformative experience to simply pause instead of immediately filling up space.*[132]

MBS often begins with a pause, as in the example below where we hear from a supervisee after a brief arrival practice.

Example – finding space

In the short inquiry that followed the brief arrival practice, the supervisee reported feeling settled, a sense of relief, *"It's so different to the rest of my day where I've been going from one thing to the next with no space. I've literally been on the edge of my chair. I can now sit back, my face feels lighter and less tight, my mind is still jumping around, but I can see it, and there are some spaces between all the thoughts"*. Then, the supervisor moved into setting the agenda with the supervisee for the rest of the session. The agenda might be the topics and themes that come in, but this spacious way of arriving is also the 'agenda'. If we return to our poem, *"then we can come to see how it is fuel, and absence of the fuel together, that make fire possible"*. We can see in this example how the impact for the supervisee from that initial practice and inquiry was that they had more awareness of their internal experience, they found more space in the body as it opened and relaxed, and this too extended into an openness in the supervision session.

During our MBS training, we repeatedly hear people talk about how pausing is incredibly transforming within the supervision dialogue – *"The power of the pause"*. We start by doing this formally, systematically, where we, as the trainers, bring the pause in with a bell or zoom broadcast message. Although this interrupts in the middle of a sentence or stream of thought, people are still surprised at how useful it is, often reporting, *"It came at just the right moment"*. As a new supervisor it is supportive to pause when not sure what to 'do', checking in and discerning where next, but also, as a supervisee, having the space to let things land, shift more into awareness of what is happening, coming more to the felt sense and maybe the body. When the supervisor or supervisee begins again after the pause, they sometimes pick up where they left off with a bit more space and perspective around it, and sometimes something new has been seen or felt.

We then invite supervisors on the training to find their own ways of bringing pauses and space into MBS, knowing that for many, the default is to fill the space and 'make the most of the time', as if space is a waste of time. Within MBS, we work with our

---

[132] Chodron, 2000, p. 46

own and supervisees' habits and patterns, often cultural ones. I (Alison) know this well, especially when I am excited, passionate, interested in a topic or narrative, and want to know and learn more ... The space is quickly forgotten in the midst of busy work and life schedules. Personal mindfulness practice supports finding space, and space supports mindfulness practice and a mindful approach to life.

Summary

1. Space is one of the three warp threads of MBS, which can easily be lost, forgotten, or filled up.
2. Creating space supports:
   - Bringing awareness to experience, both internally and externally.
   - The ability to move out of habitual reactions.
   - Shifting into a different mode, allowing for more contact with the body and a felt sense.
   - A reflective process, moving more into connection with each other in MBS.
   - Widening the perspective.
   - Making skilful choices.
3. We offer a variety of ways to cultivate and build space before, after, within and between MBS, such as mindfulness practice, time to reflect, moments of pausing and protecting space in our environment and schedule.

Reflective questions

We invite you to have an extended reflection to explore what finding space means for you in your day. What creates space in body, heart and mind? And to be curious about those moments when there doesn't feel as if there is space, how does this feel? What is the impact of having moments of space?

What do you notice when you take a pause during a conversation with another? What are the different ways you pause? What supports you to remember to pause and make space?

Do you notice others creating space within relationships and dialogue, in groups and 1:1 encounters? Maybe your supervisor? How is the space created? What is the impact?

How might you bring more space into supervision? As a supervisor? As a supervisee? Are there any suggestions we have made that you might 'play' with?

What prevents you from creating space and taking pauses? And what might support you in working with any obstacles?

References

Chodron, P. (2000). *When things fall apart: Heart advice for difficult times*. Shambhala Publications.

Kabat-Zinn, J. (1994). *Wherever you go, there you are: Mindfulness meditation for everyday life*. Piatkus.

Segal, Z. V., Williams, J. M. G., & Teasdale, J. D. (2013). *Mindfulness-based cognitive therapy for depression* (2nd ed.). Guilford Press.

Sofer, O. J., & de Haan, S. (2023). Nonviolent communication: Mindfulness and compassion in relationships. In F. Koster, J. Heynekamp, & V. Norton (Eds.), *Mindful communication: Speaking and listening with wisdom and compassion* (pp. 16-35). Routledge.

Woods, S. L., Rockman, P., & Collins, E. (2019). *Mindfulness-based cognitive therapy: embodied presence & inquiry in practice*. New Harbinger Publications.

Chapter 6

The Petals

In our weaving metaphor, we are now moving into the weft. These are the horizontal threads woven in and out to create the weave. Weft threads are flexible and varied; using different coloured wefts with the same warp will create different weaves. Weft threads can also be woven differently, passing through each warp thread or passing over more than one at a time, creating different patterns.[133] So within MBS, the content, the Petals, will be varied.

These Petals are the topics of supervision as opposed to the process. We name five different Petals: Contexts, Mindfulness-Based (MB) Work, Group and Individual Processes, Personal Mindfulness Practice, and Theory and Understanding (Figure 6.1). These Petals cover the broad scope of what might come into MBS, capturing the various content, topics, subjects, material, themes, threads, issues, and questions brought to MBS. The Petals are what the supervisee brings to the agenda and wants to know and learn more about, as well as what the supervisor has knowledge and skills in (not necessarily an expert).

---

133 You may like to refer back to Figures 1.5 and 1.6 in Chapter 1

Figure 6.1 The Petals in the MBS framework

Many factors affect and influence the content of MBS, and how it is structured. As we have already seen, MBS is a relational process that considers the individual developmental needs of the supervisee as well as what is emerging through the mutual inquiry process, so a different weave is created with each supervisee and within each session. Other factors are the supervisee and supervisor's geographical and cultural context, the setting the supervisee is in (e.g. workplace, health and social care, education, third-sector/charity, local community, the criminal justice system) and the mode of work (e.g. curricula-based, MBP, supervision, training, leadership, 1:1 work).

In this chapter, we offer a flavour of the possible content for each Petal to show the scope of what can be brought to MBS. We illustrate how these topics come into MBS in different ways and how there is movement around the different Petals within a session. Finally, we discuss what resources supervisors to work with this varied content.

Contexts

This is an enormous Petal which covers:

Supervisee's training context. There may be specific needs and criteria according to the training programme, such as being aligned with particular approaches or curricula. There may be an assessment process the supervisee is working towards, and the number of required supervision sessions might affect how much content comes into each session. Where a supervisee is in terms of their developmental pathway will impact the topics and how the weft gets woven.

Supervisee's own context. Supervisors don't need to know everything about the supervisee, but part of the restorative function of MBS is to be able to support supervisees. This might include helping the supervisee explore the interface between navigating their own health and well-being and challenging times in life and their MB work. It may link with explorations about personal practice in the midst of life events.

Application context (the nature of the work). Having a clear understanding and knowledge of the specific client or group to which the supervisee is offering their MB work and the expertise necessary for that particular application. It also includes exploring the challenges and joys of teaching in-person or online.

Organizational context. Clarity around the impact of the organization/system in which the supervisee works, e.g. health and social care, workplaces, educational establishments, charities, prisons/criminal justice, community groups, etc. MBS can support explorations about how to work within that setting, how to adapt and modify where needed, and what the issues and cultural threads are in that setting. The organizational context can also bring personal challenges for the supervisee.

Cultural context. This will include explorations about culture, finding ways of bringing that awareness and knowledge into teaching, and exploring adaptations needed. This includes diversity and inclusion, bringing awareness of issues relating to systemic trauma, inclusion/exclusion, and justice/injustice. The supervisor and supervisee are willing to work with assumptions and biases (conscious and unconscious).

Wider mindfulness field. Awareness and exploration of the changing trends, knowledge, research and how these relate to the supervisee's MB work. At times, this might be broader than the mindfulness field and be connected to more global issues, such as social unrest or world disasters.

Supervisory context. Depending on whether it is short-term or long-term, part of training, mentoring, or co-working may impact the content, how much, and which direction to go in.

All these things can be brought directly into MBS as content. Contexts can bring about what we refer to as professional and ethical dilemmas for supervisees. These questions link to some of the areas of the Belt and Integrity. Some of these aspects of contexts are present in other elements of the MBS framework, such as cultural context, which ripples all the way through MBS. Some of the aspects around contexts may or may not be in the supervisor's knowledge and scope of practice. There are likely times when supervisees are more knowledgeable about their context than the supervisor, and act as a resource to the supervisor to aid their understanding.

Mindfulness-based work

This Petal includes the wide range of skills that supervisees might need in their area of work. Referring back to Chapter 2, this is the learning aspect of MBS, supporting the *what* and *how* learning. In MBS, supervisors support supervisees in working with their strengths and growing edges. This includes reflection on what skills are needed and ways of enhancing existing skills and developing new ones. It can be a place for ideas and suggestions, supporting MB work to be alive and creative. This skills development may utilise a framework or map to guide the explorations, such as the MBI:TAC or MBI:TLC. Supervisees might be engaged in a range of MB work, such as:

- Curricula-based, e.g. MBPs – eight-week courses such as MBSR, MBCT, and other curricula-based courses of varying lengths.
- Sharing MB practice, such as introductory sessions with friends and family, within a workplace setting or regular practice sessions within a community.
- 1:1 work, which might be MBP-based or other forms of 1:1 work.
- Expanding from the above into new areas such as MBS, mentoring, and training.
- Mindful approach to work, e.g. within leadership.

Mindfulness-based teaching skills

Originally, MBS was linked to supervising teachers of MBPs. It is often the main Petal that new supervisees bring to supervision, as they have many questions about their work and how to do it. The content for this Petal might include all the preliminaries needed before beginning to run a course, details of the appropriate curriculum, what to teach, how to lead practices, working with inquiry, making recordings, handouts/workbooks, timing issues, ways of conveying teaching, resources, feedback on teaching, and ongoing development of all the teaching and inquiry skills. The MBI:TAC and MBI:TLC are often utilized as a framework/map to support the supervisee in reflecting on their teaching. Part of the supervisor's role is educational, helping the supervisee learn the variety of skills needed for this work. There are opportunities for reflection and feedback. Bringing in live teaching or video/audio recordings can support this feedback process.

The domains of the MBI:TAC might still be helpful for anyone sharing mindfulness practices. For those supervising, the MBS framework can be used to explore supervision skills. For other areas of MB work, there may be frameworks that support skill-building in that arena. For example, within mindful leadership work, exploring leadership competencies and the skills of mindful leaders may support the supervisee's skill development.

Group and individual processes

This Petal covers understanding the learning and developmental processes of groups and individuals. For supervisees working within a group context, this Petal will include supporting them in forming relationships and establishing the group. Trish Bartley and Gemma Griffith's Inside Out Group model,[134] describing how inside-out embodying can support attending to reading the group, holding the group and befriending the group, covers much of the territory of the group aspect of this Petal. Common questions about groups are: How do you work with individuals in the group who are quiet, overtaken, non-engaged, or distressed? How do you work with groups that struggle to be a group? How do you engage a group when working online? How to make the most of being in a group?

Safety and inclusivity are essential aspects of this Petal for groups and individuals. Safety includes establishing a safe group/relationship from the initial orientation phase to clarifying clear boundaries in grounded and friendly ways. Inclusivity includes all the ways the supervisee can cultivate respect and facilitate healthy and sustaining connections within the group, including any adaptations that might be needed. The paper 'Mindfulness-based stress reduction for our time'[135] invites a re-examining of the pedagogy of MBPs to explore how the theme of diversity and inclusion can be embodied and brought alive for all demographics of society. They suggest a particular emphasis on awareness of oppression and power dynamics, and creating spaces that nurture psychological safety and a sense of belonging. These might be examples of what supervisees are bringing into supervision.

The supervisor will support and encourage the supervisee to work in ways that are trauma-sensitive and neuro-inclusive in all aspects of their work, as well as exploring in more detail the specific vulnerabilities and needs of individuals. This might involve discussing trauma sensitivity, how it relates to the individuals the supervisee is working with, and could also be related to the supervisee and their own vulnerabilities. This includes working in neuro-inclusive ways with supervisees and ensuring they do the same with those they are working with, e.g. exploring supportive ways of practising, being in a group, being on screen, etc. There are also times when supervisees experience challenges in their relationship with those they are working with and wish to unpack this within MBS. Working with ending processes is part of this Petal.

The supervisee's personal process within their MB work is explored through the mutual inquiry process. Supervisees may be working solo or with a colleague/co-worker, and each can present both joys and challenges that can be brought to supervision. The supervisee may have joint supervision with their co-worker,

---

134 Bartley & Griffith 2022; Griffith et al., 2019
135 Crane et al., 2023

allowing their working relationship to be a topic of discussion with both present, and they may need to have some space on their own to discuss things, especially if the working relationship is more challenging.

Personal mindfulness practice

As a personal mindfulness practice forms a foundation for MB work in all its forms, it follows that MBS includes time to focus on practice. This includes what might be referred to as formal practice, where there is a clear intention to practise for a certain length of time, in a certain way, through to more informal practice, where mindfulness is integrated into the activities of the day. This might include mini moments of mindfulness. Within MBS, the supervisor may support the supervisee's practice, explore obstacles and blocks, know the joys and delights of practice, inspire them, share resources, check in with intention, and help them find time and motivation to practise. Having a depth of practice allows the supervisee to know some of the experiences that participants might meet if they are teaching or sharing mindfulness practices in some form. An established practice also supports a growing confidence in an MB approach to different aspects of life.

The supervisor is helping the supervisee to link their practice with their MB work, asking the supervisee to reflect on aspects of their own practice and how it informs their MB work with inquiry questions such as, *"I am wondering about this in terms of your practice"*, *"How might this inform you?"*, *"What are you recognising through your own practice that you might bring to the class?"* Talking about practice can be a sensitive topic, so supervisees might not bring it to supervision, as they may hold expectations of themselves around how they should be practising. The supervisee may have a different personal practice from the one they teach, so some conversation about how to work with this can be supportive.

Theory and understanding

This Petal covers the *why* aspect of learning referred to in Chapter 2. It can be an area that supervisees bring into MBS as an agenda item, but it is often an area that gets woven into the dialogue. It relates to understanding why things are taught and done the way they are in MBAs, a particular exercise or practice, and understanding the intentions and rationale. The supervisor may ask questions about what the supervisee thinks the intentions are of specific aspects of a curriculum. They might ask about what is informing their understanding of their MB work. They may be linking the supervisee's experience to a particular theory that underpins the aspect of mindfulness being explored at the time, e.g. turning towards, a compassionate response, working with thoughts, and coming to the body.

Supervisees will also bring how to convey theory within their work, didactically or more implicitly. The supervisor might begin by checking out the supervisee's understanding of the theory. Then the supervisor might explore ways the supervisee could convey this theory in their work. The supervisor might share how they approach this themselves and give an opportunity to practise in the session.

Theory includes a broad and deep understanding of the human condition from different angles that underpin MBAs and inform all aspects of how mindfulness is taught, including psychological principles, theories, and Buddhist teachings. It also includes social models as a basis for understanding the world we are living in and how those conditions are experienced. The theory could also include expanding to other frameworks and models that widen the lens of understanding for both the supervisor and the supervisee, such as understanding theories that support social justice, equality, diversity and inclusion, and learnings rooted in ancient traditions. The theories drawn upon will also be linked with the context of the MB work and the supervisee's cultural experience and background. The content within MBS is not so directly about the actual theory but more about its application within the MB work. How does the theory get translated and applied? It needs to come from a basis of understanding, often cognitively and experientially.

How does this content come into MBS?

Usually, the initial bringing in of content comes from the supervisee. Supervisees will set the agenda for the session and name what they would like to focus on. They may send this agenda before the session or name their topics at the beginning of the session. The supervisor may also add things to the agenda, such as suggesting revisiting something from a previous session or something they think is essential to cover. Supervisees may send in more detailed information before the session in the form of a written reflection, which includes naming areas they would like to bring to the session. As the supervisee begins with each of their agenda items, the supervisor might invite them to say a bit more; it is a balance so there is room for inquiry rather than a lengthy description of the situation, using phrases such as, *"Can you give me a brief idea of ..."*, *"Could you give a little bit of a sense of ..."*, or *"In that specific moment ..."*. Then there is plenty of room for inquiry and seeing what unfolded at the time and what unfolds in the supervision session.

Increasingly, supervisees are bringing video or audio recordings to MBS. The supervisor might watch a section of the recording before the session, or they might watch a clip together within the session. These recordings provide material for exploring the different Petals. Similarly, there may be opportunities for live teaching within MBS, with either the supervisee guiding a practice and/or inquiry or vice versa.

Moving around the Petals

Part of our intention in this chapter is to convey the scope of MBS's content. We are keen that it is not limited to thinking it is just about teaching skills. Both the supervisor and supervisee can move around these Petals during a session. A supervisor, in particular, will be holding the span of all the Petals; they may direct to different Petals as part of a more expansive exploration and, at other times, invite zooming in closely on one particular area.

Example – moving around the Petals

A supervisee has put on their agenda that they want to know how to develop their skills in guiding a body scan practice. So, within the session, the supervisor might explore guiding practice skills, using the key features of domain four of the TLC/TAC (guiding mindfulness practice) as a backdrop. The supervisor might also move to other Petals, bringing in questions and areas of exploration such as: What is the supervisee's own practice and experience of the body scan? (Personal Mindfulness Practice Petal); What do they think the intentions are for this practice? (Theory and Understanding Petal); What is the context within which they are teaching? (Contexts Petal); Are there any specific considerations they might need to make for the individuals within their setting to feel safe and included during the practice? (Group and Individual Processes Petal).

Over a more extended period, the supervisor and supervisee might check in with the whole breadth and depth of supervision to see if any areas need to be covered within MBS. Both supervisors and supervisees have their more familiar and favoured topics. Might there be any merit in spending time with another Petal? We encourage moving around the Petals within a supervision session and across sessions. This doesn't mean that every Petal has to be covered every session, but we might expect each one to be touched upon over a period of MBS.

How can you resource yourself as a supervisor to work with these Petals?

We mentioned in our introduction that these Petals are what the supervisee brings to the agenda and wants to know and learn more about, as well as what the supervisor has knowledge and skills in. Whilst this is not about the supervisor needing to be an expert in all areas, it is part of the role of a supervisor to equip and resource themselves to meet their supervisee's needs. We have created a list for supervisors identifying ways to keep up to date and relevant for their supervisees:

- Your own teaching and MB work and accompanying reflective processes.
- Ongoing experiential learning from supervision both in the delivering and receiving.
- Supra-vision (supervision of supervision).
- Your mindfulness practice – regular and extended periods of practice, a depth and range of practice, the knowledge that comes from practice, such as knowing struggles, knowing how practice supports life, the insights and inspirations.
- Recording your own work and having feedback.
- Keeping up to date – with new programmes and forms of offering MB work, deepening your experiential knowledge (you cannot do this in every area of mindfulness so you may concentrate on your field and specialisms).
- Linked with the previous point, training and ongoing professional development may fill specific gaps in your knowledge, skills and experience or go deeper into different areas.
- Using a variety of resources for new learning:
    - Reading – books, research, articles, blogs.
    - Podcasts, videos.
    - Mini database searches to delve into research.
- Connection and contact with others in the field, e.g. via conferences, peers, and peer communities.[136]
- Familiarity with frameworks such as the MBI:TAC and MBI:TLC.
- Knowing about the needs of different populations and what kinds of adaptations might be needed – this might require extra research.
- Developing skills in giving feedback on teaching; this might also include skills in managing technology and approaches to watching/listening to clips of MB work.
- Knowledge of good practice in creating and maintaining safety, including safeguarding processes.
- Awareness of diversity and inclusion – includes your own work around blind spots and bias, and you may need others to help you see your assumptions and bias, e.g. supra-vision and peers.
- Knowledge about group processes and dynamics through courses, reading (mindfulness-based and other resources about group work), knowing the importance of the orientation processes in setting the group's culture.
- Knowing your limits and not practising outside your scope of practice and experience: Can I supervise ethically and competently? Can I supervise this particular supervisee ethically and competently?.

---

136 For example, Support for Integrity in Teaching and Training (SiTT) https://www.sitt.community/

This looks like a long list, and it is, because the role of being a supervisor is an important and multidimensional one. This means that supervisors must be experienced practitioners and equipped to work with the different topics and experiences that their supervisees encounter. It doesn't mean supervisors have to be perfect and have the answer to everything, but they do need knowledge, skills and experience. We return here to our dance metaphor and the linkage with this concept of knowing how to dance. In terms of the creativity and flow of the dance, supervisors meet this content with the processes described in Chapters 3, 4 and 5, the warp, drawing upon the Container, a personal mindfulness practice, the attitudes of mindfulness, all the aspects of the relational inquiry, and giving space to the process.

Summary

1. The Petals cover the broad scope of the content, topics, themes and questions within MBS, which we have organized into five areas:
   - Contexts
   - Mindfulness-Based Work, which includes teaching skills
   - Group and Individual Processes
   - Personal Mindfulness Practice
   - Theory and Understanding
2. The Petals are part of the weft and will differ for each supervisee and within each supervision session, depending on factors such as the mode of work, the setting, the supervisee's developmental stage and the cultural context.
3. Usually, the supervisee decides what topic, themes, and questions to bring to MBS. The supervisor might also invite reflection and inquiry in other Petals, encouraging moving around and a broader view.
4. Supervisors are required to keep themselves equipped and resourced as supervisors to meet these many different topics of supervision; we give some ideas of how to do this.

Reflective questions

What topics have you taken to your own supervision and supra-vision over the years? Are there any aspects of these Petals you haven't taken to supervision? Do you have your more familiar places and preferences?

From your experience can you see any other Petals missing in our framework?

As a supervisor, which Petals have you noticed supervisees bringing? Do you ever encourage the supervisee to move to another one, as another angle to explore the topic being brought to MBS?

In what ways do you equip and resource yourself to work with each of these Petals? You might like to take each one separately, as there may be some general ways you keep resourced and some more specific.

As you reflect now, is there anything useful to support you as a supervisor in meeting your supervisee's needs?

References

Bartley, T., & Griffith, G. (2022). *Teaching mindfulness-based groups: The inside out group model.* Pavilion Publishing.

Crane, R. S., Callen-Davies, R., Francis, A., Francis, D., Gibbs, P., Mulligan, B., O'Neill, B., Williams, N. K. P., Waupoose, M., & Vallejo, Z. (2023). Mindfulness-based stress reduction for our time: A curriculum that is up to the task. *Global Advances in Integrative* Medicine and Health, 12. https://doi.org/10.1177/27536130231162604

Griffith, G. M., Bartley, T., & Crane, R. S. (2019). The inside out group model: Teaching groups in mindfulness-based programs. *Mindfulness,* 10, 1315–1327. https://doi.org/10.1007/s12671-019-1093-6

Chapter 7
The Belt

Teaching mindfulness is a great privilege, providing the opportunity to connect with the full range of human experience. With this comes the call to make ethical commitments to meet each participant in our teaching and learning communities with as much sensitivity as possible.[137]

This inner ring of the Belt is one of the weft threads and consists of five elements: Contracting for MBS, Diversity and Inclusion, Safety, Competency, and Good Practice. The Belt holds guiding principles, legislation and frameworks that are part of a duty of care. Duty of care is concerned with well-being, compliance and good practice, described by the International Committee of the Red Cross as "... *a legal concept that comes from common law and can be defined as a legal obligation requiring adherence to a standard of reasonable care while performing any acts that could foreseeably harm others.*"[138] In the context of MBS, this duty of care applies to MB work itself and to the supervisory relationship, so we suggest that Rhonda Magee's call in the opening quote be extended to include how the supervisor meets each supervisee.

MBS is part of a much bigger context, so the issues that are alive within communities and society and within the mindfulness field impact MBS and come into the space of supervision. This includes the whole arena of mindfulness as a profession, what that means in practice, and the many ethical issues the field

---

137 Magee, 2016, p. 244
138 International Committee of the Red Cross, (n/d), p. 1. Duty of care: elements of a definition. https://unsceb.org/duty-care-policy-framework-and-guiding-principles-irc

grapples with. It also includes awareness of wider societal ethical themes such as diversity and social justice, ensuring that the supervisee's MB work is congruent with current social policy in their context.

The use of the term *Belt* for this part of the framework conveys this sense of upholding and adjusting to ensure it is not too tight or too loose. You might imagine that if you are wearing a belt and it is too loose, your clothing will slip down, but if it is too tight, it will be uncomfortable and restricting, so there is a need to readjust accordingly. As part of the weft, the Belt is woven into the fabric of MBS, nestled within the warp threads, so decisions around when and how to draw on the Belt are held in the wider relational and embodied process of MBS. For example, if the supervisee's competency is the focus of a supervision session, the supervisor will be holding in mind elements of the Container, such as Intention and attitudes of Compassion/Wisdom, and they will also be attending to the processes within Mutual Inquiry.

In MBS research, it was recognized that MBS sits balanced on the wider context of professional and ethical issues and practice; the use of the word balance again conveys this idea of not leaning too heavily in one direction or the other.[139] This aligns with our concept of the Belt, with the supervisor taking care not to hold these issues too tight or too loose. Of course, the particular legislation and frameworks that are drawn on will be informed by the context within which the supervisee's MB work takes place. This is also why it is considered part of the weft, the part of the framework that is adapted and tailored to meet specific needs and contexts.

This chapter is practical, pointing to ethical and professional issues and key frameworks to consider adherence to. Without a formal regulatory body for MB practitioners, a commitment to professional practice requires lifelong reflection and engagement around three main areas, outlined by Pamela: (1) the personal values and ethics of the practitioner, (2) MBA factors such as the ethos of MB programmes, robust teacher training and professional practice guidelines, and (3) wider societal issues.[140] We point to a range of resources and recommend you follow these up, or investigate resources pertinent to your context. You will also see elements of the Belt woven into Part Three.

Let's pause at this point for a brief reflection.

---

139 Evans et al., 2024
140 Duckerin, 2021

Pausing for self-reflection
Intention around ethical practice

Taking a few moments to drop into stillness and silence, feeling into your posture and the body supported by the earth underneath, and being aware of the movement of breath.

Inviting you to drop in some questions into this practice space, to support reflection and explore your relationship around good practice and the ethical dimensions of your work. The answers are not as important as just opening to the questions and listening for any response or resonance – it may be a response from the mind (ideas, thoughts, words), or more of a felt sense within the body, or perhaps for you it is more of a connection to the heart.

Pausing with each question for a while, repeating it a few times, before moving on to the next question:

What matters to you within your MB work? What matters the most to you?

What matters to you around your role as a supervisor? What feels most important to you in this role?

What is your intention around good practice? What ethical commitment would you like to make?

Staying with this reflection as long as feels supportive for you. Ending with a few moments of returning attention to a wider awareness of the whole body.

Contracting

All models of supervision from other professions emphasise the importance of clear methods of professional contracting. There are two contracting processes: the overall supervisory contract and the session contract.

The overall supervisory contract

The overall supervision contracting arrangements lay out what supervision is and is not, the framework used, the relationship of supervision to the work undertaken, and the practicalities. Alongside this contracting phase are the beginnings of building the supervisory relationship. As well as clarification that supervision is related to their work, the supervisee's personal mindfulness practice formally and in life will also be part of the discussions in MBS in order to integrate practice into their MB work. So, contracting combines a commitment to a written agreement and the start of a collaborative conversation. Depending on the context of their MB work, the contracting stage may also need to include the supervisee's employing agency and any external agency. We offer a contracting checklist (Appendix A) and a sample MBS contract (Appendix B) in the Appendices.

Taking this time at the start to orient the supervisee to the breadth of MBS, to reach agreements and make commitments holds the integrity and the process of supervision, clarifies expectations and is a place to come back to, particularly if difficulties arise. The process will likely include some initial communications between the supervisor and supervisee, the supervisor sending a draft contract for the supervisee to review, and then a more structured conversation, including finalising the written contract. Below is a list of topics to include within this contracting phase:

- Gathering information about the supervisee's experience, including personal practice, teacher training, teaching/conveying mindfulness experience, previous experience with supervision, context, and population they are working with.
- The supervisee's goals, expectations, learning needs and whether there is a good match with the supervisor's experience, skills and knowledge.
- Beginning to explore the cultural background of the supervisee and supervisor, and what this contributes within the supervisory relationship/space, as this will also be relevant in relation to their MB work.
- The supervisee's needs such as communication needs and physical condition.
- The supervisee's learning style which will link with their neurocognitive functioning and may also be influenced by their culture, previous experience with the education system or previous supervision experience.
- How the supervisor and supervisee will work together: the nature of MBS, which could include sharing a copy of the MBS framework, what it is not, the way(s) the supervisor works and the way the supervisee likes to work, boundaries and flexibility, methods of supervision such as pre-supervision reflections and preparations, use of video or live teaching within the sessions, use of MBI:TLC or MBI:TAC.
- Agreements: frequency and duration, which may be linked to their stage of training and have specific requirements, fees and how to pay, arrangements (e.g. who sends the Zoom link), cancellations, missed sessions, sending agenda items ahead of supervision or not, time for review, and when it will end.
- Responsibilities: legal frameworks such as safety, confidentiality agreements, data protection, having appropriate insurance in place, offering and receiving feedback, responding to ruptures, and complaints procedures.

Supervisors need to be aware of the inherent power imbalance, ensuring that this contracting phase embodies the collaborative nature of MBS right from the start.

Openness and transparency are essential in this contracting phase, allowing either the supervisee or the supervisor not to take supervision forward if it does not feel like a 'good fit' between them. Factors such as knowledge and skill in a particular context, ways of working, or the felt sense are all aspects to consider regarding this good fit.

Establishing ground rules and boundaries at the start of the relationship supports both the supervisor and the supervisee in making the required commitment to the process. It also helps the supervisee make the best use of supervision and establishes this as a safe space for their support, learning, and development.

Reviewing supervision

Along with the attention given to the initial contracting phase, periodically revisiting the intentions and arrangements contributes to effective supervision by embedding feedback and responsivity into the process; agreeing on a date to review the supervisory relationship can be included in the initial contract.

Here are some considerations around reviewing supervision:

- Sometimes, it takes two or three supervision sessions to get a real feel for the process and the relationship. It can be helpful to suggest a first review after three or four sessions, allowing for any fine-tuning of the contract and the relationship at this early stage, or indeed for either the supervisee or supervisor to end the contract at that stage.
- Ending every supervision session by checking in on what has been most useful for the supervisee and inviting feedback on anything that could have been done differently or that would be helpful to pick up next time ensures there is a continual review and feedback process.
- Agree on a date for review that is either linked to a certain length of time/number of supervision sessions or linked to the supervisee's development stage, such as after completion of the close supervision required during training.
- A review may also be triggered by a change in circumstance, such as a change in the supervisee's needs, a change in their MB work context, or differences becoming apparent between supervisee and supervisor around intention or focus for supervision.
- As part of the review process, using a tool like the MBI:TLC can provide the supervisee with a structure to reflect on their strengths and areas for growth, which can be explored within the supervision session.
- To support the supervisee in offering feedback to the supervisor, using a simple feedback form can help, such as rating whether each aspect of supervision is 'about right', 'would like more of', or 'would like less of'.

The session agenda

Setting up a jointly agreed agenda at the start of each session provides direction and guidance and ensures that the supervisee's needs are best addressed within the session. It is a form of contracting for this particular session. There are different ways of setting the session agenda:

- The supervisee may send a list of items ahead of the session and/or the agenda may come out of discussion at the start of the session.
- The supervisee may send a more structured review of their MB work, perhaps free reflections or following an agreed format, or sending audio/video clips for review.
- Starting with a brief practice and then inviting the supervisee to drop into this practice space a sense of what feels important to bring to supervision, or what is alive for them in their MB work, sometimes reveals other items than the ones they had planned to bring.
- The supervisor can also add items to the agenda, perhaps picking up on items discussed last time.

Once the agenda is agreed upon, it is also possible that the supervisor and supervisee will mutually agree to make adjustments once they move into their inquiry together. Allowing time at the end of the supervision session for a brief reflection supports movement through the learning cycle, highlights key learning, what will be taken forward, and any actions for the supervisee or supervisor in preparation for the next session.

Ending of supervision

This commitment to the contracting process also includes preparing for and supporting endings for the supervisor and supervisee. As much as possible, planning for and acknowledging an ending of the supervisory relationship allows both supervisee and supervisor to mark the conclusion of their work together, honouring the process they have shared and offering appreciation, e.g. through words, a poem, images. To support a planned ending, it can help to include a clause in the initial contract stating that the supervisee agrees to say if they are considering ending rather than just dropping out of contact. Another helpful addition to the initial contract is that the supervisor, in the absence of any specific agreement, will assume the contract has ended if there is no contact from a supervisee within a certain time period, such as six months. This way there is a definite end to the process for both the supervisor and supervisee – if a supervisee gets in contact after this time, a new contracting process can be considered.

Here are a few common reasons why supervision may end:

Time-limited agreement: Supervision may be for a specific purpose, for example, during a supervisee's teacher training or as part of a certification process. In this case, there may be a formal supervisor statement that needs to be completed at the end or the use of the MBI:TLC as a way for the supervisee to reflect on their learning from supervision that they submit as part of a learning portfolio. Agreeing the procedure for these processes and being transparent about what is written supports a sense of openness and mutuality within the relationship. Other reasons for a time-limited contract might be when the supervisee's MB work is time-limited, e.g. they have a brief opportunity to offer an MBA within a particular setting/context but do not plan to continue to do so on an ongoing basis.

Changing needs of the supervisee: The supervisee may be moving into a different stage of their development or into a new or different area of MB work that is not the supervisor's expertise. In these circumstances, the supervisor can offer support as the supervisee decides what is needed next regarding their supervision, which may include supporting them in making contact with another supervisor.

Relationship factors: Sometimes it becomes apparent that there is not a 'good fit' between supervisor and supervisee in terms of the relationship or an incompatibility around ways of working. This can be a subtle recognition, tension, or a rupture within the relationship. Although these circumstances can be worked through, there will be times when it results in a decision to end the supervisory relationship, and of course this is already a part of the contract agreement that either supervisor or supervisee can decide not to continue to proceed. It may coincide with the time of reviewing the contract or outside of a planned review. Extending openness, kindness and mutuality to this tender moment can allow it to be named and acknowledged, and agreeing an ending plan.

An unexpected event: This might be ill health or some other significant life event. It is good practice for supervisors to have a therapeutic executor in place. A therapeutic executor is someone, usually a trusted colleague, who in the event of a serious accident, sudden illness or death of the supervisor, has the responsibility to contact and sensitively inform the supervisee and support them in navigating the impact of the experience.

Diversity and Inclusion

In other chapters, we point to the inner work of the supervisor in terms of their personal responsibility for reflection and development around themes of cultural responsiveness, diversity and inclusion and how this forms the bedrock of their way of being in relationship to their supervisees and their work. Here, we point to legal frameworks, which vary worldwide and in different contexts. Hence, it is important that both the supervisor and supervisee work in accordance with the relevant laws, frameworks and guidance in their context. If the supervisee works in a different country from the supervisor, it is especially important to consider points of reference.

Both the supervisor and supervisee will need to access relevant training to ensure they are aware of and comply with current laws, frameworks and understandings that support non-discriminatory practice. If they are part of an organization, they may already have access to training. Otherwise, they are responsible for seeking out training as part of their ongoing commitment to supporting integrity within the field.

Here are a few points of reference around the themes of diversity and inclusion:

- Starting from a broad perspective, the United Nations has created a comprehensive body of human rights law that provides a universal point of reference for promoting and protecting the rights and freedoms of individuals and groups.[141] The Universal Declaration of Human Rights, adopted in 1948, can both enlighten and challenge in considering one's own part in upholding the dignity and worth of all human beings to have the same basic equal rights. It can act as a guiding framework for all individuals within their work and communities, within all the ways that they interact and impact on their fellow human beings.
- In the United States of America, in the Bill of Rights,[142] the first ten Amendments of the Constitution spell out citizens' rights in relation to the government. They guarantee civil rights and liberties like freedom of speech, press, and religion. The Americans with Disabilities Act also prohibits discrimination based on disability.[143]
- In the UK, the Equality Act 2010[144] is a key legal framework to protect the rights of individuals and advance equality for everyone. It outlines nine protected characteristics that must be considered to prevent discrimination: age, race, religion or belief, disability, gender reassignment, marriage and civil partnership, pregnancy and maternity, sex, and sexual orientation.
- Many MB associations bring universal principles directly into MB work. For example, the work of the European Associations for Mindfulness (EAMBA) on diversity, equity and inclusion offers MB practitioners another point of reference in their commitment to non-discriminatory practice.[145]

---

141 United Nations Human Rights, https://www.un.org/en/global-issues/human-rights
142 United States of America, Bill of Rights, https://www.archives.gov/founding-docs/bill-of-rights/what-does-it-say
143 Americans with Disabilities Act, https://www.ada.gov/resources/disability-rights-guide/
144 UK Equality Act (2010), https://www.gov.uk/guidance/equality-act-2010-guidance
145 European Association of Mindfulness-Based Approaches statement on equity, diversity and inclusion, https://www.eamba.net/

- MB associations often draw on their specific country-of-origin legal frameworks and policies to inform their guidance. For example, the British Association of Mindfulness-Based Approaches (BAMBA) links the UK Equality Act to MB work through their vision and mission around equality, diversity and inclusion, and for UK-based practitioners is a key point of reference.[146]
- In many contexts, such as business, education, healthcare and third-sector organizations, articulated policies related to equity, diversity and inclusion will exist, and all professional regulatory bodies include guiding principles around non-discriminatory practice. We recommend supervisors encourage their supervisees to seek out the relevant frameworks and explore within supervision how they relate to their MB work.

For supervisors and supervisees working in countries without a mindfulness-based organization that articulates principles and frameworks, we encourage them to refer to the resources listed above to develop their own points of reference that will underpin their commitment to non-discriminatory practice.

It is essential that supervisors keep abreast of the rapidly growing body of work from innovators within the MB field who are placing social change right at the heart of MB work; their work can both challenge and inspire as the MB field intersects in an authentic way with current societal ethical themes. Below we share some resources we have found helpful and relevant as supervisors and MB supervision trainers:

- The Mindfulness Initiative leads on developing publications to influence policy around social and political issues.[147]
- Rhonda Magee is a key figure within the MB field and author of *The Inner Work of Racial Justice*.[148]
- The Urban Mindfulness Foundation provides social mindfulness teacher training to widen access for marginalized, underserved, and disadvantaged communities.[149]
- The accompanying resource pack from the paper, 'MBSR for our time: A curriculum that is up to the task'.[150]

You may like to follow up on some of these resources or find your own within your geographical location and context.

---

[146] British Association of Mindfulness-Based Approaches policy on equality, diversity and inclusion, https://bamba.org.uk/
[147] The Mindfulness Initiative https://www.themindfulnessinitiative.org/
[148] Rhonda Magee, 2021; https://rhondavmagee.com/
[149] The Urban Mindfulness Foundation https://www.urbanmindfulnessfoundation.co.uk/
[150] Resources for socially engaged MBPs https://home.mindfulness-network.org/mbsr-for-our-time-resources/

Safety

Good practice guidelines for MB teachers generally include a requirement for a qualification or equivalent life experience within mental or physical healthcare, education or social care, and knowledge and experience of the populations that they will encounter within their MB work. Among other factors, this supports understanding around themes of safety and vulnerability within their context: knowledge about how harm can occur, understanding the risks, knowing their responsibility in minimising harm and responding if they recognise the risk of or actual harm taking place.

In Europe and the UK, the term *safeguarding* is used to outline actions that promote welfare and protection from harm, abuse and neglect for children, young people and adults at risk. The term is also used by the United Nations, particularly in relation to children. Within other countries, legal frameworks promote well-being and freedom from harm which supervisors and supervisees can refer to for guidance. For a direct reference to MB supervision work, the Mindfulness Network's safeguarding policy offers an example of a UK-based application of the duty of care around preventing harm and abuse.[151]

Practitioners working within an organizational structure will be required to comply with policies and procedures, which will be supplemented by regular training. For independent MB practitioners, it is important that supervisors offer guidance around points of reference that can support the supervisee's knowledge and understanding of safety and vulnerability and encourage them to access relevant training. Supervisors themselves will also need to access regular training.

Safety and well-being

Themes of safety and vulnerability should regularly be discussed within supervision. They are directly linked to the recruitment processes for MBPs and to ensuring the well-being of participants as they engage with any MB practice or programme. This connects with themes of informed consent, where the potential participant clearly understands what to expect from the MB programme/intervention and any possible risks or harm.

This will include exploring:

- How the supervisee advertises/promotes their MB work.
- Their screening process – depending on the context, this initial review of expressions of interest from potential participants or review of an application form or referral form.

---

151 the Mindfulness Network safeguarding policy,
https://home.mindfulness-network.org/our-policies/

- Their assessment and orientation process.
- Knowing when it is appropriate to make onward recommendations or referrals if needed.

As well as exploring safety and vulnerability around their work, MBS will also be holding in mind the safety and well-being of the supervisee, with the supervisor drawing on these same frameworks if there is concern about the supervisee's well-being. This is where supra-vision (supervision of supervision) can be extremely helpful to support the supervisor in supporting the supervisee.

Trauma-sensitivity

With increasing awareness of the impact of trauma on individuals, communities and society, there are now much clearer guidelines for MB practitioners around trauma-sensitive MB practice. This includes a necessity for practitioners to be aware of the prevalence and impact of both individual and systemic trauma, how mindfulness can affect the sequelae of trauma, skills in offering trauma-sensitive practices that support all participants, and knowing how to support participants who may be impacted by past or current trauma. Supervisors can direct supervisees to appropriate training and frameworks that can inform their MB work, particularly if the supervisee is not a clinician.

Here are some points of reference in relation to individual trauma:

- It's incredibly helpful to have some understanding of how the human nervous system functions and an appreciation of the essential skill of self-regulation to support staying within an optimal level of arousal. Frameworks of understanding such as Daniel Siegel's window of tolerance[152] and Stephen Porges's polyvagal theory[153] are a useful place to start.
- For a concise review of trauma-sensitivity within MB work, refer to Eluned Gold's work on trauma sensitivity.[154]
- David Treleaven, a trauma professional and MB teacher with direct personal experience of the impact of meditation on trauma symptoms, has gathered extensive resources and training on trauma sensitivity within MB work. As well as a book, he also currently has a website that includes free resources and access to training.[155]

In relation to systemic trauma this involves moving beyond attributing problems to the individual and instead being willing to acknowledge the impact of oppression,

---

152 Siegel, 2020
153 Porges, 2022
154 Gold, 2021
155 Treleaven, 2018; https://davidtreleaven.com/

prejudice, abuse and marginalization. Supervisors can seek out resources and training that support themselves and their supervisees. We have found that the social change resources already listed and Resmaa Menakem's work[156] around the theme of systemic trauma have supported our development and MB work.

Mental health and well-being

Another key area linked to supporting the safety of vulnerable individuals is having a general understanding of mental health and mental ill-health. For example, Mental Health First Aid,[157] originating in Australia in 2000 and now offered internationally, provides training for individuals on how to identify, understand and respond to signs of mental ill-health and substance misuse. It is about providing initial help and support to a vulnerable person and assisting them to access the ongoing support that they need; it is the equivalent of calling for an ambulance, starting chest compressions and rescue breath (CPR) or offering other physical first aid if one comes across a person in a physical health emergency. Within MBS, this may be in relation to the people that the supervisee comes into contact with through their MB work, and also in relation to supporting the supervisor in responding to the needs of the supervisee and their mental well-being.

Safety within the supervisory relationship

With the inherent power difference between the supervisor and supervisee, the themes of safety and vulnerability relate directly to the supervisory relationship itself. The concept of psychological safety, considered essential in fostering an effective and collaborative learning environment, offers a helpful framework. It is about the supervisor creating conditions that reduce the supervisee's interpersonal risk so that they feel safe to ask questions, learn through trial and error, explore provisional ideas, make mistakes, disagree, and point out mistakes of the supervisor, without concern for negative consequences. Although developed in the context of clinical supervision, the framework developed by Lee et al. seems to map well onto MBS.[158]

They outline three stages or phases that build psychological safety:

- **Phase 1** – setting the stage, which is linked with the features we have named within the contracting stage.
- **Phase 2** – developing an educational alliance which includes clarity around methods of feedback and understanding cultural differences between supervisor and supervisee.

---

156 Resmaa Menakem is a therapist, trauma specialist and an author and leading voice on racialized trauma https://resmaa.com/
157 Mental Health First Aid International https://mhfainternational.org/international-mental-health-first-aid-programs/
158 Lee et al., 2022

- **Phase 3** – working collaboratively towards autonomy, which draws on developmental theory, fostering an open and curious stance, a genuine concern for the supervisee's well-being, and conveying a sense of mutuality through self-disclosure, being open to feedback and engaging in mutually respectful dialogue.

The concept of safe spaces within learning environments has been critiqued, as safety may be synonymous with no risk taking or discomfort.[159] Instead, the call is to create brave spaces, a concept from social justice literature. A brave space requires courage and respect in the face of conversations where there is a degree of challenge or discomfort. We encourage you to engage with the current debates around this topic, perhaps starting with the authors we have named – see how this resonates for you and what you find helpful as guiding frameworks within your supervisory relationships.

Competency

Competency is concerned with the supervisee's demonstration of the knowledge, skills, attitudes, abilities and behaviours that ensure the integrity of their MB work. The formal assessment of a supervisee's competency is usually part of the role of MB training organizations, but the supervisor also has a key role around supporting the development of competency. We recommend that supervisors consider what frameworks and processes might be most useful and supportive for each supervisee. In Chapter 10, under the section using the MBS framework through the developmental journey, we provide a detailed description of developmental learning and how this informs the processes within MBS.

Frameworks

The MBI:TAC is to date the main tool for assessing competency for MBP teachers, and we have discussed this and its companion, the MBI:TLC in other chapters (see Chapters 2 and 6). Within MBS, they can provide tools to dialogue around competency, helping to create a shared language and offering benchmarks. When the supervisee's MB work does not involve teaching a structured programme such as MBSR or MBCT, the supervisor and supervisee can explore together which domains or key features are still relevant for this context. For example, embodiment, articulated in domain three, is central within any MB work.

Rebecca Crane and Barbara Reid, in the context of MB teacher training, also acknowledge the central role of the MB practitioner's embodiment and suggest a balance between doing mode and being mode is important when considering skill development. For example, they describe that alongside demonstrating doing mode

---

159 Arao & Clemens, 2013; Brown, 2018; Brown & Guillen, 2022 https://brenebrown.com/podcast/building-brave-spaces/

skills such as *"connecting direct experience with conceptual understandings"*, the trainee is also demonstrating *"being in touch with direct sensory perception moment by moment"*.[160] So, within supervision, using the language of doing mode and being mode could provide a framework for considering the supervisee's development of competency. Naming this balance and seeing the Both/And nature of how competency is defined.

I (Pamela) have often used, as a framework, the approach Jon Kabat-Zinn names in his Foreword to a book focused on teaching mindfulness.[161] Like Crane and Reid, he defines competence as a balance; for example, he describes it as a combination of knowing and not knowing. He talks about *"the koan of good-enough"* teaching and offers a set of statements that are all prefaced with, *"It is good enough* for now *if ..."* His five statements point to preparation, practice, skills, knowledge and attitudes, while the use of *for now*, acknowledges both the present state of the supervisee's competence *and* that ongoing learning is necessary. I find it particularly helpful in framing the development of competency when a supervisee is being very critical of themselves or is anxious about their skill development. It provides a counterbalance to a tool such as the MBI:TAC which some supervisees can find intimidating and overwhelming.

Processes

As part of the role of supporting a supervisee's skill development and competency in teaching or conveying mindfulness, it is recommended that periodically the supervisor actually sees the supervisee's teaching via a recording or with in vivo opportunities in supervision (e.g. for the supervisee to guide a practice and engage in an inquiry of the supervisor). Prior to doing this, the supervisor and supervisee can discuss what framework would be most helpful to draw on as they consider the supervisee's skills and knowledge. For example, if the supervisee is currently engaged in an MB teacher training, they may want to focus on specific aspects that they are learning within this stage of their training. Or for a supervisee who has had a competency assessment, they may want to focus on areas of growth and development that were highlighted in the assessment. Offering feedback is an important part of the process of skill development and we offer guidance in Chapter 10.

What we want to highlight here is the importance of bringing awareness to the frameworks and processes that you draw on and to consider what will be most helpful for *this* supervisee – we come back to the concept of the Belt being not too tight, not too loose, with adjustments needed depending on the context.

---

160 Crane & Reid, 2016, p. 124
161 Kabat-Zinn, 2010, pp. xxi-xxii

Good practice

Within the MB teaching field, specific guidelines around good practice are articulated by international, country-specific and regional MB associations. Guidelines support consistency within the field around the skills, frameworks and embodied presence necessary for MB practitioners to offer MBPs that support growth and flourishing. These guidelines lay out ethical codes of conduct and specify requirements for training, supervision (during training and ongoing), ongoing MB teaching and work, ongoing personal practice, and ongoing personal and professional development. We value the concept of 'living documents', as described in the peer-reviewed paper, which points to the changing nature of guidelines as the field develops.[162] Part of supervision is ensuring that the supervisor and supervisee are keeping abreast with current thinking around good practice.

As part of professional practice, many external organizations require MB practitioners to keep a record each year of their adherence to these good practice guidelines. We recommend supervisees keep a record even if there is not an external requirement; in this way, the supervisee is holding their own personal ethical standards, and this record-keeping supports reflection on their learning and development. Supervision is a place to share these reflections and agree on areas for further development, which will link to the practitioner's supervision goals.

The recorded good practice, includes:

- initial MB training
- training/background prior to teaching mindfulness
- MB teaching and work
- supervision – ongoing, includes feedback on recordings/live teaching
- engagement with peers to share and learn
- ongoing mindfulness practice, including longer periods of practice and retreats
- other continuing professional development
- evidence of adherence to an ethical framework

---

162 Kenny et al., 2020

Example – conversations to support good practice

A supervisee brought choosing a 'suitable' retreat to supervision. They wanted to fulfil the requirements of the good practice guidelines whilst also meeting their personal practice intentions. There were issues around context – time, cost and setting to consider. Within the reflective space of MBS, the supervisor supported the supervisee in taking a considered approach to their decision making. Here are some of the aspects they explored together:

- They began by exploring the supervisee's current personal practice and what would be most supportive. This helped clarify the primary intention of deepening their practice rather than doing something to 'tick a box'. They reflected on whether there was a theme they had been exploring and would like to explore more, such as compassion-based practices, that could help provide a focus for their choice of retreat.

- They also considered recent retreats or other ways of deepening practice. What have they found nourishing? What less so? What have they discovered from previous experiences that could inform their choice this year?

- They considered current circumstances, factors that limit their ability to attend an in-person retreat and their personal vulnerability. Holding in mind the question 'Are there ways of navigating these circumstances?' For example, this supervisee had caring responsibilities, so they explored attending two shorter online retreats rather than one longer one.

- They also held in mind a longer view. For example, there were particular conditions this year that impacted choices for them which might not be there next year. They felt they might be able to commit to a longer retreat next year.

It was important for the supervisor to have an up-to-date knowledge of organizations that offer opportunities for deepening practice, including those that offer one-day practice sessions, two-to-three-day retreats and longer retreats. It was also helpful to know about donation-based events and the availability of bursaries that could support a supervisee within their financial means. Knowing about in-person and online opportunities supported the conversation. The supervisor also had some knowledge about personal retreats, as another option, with awareness of particular centres that provide nurturing conditions for a solitary or semi-solitary retreat.

As well as the supervisor's direct experience of being on retreats, over time they had gathered understanding from peers, their supervisor, and from supervisees, which helped to build up a bank of possible options.

Here are some examples of MB organizations which articulate good practice:

- International Mindfulness Integrity Network (IMI)[163]
- European Associations for Mindfulness (EAMBA)[164]
- Mindfulness Teachers Association Ireland (MTAI)[165]
- British Association of Mindfulness-Based Approaches (BAMBA). Alongside general guidelines for MB practitioners, they have also developed specific guidelines for teaching in the workplace and teaching people with learning disabilities[166]

Supervisors and supervisees may also have a core profession and will be guided by their good practice guidelines and professional codes of ethics.

The MB field is responding to the changing landscape by recognising the need for new MB programmes and adaptations to existing programmes while still upholding safety, integrity and good practice. For example, the International Panel for the Acknowledgement of Mindfulness-Based Programs is a pool of international mindfulness professionals responsible for evaluating newly developed or adapted MBPs that have been submitted for evaluation.[167] They operate independently under the umbrella of EAMBA.

For many MB practitioners, the adaptations and learning within real-world contexts will likely take considerable time, and applying for acknowledgement through the IPA may not be relevant or possible. As the diversity increases in terms of the way MBAs are conveyed, supervisors and supervisees will be exploring together how good practice guidelines can be applied in their context, including when adjustments are needed. Within the MBA field, peer-reviewed papers support practitioners in navigating this balance between fidelity and adaptation. Here are three papers which speak to these issues:

- Crane et al.[168] outline the essential elements and the flexible elements within an MB programme.
- Loucks et al.[169] offer a sequel to the previous work, with a framework to examine the different factors that can be adapted, the weft, to suit the context. The authors identify four influences on the weft: the culture, values and communication

---

163 IMI, https://iminetwork.org/wp-content/uploads/2024/02/Ethics-and-standards-for-MBP-Feb-2024.pdf
164 EAMBA, https://www.eamba.net/good-practice-guidance-for-teachers/
165 MTAI, https://mtai.ie/standards/; https://mtai.ie/wp-content/uploads/2021/07/MTAI-Supervision-Guidelines-2021.pdf
166 BAMBA, https://bamba.org.uk/good-practice-guidelines/
167 IPA Programs https://www.eamba.net/ipa-acknowledged-mbps/
168 Crane et al., 2017
169 Loucks et al., 2022

patterns of the target population, the setting and system within which the MBP will be offered, current interventions that support people within this context, and the intentions of the MBP in relation to this context.

- Crane et al.[170] explore how to retain fidelity to the MBSR programme while adapting it in ways that open the MB approach to the full societal demographic, including anti-oppression teaching methods and recognising all the conditions that influence distress and well-being within society and the communities where we live and teach.

As well as good practice guidelines for MB practitioners, some organizations also articulate guidelines for supervisors and trainers.

Other aspects of good practice include adhering to guidance on data protection, copyright laws and insurance such as professional indemnity and public liability. The supervisee is responsible for being aware of and complying with the relevant requirements within their country and context. Adding a statement within the written contract to this effect ensures that this is addressed right at the start of the supervisory relationship, and the supervisor can support the supervisee if they need help to comply. These aspects also apply directly to the supervisor, such as ensuring they have professional indemnity covering their supervision work and having a statement about their data protection policy in the supervision contract.

In conclusion, the Belt holds the integrity of MBS through principles, legislation and frameworks that attend to duty of care. Supervisors are key in supporting and guiding supervisees to practise safely, competently and effectively in the evolving and expanding scope of MB work. As part of the weft, the actual content and detail of the Belt will be determined by the context of the supervisee's MB work, but all five elements need to be an active and regular part of MBS. The elements of the warp (the Container, Mutual Inquiry and Space) ensure the Belt is held within an embodied relational process and help inform how taut the Belt needs to be as the supervisor discerns how tight or loose to hold the principles and frameworks depending on the specific circumstances.

Summary

We explored each of the five elements of the Belt.

1. Contracting
    - Contracting conversations and completing a written contract set the foundation for a boundaried professional relationship and maintain the supervision sessions' integrity.

---

170 Crane et al., 2023

- A session agenda provides direction and ensures that the time is used to the best effect to address the supervisee's needs and goals for supervision.
- Periodic review of supervision supports a process for feedback and ensures that the needs of the supervisee are being met.

2. Diversity and Inclusion
    - The MB Supervisor supports non-discriminatory practice by ensuring they and the supervisee know and understand relevant and context-specific laws and frameworks around themes of diversity and inclusion.
    - For MB approaches to develop in line with social policy and broaden their accessibility, it is important that all MB practitioners engage and participate in dialogues around broader themes such as social justice. The supervisor will be doing this work for themselves as well as encouraging their supervisee to consider these themes.

3. Safety
    - MBS recognizes the need for regular discussion around the theme of safety and acknowledges that it is the responsibility of all MB practitioners to be aware of their responsibility in terms of minimising harm and knowing how to take action if needed if there is a risk or actual act of harm. This includes trauma-sensitivity.
    - As well as the safety and well-being of those the supervisee comes into contact with during their MB work, the supervisor is also concerned about the safety and well-being of the supervisee. Accessing supra-vision is one way the supervisor resources themselves to support their supervisee.
    - Safety within the supervisory relationship includes establishing conditions to support psychological safety, including being aware of the power imbalance, cultural sensitivity and supporting mutuality within the relationship.
    - Critics of the use of the term *safe space* argue instead for the creation of brave spaces, where there is a willingness to be courageous in stepping into challenging conversations that might not always feel comfortable but are necessary within the learning environment.
    - The example above highlights the need for supervisors to stay connected with the evolving nature of guiding ethical frameworks, including these shifts in how we use language and define key concepts.

4. Competency
    - Whilst supervision is not about assessing competency, it is part of the role of MBS to support the supervisee's growth, teaching skills and competency.
    - Supervisors are encouraged to consider what frameworks and processes best support them and their supervisee in considering competency and how it can

be explored within MBS. Each supervisee will benefit from a balance of using empirical frameworks, with a more nuanced approach that is attuned to their specific needs. In this way, the supervisor is checking that the Belt is not too loose and not too tight around this theme of competency.
- It is recommended that supervisors see the supervisee's teaching/MB work periodically, which includes in vivo opportunities in supervision.

5. Good Practice
    - There are several guidelines around good practice and codes of conduct laid out by international and country-specific MB associations. The supervisee may also have their own core profession that articulates standards for good practice.
    - The supervisor supports the supervisee in accessing the most relevant frameworks for their MB work and encourages them to keep a record of their compliance and plans for compliance in the upcoming year.

Reflective questions

You may like to revisit the practice at the beginning of the chapter – what are your intentions around ethical practice and the elements of the Belt?

What is your relationship with guidelines, policies and procedures? Are there places you find them helpful, supportive, or resourcing? Are there places you find them restrictive or constricting?

Where are the gaps in your knowledge? Is there an area of the Belt where it would be useful to consider further training or study? E.g. safeguarding, trauma-sensitivity, diversity and inclusion.

Is your process for contracting robust and helpful? Are there any changes you might like to experiment with?

When was the last time you reviewed the contract with your supervisee? If it was a while ago, what gets in the way? How might you conduct a review?

When was the last time safety and vulnerability were part of the explorations within a supervision session? Did you draw on aspects of the Belt to support you and your supervisee?

How might you bring the themes of diversity and inclusion into supervision? How do these relate to the supervisory relationship and the supervisee's MB work?

How do you explore competency with your supervisee? Do you use tools, recordings of their teaching or live teaching within supervision to explore their skills? If not, what gets in the way?

If your supervisee offers MB work in new and innovative ways, what do you draw on for guidance around good practice?

References

Arao, B., & Clemens, K. (2013). From safe spaces to brave spaces: A new way to frame dialogue around diversity and social justice. In L. M. Landreman (Ed.), *The art of effective facilitation* (pp. 135-150). Routledge.

Brown, B. (2018). *Dare to lead: Brave work. Tough conversations. Whole hearts.* Vermillion.

Crane, R., Brewer, J., Feldman, C., Kabat-Zinn, J., Santorelli, S., Williams, J., & Kuyken, W. (2017). What defines mindfulness-based programs? The warp and the weft. *Psychological Medicine, 47*(6), 990-999. https://doi.org/10.1017/S0033291716003317

Crane, R. S., Callen-Davies, R., Francis, A., Francis, D., Gibbs, P., Mulligan, B., O'Neill, B., Williams, N. K. P., Waupoose, M., & Vallejo, Z. (2023). Mindfulness-based stress reduction for our time: A curriculum that is up to the task. *Global Advances in Integrative Medicine and Health, 12.* https://doi.org/10.1177/27536130231162604

Crane, R. S., & Reid, B. (2016). Training mindfulness teachers: Principles, practices and challenges. In D. McCown, D. Reibel, & M. S. Micozzi (Eds.), *Resources for teaching mindfulness: An international handbook* (pp. 121-140). Springer.

Duckerin, P. (2021). Professional practice. In R. S. Crane, Karunavira, & G. M. Griffith (Eds.), *Essential resources for mindfulness teachers* (pp. 167-178). Routledge. https://doi.org/10.4324/9780429317880

Evans, A., Griffith, G. M., & Smithson, J. (2024). What do supervisors' and supervisees' think about mindfulness-based supervision? A grounded theory study. *Mindfulness, 15,* 63–79. https://doi.org/10.1007/s12671-023-02280-8

Gold, E. (2021). Trauma-sensitivity. In R. S. Crane, Karunavira, & G. M. Griffith (Eds.), *Essential resources for mindfulness teachers* (pp. 177-188). Routledge. https://doi.org/10.4324/9780429317880

Kabat-Zinn, J. (2010). Foreword. In D. McCown, D. Reibel, & M. S. Micozzi, *Teaching mindfulness: A practical guide for clinicians and educators* (pp. ix-xxii). Springer.

Kenny, M., Luck, P., & Koerbel, L. (2020). Tending the field of mindfulness-based programs: The development of international integrity guidelines for teachers and teacher training. *Global Advances in Health and Medicine, 9.* https://doi.org/10.1177/2164956120923975

Lee, E. H., Pitts S., Pignataro, S., Newman, L. R., & D'Angelo, E. J. (2022). Establishing psychological safety in clinical supervision: Multi-professional perspectives. *The Clinical Teacher, 19*(2), 71–78. https://doi.org/10.1111/tct.13451

Loucks, E. B., Crane, R. S., Sanghvi, M. A., Montero-Marin, J., Proulx, J., Brewer, J. A., & Kuyken, W. (2022) Mindfulness-based programs: Why, when, and how to adapt? *Global Advances in Health and Medicine, 11.* https://doi.org/10.1177/21649561211068805

Magee, R. V. (2016). Teaching mindfulness with mindfulness of race and other forms of diversity. In D. McCown, D. Reibel, & M. S. Micozzi (Eds.), *Resources for teaching mindfulness: An international handbook* (pp. 225-246). Springer.

Magee, R. V. (2021). *The inner work of racial justice: Healing ourselves and transforming our communities through mindfulness.* Penguin.

Porges, S. W. (2022). Polyvagal theory: A science of safety. *Frontiers in Integrative Neuroscience, 16,* 871227. https://doi.org/10.3389/fnint.2022.871227

Siegel, D. J. (2020). *The developing mind: How relationships and the brain interact to shape who we are.* Guilford Press.

Treleaven, D. A. (2018). *Trauma-sensitive mindfulness: Practices for safe and transformative healing.* W. W. Norton.

Part Three:
Using the Mindfulness-Based Supervision Framework

Part Three introduces you to various contexts of applying the framework. We have developed the framework to be versatile and allow supervisors and supervisees to be flexible to meet the needs of the conditions that arise wherever MBS occurs. This might call for different parts of the warp of the framework to be emphasized. Aspects of the weft will vary, such as the frameworks that hold the standards within the Belt and the content brought to supervision within the Petals, which are shaped by a multitude of factors. We give examples within each chapter of ways of using the framework. These examples offer an illustration but are not exhaustive. Our interviewees, Uz Afzal, Debbie Hu, Jem Shackleford and Martin Summerfield, have supported us greatly in this part of the book, helping us to think through possible modulations and offering their insightful experiences and examples.

Our interviewees

We introduce our interviewees in the order in which they appear in the coming chapters.

Uz Afzal (she/her) is a mindfulness supervisor, practitioner and author. She is of South Asian descent and is London-based. She teaches mindfulness to children, and to adults in various contexts, including in mental health spaces, with communities of colour, LGBTQ+ folks and refugees and in corporate, arts and educational settings.[171]

Debbie Hu (she/her) is a senior consultant psychiatrist in Taiwan. She teaches, trains, and supervises a range of mindfulness-based programmes and diverse populations with organizations such as the Oxford Mindfulness Foundation (UK), Mindfulness in Schools Project (UK), and the Mindfulness Network (UK). Her commitment to mindfulness extends to volunteer service across different regions, e.g. as President of the Taiwan Clinical Society of Mindfulness-Based Approaches and a trustee at the Mindfulness Network (UK).[172]

Jem Shackleford (he/him) is a mindfulness teacher, supervisor and practitioner. He teaches mindfulness to adults and children in various contexts. He is also a teacher trainer through the Mindfulness Network (UK) and Mindfulness in Schools Project (UK), and is the MBITAC Lead for the Oxford Mindfulness Centre (UK). He is a trustee of the British Association of Mindfulness-Based Approaches (BAMBA). Through his work and personal life, he tries, as a white British male, to use his unearned privilege to make the transformative impact of mindfulness accessible to those who are excluded. He lives with his partner in Cornwall where he can follow his other passion, surfing.[173]

Martin Summerfield (he/him) trained in MBSR at Bangor University (UK) in 2015 and specializes in applying mindfulness within commercial workplaces. He runs Anchorpoint and also facilitates for Awaris, delivering mindfulness and resilience training across the finance, IT, energy, and government sectors. Additionally, he supervises mindfulness trainers in commercial settings. Martin lives with his family near the Lake District and enjoys outdoor activities.[174]

---

171 For more information visit, https://www.beherebreathe.co.uk
172 For more information visit, https://supervision.mindfulness-network.org/choose-a-supervisor/debbie-hu/ https://oxfordmindfulness.org/people/debbie-hu
173 For more information visit, https://supervision.mindfulness-network.org/choose-a-supervisor/jem-shackleford/
174 For more information visit, https://anchorpoint.org.uk

Chapter 8
Using the Mindfulness-Based Supervision Framework with Culture in Mind

Opening a conversation about culture and difference isn't the same thing as being open to it. A good supervisor should do both.[175]

This vital chapter looks at how awareness of culture must be part of applying the MBS framework. In more recent years, there have been moves within the mindfulness field to shift the dial in terms of increasing inclusivity and diversity within MBPs. In her research into MBS in 2019, Alison found that research participants spoke of the issues around lack of diversity, with comments such as, *"I am aware of the hugely white bias in the mindfulness world and the need to address that."*[176] One of the recommendations in that research was to raise supervisors' awareness and skills in working within diversity and inclusion and increase awareness of power in relation to culture. This active consideration of culture within supervision can also be found in other fields and modalities.[177]

---

175 Hardy & Bobes, 2016. p. 79
176 Evans, 2019, p. 131
177 Vekaria et al., 2023a; Hardy & Bobes, 2016

We acknowledge that the MBS framework itself has been influenced by many cultural factors, including the cultural background and experience of those behind its development, along with the cultural influences of the settings and geographical location within which it has been developed. It makes sense that it may need some modulation as it meets other situations. Several years ago, our colleague, Uz Afzal, facilitated a training day for supervisors within the Mindfulness Network about more effectively bringing equality, diversity, and inclusion into our supervision work. This was a question that had been on our minds for some years and following that training day, we committed to making changes to the MBS framework to reflect this orientation more explicitly.

This is a massive area of inquiry and work, which we can only begin to address here. Therefore, our focus will be centred specifically on supervision and how the MBS framework can support supervisors to work actively with culture in mind. Culturally responsive supervision may be a new area of learning for many reading this book. We are very much in the process of learning ourselves, so we write this chapter as a beginning, drawing upon others' experiences in the field of supervision who have been practising cultural awareness for some time.[178]

Our interviewees, Debbie Hu and Uz Afzal, offer insights about cultural awareness within supervision from their cultural perspective. Debbie describes the country she lives in, Taiwan, as a mosaic of cultures and cultural influences, histories and heritage, including Chinese, Japanese and indigenous cultures, alongside varying degrees of Westernization. Uz describes London, where she lives, as a diverse and vibrant city. The settings in which she works include diverse aspects of culture in terms of race, sexual orientation, mental health and often intersections of all three. We could see this as the picture everywhere; we are all cultural beings, living and working in a mosaic of cultures, with our own cultural backgrounds and experiences made up of diverse factors and influences.

We begin by outlining some broader principles of what we mean by culture, culturally sensitive supervision and the MBS supervisors' role before moving into how cultural context can be held in awareness using the MBS framework. Returning to our weaving metaphor, we see how a different cloth gets woven according to culture within the Petals. Our interviewees give examples from their own contexts to illustrate how MBS might be modulated. From these examples, we encourage reflection on what holding cultural context in mind within MBS might mean for you and your supervisee(s).

---

178 Vekaria et al., 2023a, 2023b; Hardy & Bobes, 2016

What do we mean by culture?

There is a wide array of possible answers to this question, so we will outline the terrain we suggest is relevant for MBS. Importantly, we want to emphasise that culture permeates all of us and our lives; as one of our supervisor colleagues said, *"We are living in the ocean of culture"*. Culture has many nuances and ripples through all aspects of our lives.

When discussing culture in relation to supervision, Vekaria et al.[179] talk about culture being a heterogeneous construct, often conceptualized by numerous contextual variables (e.g. race, gender, class, age). In their book about culturally sensitive supervision and training, Kenneth Hardy and Toby Bobes discuss culture as, *"A worldview, an epistemology or way of thinking about the world and where we place ourselves in it."*[180] They give some sense of the many nuances that relate to culture, which we have drawn upon:

- It is a broad-based, multidimensional concept comprised of, but not limited to, class, religion, sexual orientation, gender, family of origin (over several generations), ethnicity, age, regionality, education, and socio-economic factors.
- It is dynamic, fluid and static, influencing and shaping how we navigate the world. For example, my (Alison) gender identity has remained static throughout my life as female, but the meanings I give to this and how I behave have been a more dynamic process.
- It is pervasive and influential. All aspects of our lives are affected by culture, and we all have a cultural journey.
- It is multifaceted and multipurpose, sometimes in positive and other times in negative ways, e.g. supports a feeling of rootedness, is part of identity development, can be a coping resource, brings about rules of engagement for groups and society, can be a way of delineating inclusion and exclusion, and can be a marker of pride and shame.
- There can be ways that socially constructed categories such as gender, race and class are used to discriminate. The theory of intersectionality[181] describes how these categories are best understood as overlapping or intersecting rather than isolated and distinct. Therefore, there is a cumulative way that multiple forms of discrimination combine.
- Culture is timeless. It can connect to our history and how this has shaped us, situate us in the present, and provide a foundation for how we envisage and approach our future, giving a sense of what is possible or not.

---

179 Vekaria et al., 2023b
180 Hardy & Bobes, 2016, p. 2
181 Term first coined by Kimberlé Crenshaw, 1989, 1991

Culturally responsive supervision

Culturally responsive supervision assumes that we are all cultural beings and that a supervisor's and supervisee's cultural background and experiences permeate their work and supervision.[182] We might say that we all come with kaleidoscopic identities, which impact our context of privilege, discrimination, and oppression and shape our resilience and uniqueness.

When asked, *"What does cultural responsivity mean to you?"* Uz responded that it begins with ourselves. By this, she means the process of recognising and being aware of all aspects of our identities and being open to these, with awareness of the ways in which others and ourselves have met these different aspects. Remembering it's an ongoing, evolving, changing process. Uz said: *"I approach with a wish to open, soften, accept and embrace, which helps to heal the wounding caused through aspects of my identity not being met. In supervision, I bring this awareness of identity to myself and my supervisees. I hope that this awareness ripples out from them to the communities within which they are living and working."*

Some of the ways that culture may show up within MBS relate to:

- Aspects of identity and the ways these identities are met.
- Education/learning style.
- Language and communication.
- Power within the relationship(s).
- The influence of geographical location on values and behaviour, e.g. understandings of well-being, different ways that discrimination is more apparent.
- Connection with cultural influences within the supervisee's work.

In conversations with other MBS supervisors, there has been an acknowledgement of how difficult it can feel to work within diversity, especially when it is unfamiliar. It can bring conflicting emotions, discomfort, shame, fear, sadness, and anger, along with a wish to 'get it right', not wanting to cause harm through misplaced words and actions, whilst also knowing that no words/inaction can also cause harm. There is a dance between acknowledging the concept and experience of common humanity and acknowledging difference and diversity because by not doing so, we might shut down an individual's or group's engagement and contribution.

While there are more challenging aspects of working within diversity, there are clear benefits for all in developing welcoming inclusive spaces within MBS and all aspects of MB work. Culturally diverse spaces are a rich environment for learning,

---

182 Vekaria et al., 2023b

encouraging curiosity, enlivening energy levels and interest, and widening views and perspectives as we take in a range of experiences. Diverse spaces are exciting places for personal growth and for co-creations to emerge.

So, working on the premise that culture permeates all of us, it is important to develop cultural competence. By this, we mean developing the cultural awareness, knowledge, and skills required to respond competently, sensitively, and with attunement as an MB supervisor. We will continue in this chapter to provide some ways to develop cultural competency.

Role and responsibilities as a mindfulness-based supervisor around culture

The role of an MBS supervisor includes being culturally sensitive, with the responsibility to bring conversations around culture into supervision and lead the way into this vulnerability. Hardy and Bobes name the key ingredients for being a culturally sensitive supervisor as *"... compassion, integrity and 10,000 hours of practice."*[183] This reminds us that this work requires sustained effort and commitment and is an ongoing learning process that will be taking place both within and outside of the supervision space. It requires intentionality, reflection, and dialogue with others.

Here are some of the responsibilities we suggest you hold as a culturally attuned MBS supervisor:

- Leading the way in bringing culture into MBS and continuing to open conversations and safe spaces for vulnerability to be shared.
- Being prepared by committing to your own ongoing personal work around culture.
- Developing your cultural awareness and skills in cultural humility.
- Being prepared by embedding conversations about cultural responsivity into your MB work (teaching, 1:1 work, supervision, supra-vision, peer connections).
- Specifically ensuring that supervisees know that culture is part of supervision and doing this in ways that are culturally appropriate.
- Being sensitive to the use of language, how it informs a supervisee's experience and any potential miscommunications.
- Being aware of how power dynamics are impacted by cultural experiences, values and norms.
- Being willing to make and learn from mistakes.
- Being transparent, open and collaborative.
- Being sensitive, curious, and brave.

---

183 Hardy & Bobes, 2016, p. 27

Uz spoke about her experience of being empowered as a supervisee through her supervisor and how she aspires to take this into her role as a supervisor. She describes this in the example:

Example – empowering and 'uplifting' as part of the responsibilities of the supervisor

My (Uz) experience of supervision was that my two brilliant supervisors have seen my potential, resulting in a feeling of being uplifted. It is both a felt sense and has led to positive actions.

For example, each of my supervisors has:

- Seen and acknowledged all of me.
- Sometimes seen more in me than I see in myself – strengths and potential. This is important as the opposite has often been my experience.
- Believed in me and put me forward for things.
- Invited me into the field. Opening opportunities, widening circles for me, for example, inviting me to present alongside them at a conference.
- Supported me through the anxiety of stepping into new opportunities. That anxiety, too, is fuelled by my cultural background and experiences, and the supervisor was aware of this. For example, how it felt to speak at a mindfulness conference when I had not seen many people with my cultural background in that position before.

All of this brings about a sense of, *"If my supervisor keeps on respecting me and my work that much, maybe I have to believe their belief in me."*

I, too, then want to empower supervisees to bring all of themselves into the mindfulness space – it is crucial they are there. It is important that they feel comfortable to bring all aspects of their identities into the role. There is so much that we share that is not just about mindfulness – who we are, how we see things, and how we relate to each other.

As a supervisor, I think it is important to do what I can to help others create spaces for mindfulness in their communities. I hope I can help by offering a place in which supervisees feel acknowledged, encouraged and believed in. As well, I hope to be able to give supervisees space for the tough times and the impact of damage they may have encountered. I hope to be there for them consistently with care.

I see it as part of my role and responsibility as a supervisor to play whatever small part I can in shifting the landscape of who is sharing mindfulness and who has a seat at the table.

Using the warp of the mindfulness-based supervision framework

The warp (the Container, Mutual Inquiry and Space) has already been described in detail in Chapters 3, 4 and 5. These warp threads provide a strong mindfulness base for explorations around culture. The Container helps to create a safe place and a brave space for this work within MBS, beginning with anchoring into a clear intention. In the previous example from Uz about empowering and uplifting, we can see links to all the elements of the warp. The supervisor is embodying aspects of the Container; they are fully present with the supervisee, attuning to their needs and dialoguing in ways which uplift. They make spaces for the supervisee to be seen and heard and to pause to tune into the whole of the supervisee.

Another supervisor spoke about an experience in a supervision session with interpretation. The supervisor was finding it difficult to follow at times and was not sure if it was the supervisee's expression or how the translator translated. The supervisee is very shy and reserved and can be quite concrete in their thinking. Yesterday, the supervisor really allowed space to see all of the supervisee, honouring them in their entirety, without trying to get anywhere in the discussion/exploration. It meant the supervisor slowed it down, moved in closer to some of supervisee's points, and asked more questions with the intention of helping them understand more rather than about the supervisor trying to understand. The supervisor concludes with, *"I'm so glad I did, as by the end, we had a lovely moment of clarity where we could really sense into the supervisee's authenticity and unique way of offering mindfulness to their group while also seeing how they can open to being more responsive to the needs of the participants."* In this example, we see important aspects of the warp, the attuning within the inquiry and space, coming together to support a new way of knowing.

A caution is that in this area of cross-cultural work, we do not always get it 'right', and sometimes, with the best intentions, words and actions have an impact and cause harm and upset, which we need to address. As a supervisor and mindfulness practitioner, you may think you are a good person – yes, and you can be a good person and still cause harm, remembering that there can be a mismatch between intention and impact. As best you can as a supervisor, you are embodying a willingness to be vulnerable, show courage, be brave, be humble and not know, not be sure, and maintain attitudes such as beginner's mind and curiosity. Integrity and safety are cultivated as part of the Container and the relational Mutual Inquiry. Creating safety includes knowing that race and ethnicity might be difficult to bring up for those who have had to deal with racism and discrimination, taking care not to generalise, having an openness to talk about your own ethnicity, and curiosity about the supervisee's.[184]

---

184 Vekaria et al., 2023a

Compassion and wisdom are important qualities that support connection with the supervisee. Debbie spoke about her experience of first arriving in English-speaking mindfulness settings (English is not her first language). She felt the fear of making mistakes and didn't feel confident. However, kindness and feeling included by the supervisor and senior teachers from other countries supported her in finding her way. She experienced this compassionate welcome through calmness, acceptance, encouragement, positive feedback, and a focus on the content conveyed, not the preciseness and correctness of each word that is spoken – letting the essence be conveyed and checking detail when needed.

We are advocating the making of space for cultural attunement throughout the process of MBS. One aspect of mutual inquiry we want to emphasise is how cultural power may be active within the supervisory relationship. Cultural power is where some cultural groups may benefit socially more than others; different histories and experiences of privilege and oppression may amplify power imbalance. Vekaria et al. look at the under-researched area of race and ethnicity in supervision where there is a visible difference between the supervisor and supervisee. Qualities and skills such as acceptance, permission, and flattening power are required.[185] The Mutual Inquiry of the MBS framework includes that as part of the relational aspect of MBS, there is a meeting as cultural beings, requiring attunement, reciprocal respect and sharing and modulating when needed.

Using the weft of the mindfulness-based supervision framework: the Belt

Promoting cultural responsiveness, non-discriminatory practice, safe, inclusive, and diverse cultures within workplaces, organizations, and professional practice is found in many aspects of society, as well as the mindfulness field. In Chapter 7, we outline frameworks in different geographical and organizational settings that hold this duty of care that can be drawn upon within MBS. These may be legal frameworks around non-discriminatory practice, as well as policies and practices that support equality, equity, diversity and inclusion. Supervisors encourage supervisees to find out about the relevant frameworks in their context, helping these frameworks to be on the supervisee's radar and open the conversation.

We pick up here specifically on the contracting process and creating safety with cultural context in mind.

---

[185] Vekaria et al., 2023a; 2023b

Contracting

As a supervisor, there are many things you are attending to in these early conversations. You are beginning to build the relationship, finding ways to welcome all aspects of identity and show your own, while feeling into what is appropriate in this situation. You might consider what sense of yourself as a cultural being you portray through your bio, website, staff profile, etc. And then how to introduce yourself to the supervisee. You may not go through every aspect of your identity and cultural background immediately or ever, but you might feel into what is enough to begin to give something of yourself and open the space. For example, this might include some of the following: where you live, have lived, family, pets, hobbies, language you speak, your current context, your ethnicity, mindfulness practice and influences, religion/spirituality, any other aspects of identity that feel important to name as early beginnings. You might continue to say a little about your intention in sharing this is to invite the cultural context for both you and the supervisee to be part of the supervision conversation as you recognise how it shapes who we are, how we are, how we are in relationship and the link to MB work. You may continue to say how you wish to create a safe space within supervision for conversations to be possible when it feels appropriate. And then invite the supervisee to introduce themselves.

In summary, it is part of the role of the supervisor to let supervisees know that conversations about culture can be part of supervision. I (Alison) was struck by a simple example in a recent MBS connection where a supervisor introduced themselves with the following, *"I am ..., I live in ..., originally I am from ..., I speak ... languages and arrive here open to and excited by diversity"*. It felt like a simple, practical cultural introduction with a different feel to an introduction about where we work and what we do.

Cultural awareness can also be added to the supervision review process as part of re-contracting around working together. Asking questions such as:

- Did your supervisor/I understand you as a cultural being and respond with sensitivity?
- Would you have liked more or less focus on culture?
- Is there anything about culture that would have been useful to bring into supervision?

Safety

Creating safety within MBS sits within the Container and the Belt. Safety includes awareness and understanding of systemic trauma and its impact and being able to create and maintain safe spaces for layers of oppression to be held. Uz described noticing in her work that within groups with specificity (identities in common), there is a sense of safety and mutual understanding which is both unspoken and sometimes spoken. It is both powerful and tender. She spends much time setting the Container – establishing a group culture to support safety and comfort. For her, meeting all aspects of a supervisee's social location and cultural identity is an important foundation before a safe space can be created. She said: *"The world feels entirely different when you are uplifted and celebrated for all the parts of you. You know it and feel it."*

Without the safety of being met, what might a supervisee do? Stop supervision, carry on half-heartedly, maybe even stop the whole path they are on?

Using the weft of the mindfulness-based supervision framework: the Petals

In Chapter 6, we discussed the Petals, the content of MBS, and the learning of the *what, how* and *why* of MB work. As weft threads, there are many factors that influence the variation in how these weft threads get woven, and in this chapter we point out culturally specific factors. When it comes to culture, we would also emphasise that there will be aspects of a supervisee's culture that a supervisor does not have knowledge and experience in, so they will be learning from the supervisee. As a supervisor, you need to listen to supervisees and ask questions whilst balancing not taking up all the supervision space with your needs as a supervisor to understand. You will likely need to do some work outside of supervision as well.

We look at each of the Petals with culture in mind (concentrating on the Context Petal) and what resources a supervisor to meet diverse experiences, themes, topics and issues.

Contexts

As we saw in Chapter 6, this is a vast Petal and here we point to some of the factors in relation to culture, training, geographical location, language and social context.

Training. As a supervisor, you might know less about a supervisee's training context if their training is taking place in a different country with a language you don't speak. It can be more challenging to read websites, training handbooks, and curriculum details, requiring time to investigate and understand.

Geographical location. Different geographical locations will have their own cultural context, which might influence a whole range of experiences, such as education systems and approaches, different histories and narratives passed down the generations, and different perceptions of mindfulness and values. Within MBS, we are actively seeking to understand context, history, value systems, and communication styles. This can be in very small ways; for example, I (Alison) noticed that when Debbie and I met for the interview, we both had a cup of tea. I asked Debbie what tea she was drinking, which opened a conversation about tea in Taiwan and its history. There might be moments of acknowledging holidays and festivals, seasons and weather patterns.

Language. Language is a huge part of cross-cultural supervision. The supervisor can be curious and sensitive about how language informs the supervisee's experience and the supervisory process. The meaning of words will vary in different languages and words cannot be simply translated word for word. What requires one word in one language might need a sentence in another. Debbie noticed this in her experience translating the MBS resource book into Mandarin for supervision training. For example, there are three different words for practice and two different words for integrity. She and her colleagues wanted to convey with care the specific meaning in the MBS framework and this approach to supervision.

Supervisors need to remember to pay attention to all the nuances around language and watch for misunderstandings and miscommunication, even when speaking the same language. It is easy for the subtlety conveyed through language to be missed or misunderstood. When words are not so easily understood, tone and pitch are especially important. It can be supportive to check in and clarify regularly. Also, building a supportive culture for the supervisee to be able to say they don't understand and ask for an explanation. Each language (and within languages) has its stories, phrases, verbal expressions and colloquialisms. In the words of Debbie, *"We can make real-time adjustments, clarifying about what is being expressed, not assuming, and making language adjustments".*

Debbie gave three examples that convey from several angles something of these many nuances around language within MBS.

Example – the nuances around language within MBS from Debbie

1. A supervisee brought the challenge of a participant who was not engaging. Their perception was that the participant was disengaged, not interested or motivated in the group. During the exploration within MBS, the supervisor put forward the possibility that this may be due to culture, for example, the language barrier, as the group was not being taught in the participant's first language. The supervisee hadn't considered a language barrier. They started to open up to an alternative perception – another way of making meaning together by considering the cultural issues. They explored ways to support the participants.

   The supervisor then noticed a second layer, recognising that the supervisee perceived their lack of awareness of the language barrier as a failure on their part. A strong cultural influence from their educational background to do well, get things right, and be competent was influencing a feeling of shame. This, too, was named and explored.

   In this example, we can see how the supervisor is supporting an opening of view/perception for the supervisee and bringing cultural considerations into the supervision, both for participants and the supervisee themselves.

2. The supervisor and supervisee speak different first languages. The language of supervision is the supervisee's first language and one of the other languages the supervisor speaks. The supervisor notices moments when they think they have understood but then feels there is something else that may be missed. They use subtitles as well for video material. They pay attention to voice, tone, body gesture to get a fuller picture.

   In this example, we can see the variety of ways that might be used to understand (spoken words, written words, non-verbal communication) and how patience and time support. As well as the precision in the actual words, the supervisor can often pick up something in the atmosphere. There may also be conversations needed about when it feels more helpful to find a supervisor who speaks the same language.

3. Debbie's experience as a supervisee and trainee in English-speaking contexts is that she expresses herself slightly differently, noticing that in English she is more talkative and thinks more straightforwardly, and in Mandarin she sits back more. This is not a conscious decision; it just happens. It helps her to recognise that others will have different reactions by participating in different languages, which can change the experience.

Social context. As a supervisor, you may not know everything about issues relating to systemic trauma, inclusion/exclusion, and justice/injustice, but it is part of your responsibility to be engaged in learning and updating yourself. It helps if both the supervisor and supervisee have a willingness to work with assumptions and bias (conscious and unconscious) and be open to new ways of seeing and working. This knowledge, experience, and openness are in the background of MBS as well as coming directly into the content at times. Supervisees will be working within diversity in their work and bringing it to supervision, or it gets revealed within the inquiry process. There may be factors in their life around any of these issues that impact their mindfulness practice and work. If they teach programmes or work with approaches that directly address social justice, these themes will hold a more central place in MBS.

MBS can be a safe place to explore and practice saying the words to enable conversations to take place.

Example – enabling conversations

A white supervisor new to supervising is about to supervise for the first time. Her supervisee is black. In supra-vision (supervision of supervision), the supervisor invites an exploration about how they can bring this up and talk about ethnicity in a way that leaves an open space for the supervisee but also doesn't assume what they may need. Within supra-vision, the supervisor is nervous about how to bring this up and what to say. They practise saying the words, trying out different sentences, feeling the unfamiliarity, and checking in with their intention. They take this forward, noticing that they likely would not have opened this conversation without this time in supra-vision.

Mindfulness-based work

In this Petal, supervision is focused on the development of skills within whatever MB work is undertaken. The supervisor will bear in mind different ways of learning and pedagogies that are culturally based. They may not align exactly with what they are familiar with, so the supervisor will be moderating and modulating their approach. Some of this is due to developmental stages of learning and sometimes cultural approaches to learning.

In terms of skills development the MBI:TLC and MBI:TAC can be used within this Petal, especially for those teaching MBPs. However, at the time of writing this book, there is awareness that aspects of the tools may not entirely fit across all cultures. For example, there may be different styles of inquiry, communication and ways of sharing, bringing an opportunity for conversations within MBS.

There may be a variety of ways that supervisees are adapting and modulating MBPs.[186] Supervision offers a space to explore the intentions, the rationales, and the actual modulations before and after implementation. All of this can support the supervisee in navigating the balance between adherence and being integral to longstanding approaches along with innovative and much-needed shifts. One example is that the metaphors, examples, poems and quotes used within MBPs may not be relevant or relatable. In supervision, the supervisor might be celebrating different poems, examples and metaphors and empowering the supervisee to bring relevance to their own setting as they teach, practise and convey mindfulness.

The supervisor can also pay attention to the style of communication, for example, the degree of politeness, directness and use of humour. An example from supervision training comes to mind when we were exploring offering and receiving feedback to supervisees. One supervisor expressed how, in their culture, there was a directness within communication so that feedback would be given very directly. They imagined how it would be if they worked with a supervisee less used to this cultural style; they might need to modulate. And equally if someone was supervising that supervisor, they may need to modulate to being more direct. It is the same sort of ways we are modulating and attuning all the time in MBS, just here it is with culture in mind.

Group and individual processes

This Petal provides a great opportunity to tune into the diversity of the participants or clients the supervisee is working with. If the supervisee is facilitating an MBP group, the supervisor might ask questions that invite further exploration around three broad areas of this Petal:

- Who is coming? Bringing them to mind. What is their unique cultural identity? What are the cultural factors to be aware of in the group?
- How does the supervisee relate to the people and the cultural factors– both on a more conscious level and more underneath the radar? Who do they feel more drawn to? Who do they move away from? What might not be being seen? Holding awareness of their own cultural background and experience, the supervisee considers when it is appropriate to explicitly bring that in.
- Explorations about ways of being inclusive, any adaptations required, and any actions to take in all aspects of work right through from publicity and marketing to the actual mindfulness interventions.

Culture is present within the supervisor, supervisee, participant(s)/client(s) (Figure 8.1). It is a complex and dynamic picture which can come into supervision inquiry within all of these layers.

---

186 Crane et al., 2023

Figure 8.1 The people 'present' and who is being held in mind during MBS

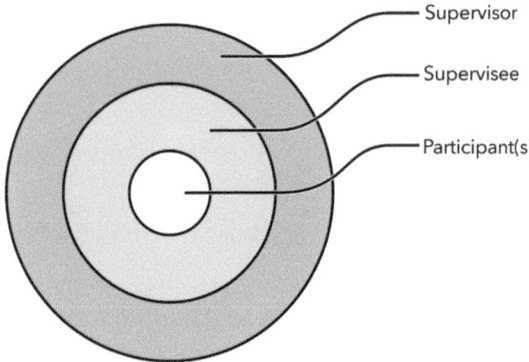

There are times when it feels safe and supportive to be in cross-cultural groups, and other times when it can be supportive to be within affinity groups with those who share some similar social/geographical/cultural locations. Within MBS, a supervisor might be encouraging a supervisee to consider signposting participants to a group where there may be more affinity with others or suggesting a supervisee seek supervision with a supervisor where they feel more affinity.

Personal mindfulness practice

Supervisees may have different traditions for their personal mindfulness practice to those underpinning an MBA. These differences might be culturally based. MBS can be a place to explore working with these different practices and possible ways practices might sit alongside each other or be integrated. This might also include explorations around conditions that create safety and support for longer periods of practice, e.g. retreat. As culture is held in mind, there may be occasions where the supervisor needs to hold systemic trauma sensitivity in mind and how this might have an impact on the supervisee's practice. This could be linked to social/political events happening around the time of the supervision session. As a supervisor, it is important to be aware and hold a space for the impact of these events, which likely go far deeper than just what is happening at that moment – sensitivity, openness, and courage may be some of the qualities required to support the supervisee in whatever way they may need.

Theory and understanding

There may be an emphasis on drawing on particular paradigms, ways of understanding and knowing that support an emphasis on cultural factors (e.g. social models of understanding, specific social justice models, frameworks of understanding from cultural traditions), exploring how to incorporate them into the supervisee's MB work. There could be an underlying leaning towards supporting the importance of critical thinking and reflection.

Ways in which these Petals (topics) might come into supervision

In Chapter 6, we identify the ways in which these topics come into supervision. Here we emphasise some culturally specific aspects:

- The supervisor and/or supervisee may use different pedagogies, such as storytelling, to discuss difficult topics.
- The supervisor may bring their own cultural background, experiences and learning as examples.
- Video sharing might need translation, either within the supervision session or using subtitles.
- There may be more use of pre-supervision reflection forms to support conveying information beforehand and cultural preferences around structured ways of learning.
- Reading, training, and listening to culturally related materials may form the basis for the beginnings of conversations.

Attuning the mindfulness-based supervision framework with culture in mind

During our conversation with Debbie, she gave an example of working with a strong cultural value, which is often the norm in Chinese-speaking countries, which we summarise in the example box.

Example – how working with cultural values/norm requires modulations to the MBS framework

Debbie described how there can be a strong cultural norm in Chinese-speaking countries: *"to do well, strive to be best you can, do this quickly, work very hard … We are told in our childhoods we need to work HARDER and HARDER, to be a useful person or respected person in your community."* Debbie recognized that whilst this is something likely in many cultures, it frequently shows up in MBS as a repeating theme in her culture. It has roots within the educational system, society, work, and family expectations. Within mindfulness-based work it is easy for the supervisee to get entangled into this striving pattern. They might miss their own striving, striving within the group, striving in supervision, as this territory is so habitual. Debbie also witnesses how participants move into blaming themselves for not getting a good result, and subsequently, the teacher (supervisee) blames themselves for not being a good teacher.

Debbie finds that there is recognition and a loosening when this striving is named within MBS. The pattern of striving is seen within the individual, the group and the culture. This recognition and loosening opens up exploration, such as considering the impact of an attitude of striving. As a supervisor, she can support the growing of confidence for MBP teachers, working particularly with seeing strengths and accumulating an atmosphere of compassion and kindness. This links to aspects of the framework, e.g. Compassion/Wisdom, Embodied Presence, coming back to body and attitudes of mindfulness, space, inquiry approach supporting empowering, allowing vulnerability, and mutuality. As a supervisor, Debbie can encourage experiential ways of knowing striving through the different Petals. For example, in the Theory and Understanding Petal, the supervisee can be supported with understanding underpinning attitudinal foundations of MBAs, especially non-striving, allowing, patience, beginner's mind. The supervisee can begin to explore these attitudes experientially in practice, teaching, and life and might be noticing how they go against a cultural norm at times.

Within the Mindfulness-Based Work Petal, Debbie might utilize tools such as the MBI:TLC, and incorporate videos that support clear, structured learning that may be a good fit with the supervisee's cultural style of learning. Debbie described how, on one occasion, she helped the supervisee to recognise that they understand themselves better than the supervisor does, which wouldn't be a cultural norm. The supervisee was initially confused when invited to make their own reflections on their teaching when watching a video of their MBP group. They were expecting the supervisor to make an evaluation and 'tell them' what to do. With encouragement, they started to enjoy the video viewing and self-reflection process. Debbie was attuning to them and their cultural context along with the pedagogy of MBAs and MBS, engaging in this dance we have been referring to, making sensitive choices and working with the supervisee in ways that empower. Overall, Debbie sees the MBS framework as being based on wisdom and respect, so rather than adaptation for different cultures, as a supervisor, she might lean particularly into some areas more than others.

Resourcing yourself to meet the cultural aspect of these Petals

All of the ways of resourcing yourself as a supervisor outlined in Chapter 6 are still relevant. Here, we also wish to bring in three ways we are finding helpful, specifically with culture in mind.

Developing cultural awareness

Not everything that is faced can be changed, but nothing can be changed until it is faced.[187]

As already stated, it is part of the role of a supervisor to be doing their own work and learning in developing cultural awareness outside of MBS. This takes time, effort, and intentionality. It is beyond the book's scope to go into all the details of how this is done, so we point to some broader ideas of the processes and activities that might support it. As supervisors, it is up to you to find the specific details and opportunities.

Uz emphasized that supervisors need to be aware of what we don't know as well as what we do. It is no fault of the supervisor – there may be things we don't see and simply can't be aware of due to our social location (for example, due to our race, gender, sexual orientation, ability and so forth). However, we can keep questions in mind, we can keep learning, and we can stay humble. When we receive feedback, we can take it on board. We definitely don't need to make it about ourselves.

In short, supervisors need to be actively and continually challenging any prejudices, latent or otherwise, that we find within ourselves.

Here are some ways we have found support in developing cultural awareness:

- **Self-reflection.** As a process to enhance learning and growth, this could be in conjunction with any of the other ideas, reflecting before, during and/or after supervision. This can include written reflections. We have been offering reflection questions at the end of each chapter and offer some culturally related questions for this chapter. You may want to give yourself time after experiences/trigger points arise to reflect, or alongside this you may decide to devote a particular period for more concentrated reflection and study.
- **Conversations/dialogue with others.** In your own supervision and supra-vision, with mindfulness peers, creating/joining groups that are dedicated to working with these themes which may be affinity groups or more diverse spaces.
- **Additional continuing development training and workshops on the many aspects of culture.** Includes training aimed at MB practitioners and a wider range of training that may be available to you.

---

187 James Baldwin quoted in Hardy & Bobes, 2016, p. 49

- **Gathering and looking out for resources that may open and expand your knowledge and perspectives.** This might include online talks, books, both novels and non-fiction, research papers, film, podcasts, art and music, travel, YouTube recordings, TED talks (and when you find something supportive, you might have others in mind who you think could benefit and pass this information onto them).

You can see from this list that we are advocating for a broad reach of what supports cultural awareness and not staying just within our professional arena of training and resources. We are not naming specific resources, but rather the principles to keep discovering and learning by keeping up to date, finding new ways of approaching, exploring new terminology, finding key authors to follow, including those who have something different to say on the subject, and generally remaining open.

Developing cultural humility

In the previous section, we spoke about the commitment to lifelong learning and self-reflection in relation to cultural awareness. The attitude with which this process is embarked upon is important. The invitation is to have the humility to say what we don't know. In the words of Matthew Mock, *"We can never truly know another person, her or his experiences, lives, and legacies, unless we are open to acknowledging what we do not know."*[188] Vekaria et al., describe a theme of cultural humility,[189] with sub-themes emphasising the supervisor's responsibility to think about their own development and learning, how they can learn from the supervisee, and to be mindful of reactions to race and ethnicity, biases and prejudices, and any power dynamics that exist.

When embracing cultural humility, supervisors can demonstrate care and genuine curiosity. It can be truly humbling to acknowledge blind spots which reflect unconscious bias. In the words of our interviewee, Debbie, *"Be humble, do your own self-evaluation, find your own bias, be willing to learn from supervisees, if uncertain, then double check"*. This needs wisdom as well; not everything is down to culture, and some behaviours may still not be appropriate even if they are cultural, so supervisors are holding this in mind. For example, Debbie spoke of a moment when a supervisee was clapping their hands when teaching each time the participant got something 'right'. During the supervision dialogue, the supervisee explained it would be culturally appropriate to do so, but when they reflected on the attitudes of accepting and allowing being cultivated in a mindfulness class versus getting it 'right' and receiving applause from the group, they concluded that another response would be a better fit. The supervisor's wisdom to inquire further rather than just put it down to 'culture' allowed for a deeper exploration.

---

188 Matthew Mock, quoted in Hardy & Bobes, 2016, p. 133
189 Vekaria et al., 2023a

Another aspect of cultural humility is knowing the limits of whom to offer supervision to and when someone closer to the supervisee's cultural background and experience might be a better fit for them. A supervisor cannot rush to any conclusions or assumptions as to what the supervisee might need, but opening the conversation and choices is part of the humility.

Developing Both/And thinking

We often find ourselves referring to Both/And thinking in relation to MBS. It is a way of thinking and being, often around the consideration of ethical issues but also when in a relationship with another to support mutual collaboration, connection, and conversation. We were curious to notice that Hardy brings this approach into his work around culturally sensitive supervision.[190] Both/And thinking is the opposite of the more binary position of Either/Or. It allows for more complexity, nuance, multiple perspectives, ambiguity, paradox and uncertainty.[191] It becomes possible for two seemingly contradictory statements to be true.

Adopting a Both/And approach allows supervisors to hold differing views, experiences and perspectives respectfully while staying connected and engaged. Both/And thinking means that we don't have to land with just one solution; we can embrace and hold multiple viewpoints. So, for example, in relation to culture, a Both/And perspective allows a supervisor to see that both being privileged and subjugated can co-exist in one person, and both reflect a person's cultural experience. We might look at different aspects of our cultural background and see this to be the case, e.g. I (Alison) see for myself the privilege that comes from being 'white' and times when being female has left me feeling at a disadvantage. This more flexible thinking style can foster greater understanding and compassion and make space for the many nuances around culture and the impact of cultural constructions.

We imagine that as you read this, it is a familiar way of approaching being with another in supervision. The attitudes of allowing, letting be, trusting, not-knowing, curiosity, compassion and wisdom all support this way of thinking and perceiving. The language that is used during inquiry invites, opens, and deepens; the use of open-ended questions, the guidance a supervisor might give is offered as one possibility, not an absolute, working with common humanity and seeking to find common ground, as well as acknowledging diversity, allowing and accepting uncertainty and ambiguity, learning to be comfortable with complexity, not having to find solutions and fix everything, and seeking out and listening to alternative experiences and perspectives.

---

190 Hardy & Bobes, 2016
191 See Michelle Buck for a discussion about Both/And thinking https://www.believeinmind.com/self-growth/either-or-vs-both-and-thinking/

With this Both/And thinking in mind, Soh-Leong Lim and Ben K. Lim remind us not to romanticise culture; it doesn't need to be glorified: *"Culture has both blessings and curses. It is a blessing when it serves as the glue or provides the platform to bring people together in traditions that have shared meaning and purpose; it is a curse when it oppresses."*[192]

Words of wisdom

We conclude this chapter with pithy words from Uz, for all supervisors and all your supervisees to help to keep culture in mind.

Remember …

You can't know the extent of the harm that you can do unintended and unwittingly.

And the opposite: You can't know the extent of the absolute treasure you can give someone when you open to all aspects of who they are. It uplifts, supports and heals the pain of non-acceptance.

Be active – it is an active thing to be an anti-racist. It's not just watching a film or reading a book from time to time by a Black director or Asian author. It's about uprooting prejudice within ourselves and within systems. (We can extend this to any other aspect of social identity)

Keep doing the work – actively and deliberately.

It's good for us and good for everyone else.

Summary

This is a massive topic, at the heart of Mutual Inquiry, and an area for ongoing investigation, discussion and learning. After a brief introductory section, we focus in this chapter on bringing cultural sensitivity into MBS, weaving in the learning and examples from our two interviewees, Uz Azfal and Debbie Hu.

1. Background introduction:
   - Culture is constructed and conceptualized by numerous variables, e.g. class, religion, sexual orientation, gender, family background, ethnicity, age, regionality, education, and socioeconomic factors.
   - Culture permeates all aspects of us and our lives. This includes MB work and MBS.

---

192 Lim & Lim, 2016, p. 123

- An MBS supervisor has a number of roles and responsibilities to hold when they keep culture in mind; it is their responsibility to bring culture into MBS, to do their own work around culture and to develop cultural competencies within supervision.

2. Using the MBS framework with culture in mind:
    - The warp: Supervisors are creating a safe container for this work, embodying a willingness to be vulnerable, courageous, humble and not know. There should be an awareness of cultural power and finding ways of working with power imbalance.
    - The weft:
        - Cultural conversations are part of the contracting process in terms of relationship building and providing clarity that themes and issues around culture can be brought to MBS.
        - Culture is a topic of inquiry within MBS through all of the Petals, especially the Contexts Petal. Supervisors are learning from their supervisees.
        - The nuances around language and how it influences experience, relationships and understandings need to be considered.
        - There is a recognition that culture influences the supervisor, supervisee and participants/clients. Sensitivity can be brought to any actions required to support inclusivity.
        - Supervisees can explore modulations and adaptations needed in their work to support cultural sensitivity.
        - Working with systemic trauma for the supervisee or their participants might be a topic of supervision, including support for personal mindfulness practice.
        - There may be culturally diverse ways of practising, retreating, and understanding mindfulness to be explored.
        - There may be a need to foreground theories and understandings that forefront culture, such as frameworks for working toward social justice.
        - Supervisors can remain open to a range of culturally appropriate pedagogies around learning and communication.
        - Supervisors are supporting supervisees to work with their own reactions, prejudices and bias, both conscious and unconscious.

3. What resources you as a supervisor to work with culture in mind?
    - Developing cultural awareness is an ongoing process undertaken through self-reflection, dialogue with others, continuing professional development training/workshops and using various resources.

- Developing cultural humility includes opening to not knowing, having a willingness to investigate your own reactions, prejudices and bias, both conscious and unconscious, being aware of cultural power dynamics, and not assuming or stereotyping.
- We have found that cultivating and using Both/And thinking helps to remain open to diversity.

4. A reminder, as Uz said, to keep doing the work actively and deliberately. It's good for us and good for everyone else.

Reflective questions

Take time to reflect on your own cultural background and how it influences you as an MB supervisor. Remember to bring care and sensitivity to this process; it is part of ongoing work and does not need to be rushed. You may also pick these reflections up with others, your supervisor, peers, and friends. We offer some ways you might like to engage in this reflection:

reflect on the multiple ways you identify socially, e.g. race, ethnicity, gender identity, class, education, spirituality, physical ability

reflect back on being in your family from a cultural perspective and your family's cultural experience; you can go back several generations if you know this detail. How have these experiences shaped and influenced you?

reflect further on your cultural background, as well as family; also include school, friendships, and specific experiences that stand out in the different phases of childhood and adult life

how have these social locations and family narratives impacted you in terms of strength, resilience, power, oppression and subjugation?

How do these cultural factors influence you in your MB work, and your MBS as a supervisee and supervisor? How do they contribute to your strengths as an MB practitioner, teacher, or supervisor?

What power do you hold as a supervisor? How will you use your cultural power as a supervisor? How might supervisees perceive your power? Do you see any potential blind spots? How do you maintain awareness of your power? How will you be held accountable?

Reflect on any small ways that you are bringing cultural sensitivity and attunement into supervision. How might you increase this?

Considering your context for supervision, what parts of the framework fit culturally? Which less so? How do you work with this? Are adaptations or translations needed?

What is your vision for inclusion and diversity within the mindfulness field? What would you see, hear, and feel when there is equity in the mindfulness field?

Are there any aspects of this chapter that you would like to explore further? How might you continue your learning and inquiry? e.g. self-reflection, dialogue, further study/training. Take a moment to consider your intention and set a realistic action to take forward.

References

Crane, R. S., Callen-Davies, R., Francis, A., Francis, D., Gibbs, P., Mulligan, B., O'Neill, B., Williams, N. K. P., Waupoose, M., & Vallejo, Z. (2023). Mindfulness-based stress reduction for our time: A curriculum that is up to the task. *Global Advances in Integrative Medicine and Health*, 12. https://doi.org/10.1177/27536130231162604

Crenshaw, K. (1989). Demarginalizing the intersection of race and sex: A black feminist critique of antidiscrimination doctrine, feminist theory, and antiracist politics. *University of Chicago Legal Forum*, 149, 139-168.

Crenshaw, K. (1991). Mapping the margins: Intersectionality, identity politics, and violence against women of color. *Stanford Law Review*, 43(6), 1241-1299.

Evans, A. (2019). *Supervisors' and supervisees' perspectives of mindfulness-based supervision: A grounded theory study* [Doctoral thesis, University of Exeter]. https://ore.exeter.ac.uk/repository/handle/10871/37542

Lim, S. L., & Lim, B. K. (2016). *Politically incorrect*. In K. V. Hardy, & T. Bobes (Eds.), *Culturally sensitive supervision and training: Diverse perspectives and practical applications* (pp. 121-126). Routledge.

Hardy, K. V., & Bobes, T. (Eds.). (2016). *Culturally sensitive supervision and training: Diverse perspectives and practical applications*. Routledge.

Vekaria, B., Harrydwar, L., Thomas, T., & Ononaiye, M. (2023a). Supervisee perspectives on improving cultural responsivity in clinical supervision. *Clinical Psychology Forum*, 1(371), 66-76. https://doi.org/10.53841/bpscpf.2023.1.371.66

Vekaria, B., Thomas, T., Phiri, P., & Ononaiye, M. (2023b). Exploring the supervisory relationship in the context of culturally responsive supervision: a supervisee's perspective. *The Cognitive Behaviour Therapist*, 16, e22. https://doi.org/10.1017/S1754470X23000168

Chapter 9
Using the Mindfulness-Based Supervision Framework within Workplace Mindfulness

> *Mindfulness meditation is not simply a method that one encounters for a brief time at a professional seminar and then passes on to others for use as needed when they find themselves tense or stressed. It is a way of being that takes ongoing effort to develop and refine.*[193]

In this chapter, we highlight aspects of the MBS framework that require particular consideration when working with supervisees engaged in workplace mindfulness. We move in closer to some specifics, mainly the weft elements of the framework, illustrating how the *fabric* of supervision looks different within this context compared to, say, supervision with a supervisee offering MBSR to a general population in a community setting. Using the Petals and the Belt to organise the themes, we consider two main questions in relation to MBS:

---

193 Kabat-Zinn, 2003, p. 149

- What are the considerations for the supervisee's MB work regarding the workplace environment, structure and culture?
- How does the workplace context inform the guiding principles, legislation and frameworks drawn upon?

We highlight two types of workplace settings, within the helping professions and the business field, and discuss issues related to supervisees offering mindfulness for individual well-being and organizational mindfulness.

Workplace settings

We use the term *helping profession* to encompass practitioners whose work focuses on supporting individuals in their personal lives through health, well-being and/or education services. This includes therapists in physical or psychological health, those involved in social work, educators, non-governmental, non-profit community work, and the criminal justice system. We focus on education as an example, drawing on the experiences and examples of our interviewee Jem Shackleford and illustrating ways of modulating the framework within this context. There are also examples from healthcare. We envisage that the issues raised and the principles offered will be supportive across other helping profession contexts.

We use the term *business* to describe an organization or company engaged in commercial, industry, or professional services for profit or non-profit. Not-for-profit enterprises include charities, arts and culture, recreational, political and advocacy organizations. Our interviewee, Martin Summerfield, shared experiences and examples within the business context.

Scope of workplace mindfulness-based work

There are three main ways of bringing mindfulness into the workplace, and each of these can be offered in a range of ways, from well-researched, evidence-based curricula to exploring new ways to widen the accessibility of mindfulness within the workplace environment:

- Mindfulness for personal well-being and resilience: for recipients of the service and staff.
- Team mindfulness to enhance relationships and working practices among team members.
- Mindful leadership, focusing on people, creativity and innovation.

MBS is a place to honour and celebrate the supervisee's work, from the more modest endeavours right through to a multi-level MB approach.

Using the weft of the mindfulness-based supervision framework: the Petals

Contexts

This Petal is concerned with understanding the internal and external factors influencing an organization. Research suggests that understanding the context is crucial in designing and implementing an effective intervention.[194]

Institutions such as schools or healthcare facilities have a clear purpose, internal governance structures, decision-making processes, and agreed-upon roles and responsibilities. In many countries, they may also be part of a wider system, such as an educational or healthcare system. As such, much of the governance and decision-making will be determined by this wider system rather than the specific facility. This is also the case in businesses where a national or international organization, such as a financial institution, has local offices or workplaces. For smaller, more independent, businesses or workplaces, general principles and processes often interface with specific workplace operations, such as within the hospitality industry, where expectations and standards exist to adhere to.

Organizational culture includes the values, beliefs, attitudes, norms and rules that shape how employees think, feel and behave. It can be influenced by the particular workplace and the wider system within which it operates. This culture is held within and potentially influenced by the broader external context within the specific country and global factors. Therefore, the supervisor needs to support their supervisee in considering all these areas of influence.

MBS is a place to examine how the context of the organization, including the culture, can bring up ethical and professional issues that link to the Container, such as Intention and Integrity, as well as to elements of the Belt. Some examples of ethical questions might be: How are mindfulness and MB approaches perceived, understood and valued within the organization? Is it part of a staff well-being initiative or a broader culture shift towards a new way of working? For staff well-being, how will staff and the employer view this? Is there a culture where employers are accepting responsibility for staff support? Are staff able to make choices to support their well-being and resilience? Will staff attend a mindfulness event within their working hours or in their own time? Will it be optional? Is the team or wider organization receptive to a mindful approach to support their collective communication and connection? How does it fit with the organization's values, mission and goals? Will there be a pilot, and how will it be evaluated?

---

194 Newman et al., 2021

Suppose the supervisee is an employee of the organization and is already familiar with the organization's mission, values, and culture. In that case, MBS can be a supportive place to explore factors to consider as they move into the MB 'teacher' role within their workplace. They may be taking up the mindfulness 'champion' role and developing different relationships with their colleagues. If the supervisee is involved in organizational mindfulness, a much more detailed and intimate understanding of the context will be beneficial in determining how best to embed mindfulness into the organization's culture.

The supervisee going into a workplace on a freelance basis must have an understanding and appreciation of that particular workplace. Jem and Martin both stressed the importance of supervisees visiting a business/organization and shadowing to get a hands-on feel of the context of the work being done, the particular skills needed and specific demands of the various job roles, the structure and culture within the organization, and current internal and external stresses – all of this provides invaluable information to help inform discussions within MBS of the most effective way of offering MBAs within that workplace context.

Understanding the flow and timing of work within the particular workplace will also assist supervisees in designing their intervention; knowing when yearly objectives are set and being aware of upcoming significant projects or changes within a workplace may all influence the supervisee's plans.

- Within education, Jem described the need to consider the school year when supervisees are planning, such as knowing the general flow of the academic year, what happens within each term, and the times of most workload demand on staff.
- Within business, Martin spoke about appreciating the impact of times of organizational change, such as a department's restructuring, a merger, or a change in leadership, and how this might influence the supervisee's MB work.

Let's briefly look at how context may inform the different types of MBAs.

Mindfulness for well-being

Mindfulness for recipients of the service within a helping profession. This may include discussions around the choice and format of the programme to be offered. There will likely be a connection between the core work of the supervisee's profession and MBA as in they are both concerned with promoting the well-being and development of others. Other factors will need to be considered such as: Is there already a precedent for offering mindfulness within this context? Can the supervisee draw on policy or research to guide their choice? What is most likely to be supported by the organization? Does the MBA support the service/organizational goals and desired outcomes? There will likely be more support for offering a programme with an already clear evidence base, such as offering MBCT in a group to clients accessing psychological therapy, offering one of the mindfulness curricula specifically designed for a particular age of school children, offering MBSR to clients within a pain management service.

Increasingly, supervisees are broadening the scope of their MB work, generally influenced by the recipients' needs, such as offering it on a 1:1 basis with clients, making adaptations for a group of individuals with a specific vulnerability, or offering short courses. These newer areas may be more challenging to implement within the established organizational structure of a helping profession, so alongside the educational function of MBS, supervision may also focus on exploring intention and integrity as the supervisor supports the supervisee in building a case to support the implementation of their MB work in new ways that are more akin to practice-based evidence than evidence-based practice.

Mindfulness for staff well-being. Here, the supervisor and supervisee will explore the format and curriculum choices that would best suit the needs of the particular staff group. This may involve discussions with Human Resources or staff committees concerned with staff well-being. Often within the workplace, supervisees start by offering tasters, brief workshops, or drop-in sessions that can be more easily accessed by busy employees or those where the nature of their work may be unpredictable, e.g. frontline healthcare staff. Discussion on the recruitment, assessment and orientation process is essential, encouraging consideration of topics such as conscripts versus voluntary sign-up, when and where the sessions will take place (within work time or not, venue for an in-person group within the workplace or not), creating an optimal learning space either online or in person, navigating attendance when staff work shifts, how to nurture safe-enough conditions for participants to share their experiences from practice in the presence of their colleagues, especially if there are hierarchical relationships (managers and staff in the same group). Discussions may also include how the supervisee can support the staff members with their ongoing practice beyond a time-limited course, perhaps through developing workplace practice spaces and shared times for practice.

Within the helping professions, MBPs are also increasingly offered to students within their training programmes. Topics in MBS may include the following: Where are the students in the training pathway? Is attendance at the MBP mandatory? Are they required to submit reflections or other academic work on their experience of the MBP, and how might this influence their participation in the MBP?

Let's take a look at an example shared by Jem that speaks to his approach in meeting particular challenges experienced by supervisees implementing an MBA for well-being within the education workplace. He makes reference to nudge theory.[195]

---

195 Thaler & Sunstein, 2008

Example – honouring the small steps

In his role as an MB supervisor with supervisees working within the English education system, Jem highlighted the significant challenges for supervisees in implementing MBAs within this demanding and pressured environment and how this informs his approach to MBS; the principles and aspects of his approach are likely to be translatable for MBS for supervisees working within other high-pressure workplace environments.

- He spoke about the importance of MBS as a place to support supervisees in being *realistic* alongside *optimistic* about what can be achieved. Where there is no scope to implement already existing MBAs for students, for example, they may be able to offer short courses for staff, where alongside personal well-being, they can explore how personal practice can influence the teacher's presence within the classroom. Jem believes the accumulative effect of teachers' moments of mindful presence, tiny shifts in awareness, is a very effective and integrated way of communicating and conveying mindfulness to students.

- He talked about encouraging supervisees to draw on nudge theory, exploring with them how they might shape the environment to support mindful awareness and ways to make it more visible, such as using posters in hallways and using shared language within classrooms. MBS also includes regular discussions of how the supervisee can support the personal practice of the students/colleagues, such as by beginning each class with a brief pause practice. He emphasized the accumulative benefit for students if three out of their five lessons in the school day include a short mindfulness practice.

- He described working with supervisees who, alongside being MB teachers, are also classroom teachers in a particular subject, and how MBS can be a place to explore how they might bring an MB approach directly and explicitly into the lesson. So, for example in an art lesson, the students are learning about mindfulness through their experience of creating artwork. He talked about how, in this context, MBS includes valuable discussions of what is mindfulness-based and what is not, and how supervisees can keep connected to the core principles of the approach while conveying it in a unique way outside of standard MB curricula.

- He observed that the supervisee could offer an MB course for parents or an education session for parents about the course their children are attending, recognising that parents are part of the 'golden triangle', which acknowledges the equal contributions of student, parent and teacher in creating optimum conditions for student learning and development.

Team mindfulness

The supervisee may support a team or organization to bring a mindful approach to their collective processes, connections and communication. As they move beyond individual mindfulness into collective mindfulness, MBS will include a discussion of their knowledge and skills and their training needs – alongside their MB teaching skills; do they also have knowledge and understanding of team and organizational processes and how to apply mindfulness within teams and organizations? This applies to the supervisor as well; do you, as a supervisor, have the necessary knowledge and skills to support the supervisee in their endeavours? The research suggests that combining team and organization processes (such as leadership, decision-making, people management, conflict management, and workload) alongside mindfulness may be more effective than just offering a standard MBP.[196] Elements of the framework linked to ethics and professional practice will be important here: Intention and Integrity within the Container and elements of the Belt. MBS may be supporting the supervisee in scoping and planning what is possible, seeking support from senior figures within the organization, which may include developing a business case, deciding on small ways of experimenting with bringing mindfulness into this context, through to guidance as they implement a more thorough system-wide approach.

Mindful leadership

The supervisee may be in a leadership position and keen to examine the role of mindfulness within their work, from bringing a personal mindful presence into their work and interactions to embedding mindfulness within the culture and core organizational processes of the whole organization. MBS may include guiding the supervisee as they access relevant training in mindful leadership, supporting them as they build an evidence base for their proposal or supporting them in implementing their learning following training. Alongside training, reading and listening to podcasts on workplace mindfulness and leadership can enhance the confidence and knowledge of both the supervisor and supervisee. In the following example, I (Pamela) refer to a short statement by Michael Carroll[197] that the supervisee and I have found really helpful to have on a Post-it note.

---

196 Rupprecht et al., 2019
197 Carroll, 2007, p. 195

Example – mindful leadership: starting with oneself

I (Pamela) offer this brief example to illustrate how the MBS framework can support a move into a new area of MB practice with a supervisee, while staying within one's level of knowledge and skill.

For some time now, I have been engaged in MBS with a supervisee who offers MBPs for staff within healthcare. They have recently moved into a leadership role within the organization and have become interested in how mindfulness can support them within this new role. Aware of the concept of mindful leadership, they are considering approaching their manager to request support to attend specific training. In the meantime, our more recent supervision sessions have begun to focus on their personal practice and their reflections on how their growing self-awareness, or at times unawareness, links to their awareness of others and the primary tasks of their new role. Their reflections include a recognition that just as in their personal practice, they are learning to open to vulnerability with a kinder, more compassionate stance, so too can they open to their and other's vulnerability as they step into this new role.

These words from Michael Carroll have been supportive to the supervisee and myself, as we recognise that starting with oneself is the cornerstone of mindful leadership and therefore fits well within the scope of our current supervisory relationship:

"Mindfulness meditation is the fundamental and indispensable practice of the mindful leader … by sitting down and remaining still, we discover our natural talents for being patient, open, and humble. And over time, the mindfulness we develop in the practice naturally unfolds on the job – indeed, throughout our entire lives – offering us the opportunity to express the talents of a mindful leader."

In terms of the MBS framework, there have been strong connections with the warp threads, links to ethics, inclusion and good practice within the Belt, and exploration around the Petals of personal practice, group and individual processes, and contexts. In this way, the MBS framework has offered a supportive structure to guide both of us in this new venture.

Supervisor skill and experience within a particular context

If the supervisor does not have direct experience working within the same context as the supervisee, it is important to consider this at the contracting stage. It may be that the supervisor and supervisee agree that the supervisee can bring this knowledge, and that the supervisor can supplement this with their own reading/study. I (Pamela) have found that having worked within the UK and Canadian public mental healthcare systems supports my understanding and appreciation of the experience of supervisees working within similar large government bodies such as education and criminal justice. Even though I have not explicitly worked within those environments, I have some appreciation of the challenges and tensions, as well as the joys, of working as part of a more extensive system with the recipient's needs at the centre. The supervisee shares with me the details and nuances within their particular setting and context, and together, we explore how this informs their MB work.

However, there will be times when a supervisee needs to seek out a supervisor with lived experience within a particular context. This may be more relevant in their early stages of offering MB work when they are less familiar with the nuances of bringing mindfulness into the specific workplace. This calls on supervisors to be clear about the scope of their supervision practice, not to work outside their skills and knowledge base.

Jem, with his personal experience of working within the English education system, expressed how important it is for him to have insight into the unique challenges and pressures that teachers, working within the same or similar educational systems are under in their day-to-day work and how this influences the supervisees' MB work within that education system. He talked about open and honest conversations in MBS concerning the feasibility of their mindfulness work within this context. From his extensive work as an MB practitioner across many business sectors, Martin deeply understands the care and skill needed to decide how best to convey mindfulness within a particular business setting and context. In contrast, an MB supervisor unfamiliar with this type of work might not know what they don't know. Of course, supervisors may expand their knowledge and skills through further study and supervision, if they decide to move into this new area of supervision work, even if they do not have lived experience.

Mindfulness-based work

Workplace MBPs for well-being typically have shorter weekly sessions and recommend shorter daily practices than MBSR or MBCT. It is also more common for mindfulness to be part of a wider programme for resilience or team effectiveness. Within organizational mindfulness, it may be less about employees coming together for mindfulness practice and more about bringing mindfulness into how they interact and engage in their work together. So, the *what* and the *how* of 'teaching' or conveying mindfulness might look different from that of delivering an MBP. Therefore, this Petal will include a detailed exploration of the supervisee's skills in bringing mindfulness to life within their specific context: what language is most likely to land with this group, how might this part of the curriculum be best conveyed within this context, how do they best support the cultivation of the attitudinal foundations. Mindfulness for well-being may include how they convey course themes within the context of occupational stress, for example, exploring the inclusion of work-related practices such as emailing in a more mindful way or creative ways of encouraging incorporating mindfulness into participants' workday. There may be discussion around more applied ways of offering mindfulness while still staying true to the underlying pedagogy. Organizational mindfulness might be about skill building and offering relational and social practices.

In the example below, Martin speaks to one aspect of skill development that he feels requires particular attention in MBS for workplace mindfulness – embodying mindfulness. He describes using the 50:50 practice[198] as one way of supporting supervisees to cultivate an embodied presence within their relationships.

Example – Mutual Inquiry: cultivating a more mindful approach

Within the business workplace, supervisees may come to supervision with a different perspective than those from a more traditional MBSR/MBCT teaching background. They may be an established workplace trainer or a Human Resources consultant, for example, and perhaps offering workshops or brief courses on mindfulness with shorter practices and less emphasis on an inquiry-led approach, which can convey a different feel about mindfulness.

Martin stresses the central role of MBS in workplace settings in supporting a deeper experience through the cultivation of an inquiry-led approach, this process of Mutual Inquiry at the heart of the MBS framework. He described how nourishing and reassuring he found it during the MBS training when he encountered the MBS framework for the first time, and he expresses his appreciation of opportunities to reconnect with this style of talking with another. He believes that MBS supports integrity through this relational inquiry, as the supervisor models this way of being. He invites his supervisees to go on a journey around cultivating embodiment within supervision and by themselves within their own practice.

He stresses the need for the supervisor to sensitively attune to each supervisee, holding in mind their developmental level, how receptive they might be, and determining what is needed at this point in time to best support them with this journey of deepening embodiment and reflective practice. This might include:

- Sharing and using the 50:50 practice within supervision.
- Deliberately bringing in pauses.
- Exploring personal practice and how to deepen personal practice, including small steps towards longer periods of practice, like a day of practice, before considering a longer retreat.

---

198 The 50:50 practice, found in the Mindfulness for Life programme, encourages bringing attention to whatever you are doing (50%) and keep some awareness in your body (the other 50%), Kuyken, 2024, pp. 64–67; and https://mindfulnessforlife.uk/practices/

- Encouraging reflective practice, inviting space to tune into themselves and their experience prior to a supervision session, then taking time to connect with intention at the start of the session..
- Encouraging the cultivation of particular attitudinal foundations that might seem counter to business culture: a not-knowing stance, patience, open-heartedness, being with vulnerability.

Our colleague Rebecca Crane describes supervision as an integrity check – the glue within the system. Here we are suggesting that embodying within inquiry forms a substantial part of this glue, particularly within workplace mindfulness where there may be less emphasis on this within the supervisee's training and MB work.

Group and individual processes

One advantage of a supervisee offering mindfulness to recipients within their own helping profession is that they will likely be very familiar with the determinants of health and well-being in this context. Within MBS, the supervisor will encourage exploration of how this informs their approach to offering an MBA.

In mindfulness for staff well-being, the supervisor invites reflection on themes such as: the impact of forming a different kind of relationship with colleagues and peers in the supervisee's role as MB teacher, including how to sensitively gather information at the pre-course assessment that provides a valuable understanding of the specific vulnerability of individual participants; the participants forming a different kind of relationship with each other than they do within their work roles; hierarchy systems and power dynamics and how to navigate this (e.g. managers and reportees in the same group, supervisors and supervisees in the same group, perceived hierarchy among disciplines, junior and senior staff in same group); how to support safe and supportive conditions for the sharing of vulnerability within this context – what group guidelines and boundaries are likely to be most helpful? This connects with the themes of diversity and inclusion in the Belt, intention within the Container, and cultural responsivity.

Although participant attendance on a course is a common focus of discussion in MBS in all contexts, within the workplace there may be added challenges if particular work demands affect the attendance of many of the participants at the same time or if there is a culture within the workplace of putting work needs ahead of personal well-being. There can be different expectations and levels of commitment if the course is free to staff and takes place within work time rather than if they had signed up independently for a course in their own time. Discussing the factors influencing attendance is important as the supervisee may otherwise assume that non-attendance is a consequence of the competency of their teaching skills.

Personal mindfulness practice

For supervisees taking on the role of champion for mindfulness alongside their primary role within their organization, this can support them in bringing their practice right into their lives in a very active way. However, it can also bring significant stress, as they do their best to advocate for MBAs within the context of a host of challenging conditions such as limited resources, lack of support within the organization, demanding targets/outcome measures, sudden change of focus or direction of the organization, fragile funding. So, within MBS, the supervisee's personal mindfulness practice, both formal and informal, will be a regular part of the agenda, exploring how their practice supports their self-care and well-being, how interpersonal mindfulness may help them in navigating difficult conversations, and ensuring that the supervisee is sufficiently resourced to be able to support others. Jem spoke about the critical restorative role of the MB supervisor, encouraging the supervisee to cultivate compassion in the face of being unable to do all they may want to within a high-pressure work environment while working with deficits in time and resources. MBS is also a place to support the supervisee to connect with their inner wisdom about where to focus their energy to make a difference, and to have an impact even if it is small.

For those choosing to work within a helping profession, there is generally a strong intention and motivation to reduce suffering, which aligns with the intention to offer mindfulness to others. It is also recognized that those who work within the helping professions are more prone to burn-out, a reaction to long-term occupational stress which can manifest as general exhaustion and lack of motivation, this is sometimes called compassion-fatigue. If their work involves exposure to others' suffering or trauma, it is important to be aware of the potential for vicarious trauma. This requires the supervisor to recognise MBS's boundaries, know when something else such as personal therapy is required, and be willing to have these tender conversations with supervisees.

Example – the power of embodied presence

Jem spoke about the power of personal practice for supervisees working as educators. He believes that bringing mindfulness right into their work through their presence in the classroom can influence the culture in small but significant ways and can be as important a contribution as explicitly offering an MBA. He described how embodied presence can influence and shape the supervisee's interactions with their students and colleagues every day and how this balances the professional culture within some education systems of *"got to get it right, got to produce results"*.

He believes that it's crucial to explore this in supervision and to support and encourage supervisees to appreciate how their personal practice supports the cultivation of qualities such as really showing up for their students, adopting a not-knowing stance, and balancing the holding the responsibility for the class and their learning outcomes alongside a sense of co-creating and co-journeying. He talked about how this shift in their way of being takes courage, and this is where the support of a supervisor can be invaluable.

Martin also highlighted this in talking about the business workplace – this appreciation of supporting the supervisee to really show up for their colleagues and customers, for workplace trainers to bring a different quality to how they deliver workplace training, including mindfulness training.

He discussed the importance of accepting the supervisee's personal practice to be what it is, accepting that it may be 'lighter' than that of MB teachers working in other contexts whilst also always encouraging them to go deeper. Here, the supervisor is tuning into the balance of Compassion/Wisdom – acknowledging the differences that can arise in the context of workplace mindfulness while also honouring the foundation of personal practice for all MB work.

By highlighting the power of mindful presence in their contact and interactions with others in the workplace, MBS can support supervisees in really valuing the contribution of their personal practice.

Theory and understanding

In this Petal, supervisors may be pointing to particular theories and understanding in relation to the supervisee's context, which, as well as being direct support for the supervisee's MB work, can also be invaluable when they are in the process of seeking agreement to implement MBAs. There are now several robust sources for supervisees to seek guidance around evidence for MBAs within the helping professions and the workplace.[199] MBS is a place to review and critique the current evidence, watch for confirmation bias, and support the supervisee in accurately representing the scope of mindfulness; this links with integrity in the Container and ethics and professional practice in the Belt. In terms of their direct MB teaching, supervisees may be directed to theory and understanding related to specific vulnerability within their context, such as burn-out, if they deliver mindfulness for staff well-being or research into MBAs with specific clinical populations.
Amy Edmondson's work on psychological safety was developed in the context of workplace teams and directly relates to individual and organizational mindfulness.[200] The supervisor may be supporting the supervisee with holding awareness of both

---

199 For example, the Mindfulness Initiative, 2016, https://www.themindfulnessinitiative.org/building-the-case-for-mindfulness-in-the-workplace

200 Edmondson, 1999, who first coined the term *Team Psychological Safety*

general and specific vulnerabilities. For supervisees engaged in organizational mindfulness, further broadening knowledge, such as systems theory, is necessary. Supervision may also include discussions about ways of measuring and evaluating the outcomes of their work.

Martin described how the MBS framework contributes to theory and understanding, using it as a guide to broaden the scope of what is explored within supervision, particularly highlighting elements that the supervisee may not consider bringing, such as their personal mindfulness practice and embodied presence.

Using the weft of the mindfulness-based supervision framework: the Belt

Good practice and competency

There will be supports and constraints out of the control of the supervisee, which will likely influence how loose or tight elements of the Belt are held. Supervision is a place to examine how the organizational elements of the Belt in the workplace meet the MB elements and to explore ethical and professional issues that arise. In my (Pamela) MB work within the UK public mental health system, I call these 'pinch points', where there are potential conflicts between what is considered good practice within the MB field and how this meets good practice within the service; these often occur when there are resource allocation decisions to be made in the context of competing demands and outcomes.

Supervisors can direct supervisees to good practice as articulated within MB organizations. For example, in the UK context, the Mindful Nation Report and BAMBA Good Practice Guidelines for Teaching in the Workplace offer a solid evidence base.[201] There may also be relevant policy and documentation within health and social care. Again, in our context of the UK, policy documents such as the UK National Institute for Health and Care Excellence guidance *Mental Wellbeing at Work*[202] that recommends all employees should have access to mindfulness, can help give weight to the supervisee's recommendations around MBA provision. We encourage supervisors to explore with their supervisee relevant guidance within the supervisee's context, and if there is not yet guidance available, drawing on existing guidance in other similar contexts can be a place to start. MBS will include discussions around fidelity and good practice – how to approach potential adaptations to evidence-based programmes while still retaining the core elements that make it mindfulness-based.

---

201   The Mindful Nation Report, https://www.themindfulnessinitiative.org/mindful-nation-report; BAMBA's Good Practice Guidelines for Teaching in the Workplace, https://bamba.org.uk/wp-content/uploads/2023/05/Good-Practice-Guidelines-for-Teaching-in-the-Workplace.pdf
202   NICE guidance, https://www.nice.org.uk/guidance/ng212

Alongside the many extensively evidenced personal benefits of taking part in an MBP for individual well-being, research also demonstrates positive changes that are likely to enhance workplace performance, which may be pretty compelling for workplace leaders and decision-makers, yet may raise ethical concerns for supervisees if there are challenging workplace conditions, such as harassment, bullying, pressure from excessive workloads or poor working conditions. MBS provides a space to examine such ethical and professional issues, including encouraging an openness to reading the work of scholars and offering critique and caution. Other supervision themes linked to good practice include how the supervisee markets mindfulness, ensuring they are being realistic about the impact of mindfulness, not over-promising, and being aware of current relevant research.

Example – drivers for workplace mindfulness: coming back to intention

For supervisees within the business workplace, Martin encourages supervisees to consider the drivers for their MB work, watching they do not to get caught up in the exponential growth and enthusiasm around mindfulness, lose touch with the emerging evidence base and research, or place too much emphasis on financial gain. This also includes supporting them in staying within their area of expertise and skill.

Supervisors might support supervisees through an intention practice and reflection, inviting a connection/reconnection with what matters most, how their MB work connects to their values, and the ethical underpinnings of their approach to their work. Martin stressed how this supports integrity within the supervisee's work and the space of MBS.

The documents named earlier that speak to good practice also help point to the specific competencies necessary in offering workplace mindfulness. Alongside the competencies for any MB work, such as those articulated in the MBI:TAC and MBI:TLC, these may help set the scene for conversations in MBS around the knowledge, skills and experience supervisees need for their work in this context. Suppose the supervisee plans to offer a multi-level model of mindfulness, which researchers Rupprecht et al. considered more effective than just offering mindfulness for personal well-being.[203] In that case, MBS will be a place to support the supervisee in assessing their competence to undertake such a project – do they have the necessary experience and knowledge of organizational theory and practice alongside their experience teaching/conveying a mindfulness-based approach?

---

203 Rupprecht et al., 2019

MBS can also support the supervisee in preparing for negotiations with their employer around their compliance with good practice for MB teachers (training, supervision, annual retreat) and how their employer may support them with time and cost.

Safety

Knowing workplace policies and procedures around safety, safeguarding, confidentiality, diversity, and inclusion is essential for staff well-being courses. For example, Human Resources and/or well-being committee staff can be helpful allies and supporters. Being aware of points for onward referral is helpful to know in advance. BAMBA workplace good practice guidelines state: *"Whilst not working specifically with a clinical population, teachers in the workplace should have an understanding of how to recognise and manage mental and physical health conditions, and any referral processes available in the organisational context they are working."*[204] If outcome measures are being used, information for potential participants should clearly state the data gathering and reporting process.

How can you resource yourself as a supervisor in relation to workplace mindfulness?

Alongside the ways of resourcing yourself as a supervisor outlined in Chapter 6, here we add specific ways in relation to the supervision of workplace mindfulness. Our two interviewees, Jem Shackleford and Martin Summerfield, highlighted the essential contribution of lived experience to resourcing them in their roles as MB supervisors, so this features at the top of our list:

- Experience and knowledge of the workplace and workplace mindfulness, which includes being familiar with the specific programmes offered.
- Drawing on the warp threads: the elements of the Container support the holding of the space, especially when there may be competing ideologies between the workplace culture and the MB approach; Embodied Presence and Mutual Inquiry are considered central, especially where the supervisee's MB work may involve less of an inquiry-led approach.
- Undertaking further study and/or training around workplace mindfulness if needed.
- A supra-visor who understands the context.
- Contact with peers in this field, joining specialist peer networks, accessing podcasts and other materials on workplace mindfulness.

---

[204] BAMBA, (n/d) Good Practice Guidelines for Teaching in the Workplace, under section B, https://bamba.org.uk/good-practice-guidelines/

Summary

1. Understanding and considering the impact of the workplace context is central to designing and delivering effective MBAs and will be a key focus in MBS.

    - Considering how an MBA will align with workplace values and how the workforce will view it is important.
    - This work will involve liaison with others within the workplace, such as senior leadership, Human Resources, grassroots staff, and staff well-being committees.

2. MB supervisors and supervisees must work within the scope of their knowledge and skill and understand the similarities and differences between workplace mindfulness and independent community MB work.

3. MBS is a place to honour and celebrate supervisees' work, from the smallest of endeavours right up to much broader ventures of embedding an MB approach into the culture and operations of an organization. Supervisors encourage a sense of optimism *and* realism.

4. Cultivating an Embodied Presence through the Mutual Inquiry process supports a deepening of practice and reflection. This is particularly important if a supervisee's training and MB work is less steeped in an inquiry-led approach.

5. MBS is a place to return to intention, support wholesome endeavours within workplace mindfulness, and draw on the growing body of research and theory to support safe and effective interventions.

Reflective questions

Is your approach to MBS around workplace mindfulness different from MBS in other contexts? What feels important to you in offering supervision in this context?

What is most rewarding and challenging about offering MBS in this area?

What supports and resources you in your work?

Are there particular areas for your development that you would like to pursue, particularly if this is a new area of MBS for you?

References

Carroll, M. (2007). *The mindful leader: Ten principles for bringing out the best in ourselves and others.* Shambhala Publications.

Edmondson, A. (1999). Psychological safety and learning behavior in work teams. *Administrative Science Quarterly*, 44(2), 350-383. https://doi.org/10.2307/2666999

Kabat-Zinn, J. (2003). Mindfulness-based interventions in context: Past, present, and future. *Clinical Psychology: Science and Practice*, 10(2), 144–156. https://psycnet.apa.org/doi/10.1093/clipsy.bpg016

Kuyken, W. (2024). *Mindfulness for life.* Guilford Press.

Newman, R., Smith, B., & Wolpert, M. (2021). *Putting science to work: Understanding what works for workplace mental health.* Wellcome Trust. https://wellcome.org/reports/understanding-what-works-workplace-mental-health

Rupprecht, S., Koole, W., Chaskalson, M., Tamdjidi, C., & West, M. (2019). Running too far ahead? Towards a broader understanding of mindfulness in organizations. *Current Opinion in Psychology*, 28, 32-36. https://doi.org/10.1016/j.copsyc.2018.10.007

Thaler, R., & Sunstein, C. (2008). *Nudge: Improving decisions about health, wealth, and happiness.* Yale University Press.

Chapter 10

Using the Mindfulness-Based Supervision Framework Through the Developmental Journey

> *"Learning to teach mindfulness with the support of a supervisor is like learning to ride a bike without stabilisers, but still having a gentle guiding hand so that as you increase the speed and risk, you still feel supported."*[205]

This chapter explores using the MBS framework with developmental learning in mind. MBS is a support at all stages of learning and experience, and whilst the main warp threads remain the same, there may be a slightly greater emphasis on some elements at times. Elements of the weft threads will vary, for example, in the Belt – using frameworks that hold competency. Within the Petals, the developmental stage will affect the supervisee's needs in relation to their skills development within their MB work, their personal mindfulness practice, and their understanding of theory and its links with their work. The types of MB work the supervisee is engaged with might vary for contextual and developmental reasons.

This opening metaphor about supervision and learning to ride a bike illustrates how different kinds of support are needed at different phases of development when learning something new. In this chapter, we draw upon four different developmental

---

[205] Broyé, 2023. From an event about mindfulness-based supervision with the Mindfulness Network Community Friends and Oxford Mindfulness Foundation https://community.mindfulness-network.org/course/view.php?id = 241

frameworks which map out stages of learning: one from the mindfulness field, two from other supervision modalities and one from learning theory. We consider the different needs of supervisees at these stages, outlining the possible varied flavours of supervision at these phases.

We offer examples centred mainly around supervisees teaching MBPs to illustrate how considering developmental needs requires variation in the weft threads. We aim to give an idea of how MBS shifts to meet what is needed, without losing its core warp and mindfulness base.

Developmental frameworks for learning
Integrative Developmental Model

Cal Stoltenberg developed a model called the Integrative Developmental Model (IDM) with colleagues including Ursula Delworth and Brian McNeill.[206] Their model looks at the developmental stages of learning for trainee counsellors and therapists during and beyond their initial training programmes. Stoltenberg and McNeill recognise that supervision is a complex process that can be viewed through stages of development whilst recognising it is not a purely linear journey. Supervisees will not necessarily develop equally in different areas at any one time. However, based on their experience and research, they have found some patterns in supervisees' needs at different stages of learning and the varying emphasis required in supervision and the supervisor's behaviour. Here are some of the characteristics of the supervisee at each stage, based on their work:

- **Level 1** – anxiety and confusion about their role, skills and ability; lacking confidence, and maybe lacking insight; highly motivated, focus on self, so the process of being videotaped can elicit negative evaluations of self.
- **Level 2** – overcome initial anxieties and fluctuates between dependence and autonomy, between over-confidence and overwhelm when aware of the complexity, beginning to be less simplistic and single focused, turning to participant focus. Realise it is a long process.
- **Level 3** – autonomous, reflective, increased professional self-confidence, greater insight – able to reflect upon self as a therapist/counsellor, more stable and intrinsic motivation, more able to work with confrontation.
- **Level 3i (integrative)** – personal autonomy, insightful awareness, personal security, high intrinsic motivation, may even be supervisors or trainers themselves so understand the process which helps to consolidate and deepen learning, able to integrate knowledge and experience.

---

206 Stoltenberg, 1997; Stoltenberg & Delworth, 1987; Stoltenberg & McNeill, 2010

Peter Hawkins and Aisling McMahon, in their book about supervision for the helping professions,[207] liken these stages of development to those of medieval craftspeople, who might have passed through being a novice, journeyperson, independent crafts person, and master crafts person. Indeed, some MB training organizations use an apprenticeship model where learning is often passed on through experienced practitioners.

Central focus of concern

Continuing with the IDM model, in their summary, Hawkins and McMahon include a description of where the supervisee's central focus of concern is at different levels of development.[208] This understanding can support the supervisor to meet the supervisee where they are and expand the supervisee's focus/view when they are ready.

- **Level 1** – Self-focused – concern and focus on their performance
- **Level 2** – Client focused – opening out to clients in more nuanced ways (for MBAs, we might use the word participant or student)
- **Level 3** – Process focused – more able to look at the process, adjust their approach, have an overview
- **Level 3i** – Process in-context focused – the ability to integrate these different foci and see connections

The MBI:TAC

Within MBAs, the MBI:TAC,[209] is often used as a developmental map and framework, as already outlined in previous chapters. Although not exact, these stages map quite closely to developmental models within other modalities and help to build a picture of the needs for beginner/advanced beginner, which shift and change once a teacher reaches the quite broad band of competency and then moves into proficient and advanced. We would recommend that MB supervisors are at a developmental teaching level of proficient.

The Conscious Competence Learning Model

We include this model as it can help supervisors and supervisees understand the stages of learning from another view. It is unclear who developed this model, and different internet searches attribute varied origins.[210] We leave you as the reader to investigate further if you wish.

---

207 Hawkins & McMahon, 2020
208 Hawkins & McMahon, 2020
209 Crane et al., 2021
210 This is the source we referred to: https://www.businessballs.com/self-awareness/conscious-competence-learning-model/#conscious-competence-theory-origins

The model is made up of two factors, namely, *consciousness* – how aware we are of what we know or what we can do, and *competence* – having the skills to do the things we need to do. The mix of these two factors forms four or five stages of developmental learning, depending which version of the model you refer to. We are using the five-stage model,[211] and have linked it to MBS:

- **Unconscious Incompetence** – *you don't know what you don't know.* In this phase, the supervisee does not understand or know how to do something and does not fully recognise their lack of skills or what is required. Because this lack is not in awareness it can be a comfortable, almost overconfident time. The supervisor is helping the supervisee to establish awareness, value a mindful approach and clarify their intention and motivation, which helps the supervisee to move into consciousness.

- **Conscious Incompetence** – *you know what you don't know.* In this phase, the supervisee might still not understand or know how to do something, but they recognise this and can see how much there is to learn. This can feel uncomfortable and difficult. The supervisor is helping the supervisee bring compassion to themselves, work with their inner critic if it arises, point out strengths, give space for 'mistakes,' and help the supervisee move into competency.

- **Conscious Competence** – *you know that you can do it now.* In this phase, the supervisee consciously understands or knows how to do something which comes with an increased confidence. It may still require some focus and effort to maintain the competency. The supervisee becomes more active in their own development and continued practice, refining their skills, reflecting and learning.

- **Unconscious Competence** – *you can do it without thinking about it.* In this phase, the supervisee has had so much practice with bringing mindfulness into their work and life that it becomes second nature, intuitive, embodied, and authentic. The supervisee may be starting to branch out and supervise or teach/train others. Skills are integrated, and they enter collegial relationships and take their place as senior practitioner within their field.

- **Reflective Competence** – This stage is described as a mature practice stage. It involves the process of continual learning through ongoing study, reflection, and supervision as ways of keeping discovering a 'beginner's mind' and opening to blind spots.

---

211 Courtesy of Will Taylor, Chair, Department of Homeopathic Medicine, National College of Natural Medicine, Portland, Oregon, USA, March 2007

Learning to ride a bike

Coming back to the metaphor at the beginning of this chapter about learning to ride a bike, we see something of the different stages of development when learning something new and the support that might be offered/needed from another, which changes as we develop.

- You begin by having the stabilisers on, with the parent/supporter close by.
- Then you venture to take the stabilisers off but still have support like your parent/supporter running along beside you, offering a guiding hand when needed.
- Eventually, you go off on your own, but you have someone to come back to and check in with.
- And in time, you have someone to ride alongside you.

Supporting learning, growth, and competency are key intentions of all these development models/frames of reference. In Table 10.1, we offer a visual representation of the different models which we find a helpful map, remembering that the stages for each framework don't map exactly.

So, why might we bear the developmental approach in mind?

- To emphasise that an important task of supervision is aiding learning, development and growth.
- To help assess and clarify the needs of supervisees at each stage of their developmental journey.
- To modulate supervision as the supervisee develops and has changing needs.
- To recognise that supervisors are also passing through stages of development which we turn to in Chapter 14.

We might summarise that an understanding of developmental stages and needs helps a supervisor to meet the supervisee where they are and patiently be alongside them, as illustrated in this little story:

> *A man once saw a butterfly struggling to emerge from its cocoon, too slowly for his taste, so he began to blow on it gently. The warmth of his breath speeded up the process all right. But what emerged was not a butterfly but a creature with mangled wings.*[212]

We also offer some cautions about considering developmental models: not to be too rigid and lose the uniqueness of each supervisee, their needs, their context, and the dynamic relationship.

---

212 Hawkins & McMahon, 2020, p. 84, abridged from Zorba the Greek

Table 10.1 Summary of the mapping of different development frameworks into four phases

Integrative Developmental Model	Central Focus of Supervision	Conscious Competence Learning Model	MBI:TAC	Riding a bike metaphor
Level 1 (novice)	Self-focused	Unconscious Incompetence/ Conscious Incompetence	Beginner/ Advanced Beginner	Stabilisers on with active support
Level 2 (journeyperson)	Client/ participant focused	Conscious Incompetence/ Conscious Competence	Competent	Stabilisers off with a guiding hand
Level 3 (independent craftsperson)	Process focused	Conscious Competence/ Unconscious Competence	Proficient	Riding on your own with someone to keep checking in with
Level 3i (integrative) (master craftsperson)	Process in-context focused	Reflective Competence	Advanced	Someone to ride alongside with

Mindfulness-based supervision at different stages of learning and experience

We now turn to considering how these developmental models apply to MBS. Table 10.2 summarizes the nature of MBS at different stages and gives examples of the role of the MBS supervisor. This is a reminder that at all stages, MBS includes all the features described in Part Two, but there may be an emphasis on some aspects according to the developmental stage. You may also notice the three different functions of supervision: Formative, Restorative, and Ethical rippled through this table.

Table 10.2 Summary of some characteristics of supervision at different developmental levels

Stage (based on MBI:TAC)	Possible nature of MBS at this stage	Examples of the MBS supervisor's role
Beginner, advanced beginner	<ul><li>Clearly structured and simplified.</li><li>Encouraging and supportive, and leaning into what is going well.</li><li>Practical skills based.</li><li>Leaning towards content and curricula.</li><li>Developing an understanding of underlying intentions.</li><li>Start to support an understanding of what MBS is.</li></ul>	<ul><li>Scaffolding to support the supervisee who may be very new to MBS.</li><li>Offering guidance.</li><li>Giving positive feedback and identifying strengths.</li><li>Supporting with extra patience and kindness.</li><li>Appropriate self-disclosure, recalling their own experience of beginning.</li><li>Encouraging the supervisee to be a reflective practitioner.</li><li>Starting to bring live guiding and inquiry into supervision.</li><li>Helping to clarify misunderstandings.</li><li>Modelling a mindfulness-based stance.</li><li>Attending to the relational side of MBS, building trust, and creating a safe space to reveal strengths and edges.</li><li>Supporting the embodying of attitudinal foundations, e.g. recognising striving and beginning to let go.</li><li>At times, expanding out to include different Petals.</li><li>Boosting confidence and remembering how scary it is to begin teaching MBAs.</li></ul>

Stage (based on MBI:TAC)	Possible nature of MBS at this stage	Examples of the MBS supervisor's role
Competent	■ Embedding of new skills. ■ Going deeper with explorations. ■ Turning more to growing edges and finding the freedom to learn from mistakes. ■ Exploration of relational aspects within mindfulness work and the supervisory relationship. ■ It is beginning to be less simplistic and single-focused. ■ Realising the supervisee is on a journey of learning and practice is a long process that doesn't end when training ends. ■ The focus of supervision might change as needed, e.g. if the supervisee is working towards competency assessment, there may be more video viewing and feedback. ■ The supervisee is more able to pinpoint their needs. ■ Post completion of training there may be a lull, with the supervisee exploring how do they fit into the field and what will their work be.	■ Holding the supervisee with their learning process. ■ Beginning to move between a structured and more collegial approach. ■ Widening out to all the different Petals to help the supervisee explore the process and content. ■ Practice can be developed with the supervisor guiding and inspiring. ■ The normalization of errors, "*I remember that.*" ■ As a supervisor, recognising one's own biases, remembering there are different ways to teach, so allowing the supervisee to find their own way. ■ Supporting experimenting. ■ Supporting the supervisee in exploring insecurities/vulnerabilities. ■ Being more fine-tuned and specific in feedback offered. ■ Opening post-completion of training explorations, e.g. finding community, normalising the possible experience of loss and change, resourcing, inspiration and practical steps.

Stage (based on MBI:TAC)	Possible nature of MBS at this stage	Examples of the MBS supervisor's role
Proficient	■ More reflective. ■ More exploratory. ■ Don't get to this stage and think that's it. There are still things to learn, including coming back to the 'beginner's mind' and humility. ■ Broader themes, wider context and perspective. ■ The supervisee might have increased professional self-confidence, greater insight, more stable motivation, and more able to work with challenge. ■ Collegial relationship which might be peer-based with two supervisors contracting MBS together (different to peer-based groups).	■ Moving into a more collegial approach. ■ Looking out for the supervisee thinking they have reached an endpoint, and helping to keep learning alive. ■ Supervisee may be proficient in one area of their mindfulness work but more of a beginner in other areas – holding these different needs. ■ Holding the space for inquiry and deepening levels of exploration. ■ Holding up a mirror for the supervisee, the supervisor being that reflector. ■ Expanding the scope of what to explore, e.g. deepening personal practice. ■ Maybe more challenging questions within the inquiry process to help grow, to see blind spots, to shake things up a bit.

Stage (based on MBI:TAC)	Possible nature of MBS at this stage	Examples of the MBS supervisor's role
Advanced	■ An extension to the previous level with many of the same needs and considerations. ■ The scope of mindfulness work moves beyond teaching into training, supervision, supra-vision, a more meta-level in the field. ■ The supervisee brings personal autonomy, insightful awareness, personal security, and stable motivation. They may be a supervisor themselves so understand the process, which helps to consolidate and deepen learning.	■ Collegial at this stage, but important that the supervisor holds boundaries and the container. ■ Holding the space and inquiry is not so much about acquiring new knowledge but allowing learning through deepening and integration and developing wisdom. ■ Bringing humility to the space. ■ Helping the supervisee to keep coming back to beginner's mind, reducing the sense of expert, keeping freshness. ■ Helping supervisees appreciate their level of experience, what they know, and what they have to offer – not overusing humility. ■ Supporting the supervisee with widening their work to new areas, e.g. writing, research, and other projects.

Bearing development in mind in relation to the warp

In the early stages of development, or with a supervisee new to MBS, the supervisor will be orienting them into the culture of MBS. This might be a mix of explicitly describing and sharing the MBS framework or implicitly by how they offer MBS and guide the process. The supervisor will likely hold the Container to begin as the supervisee finds their way into mindfulness and embodying it. The metaphor about riding a bike points to the changing relationship within MBS. The supervisor is attuning to the supervisee within the inquiry, sensitive to different factors that will influence how they learn and grow, such as neurodivergence, past learning experiences, and current context. Over time the inquiry often becomes increasingly collegial. The supervisor brings an encouragement to allow space: moments to wonder. Early on, this might include doing one thing at a time, not thinking too far ahead, learning and developing in bite-sized pieces. Supervisees new to MB work bring many agenda items to supervision and lots of questions, so the supervisor is helping them make choices about how to manage time and space.

Using the weft of the mindfulness-based supervision framework: the Belt

We would like to emphasise two aspects of the Belt with development in mind. One is the competency aspect and the need to hold this in a way that supports the supervisee's growth and learning, so not too tight and not too loose. We explore the use of the MBI:TLC and MBI:TAC later under the Petals.

The other aspect is a reminder from Chapter 7, to regularly review the contract as the supervisee's needs and expectations change with their learning and development. Re-contracting verbally and/or in writing can help keep supervision fresh and developmentally appropriate. It may also be time for the supervisee to find a different supervisor as needs shift.

Using the weft of the mindfulness-based supervision framework: the Petals

Whilst each Petal will potentially be relevant in all the different developmental stages, there can be different flavours of how things get explored and we are going to focus on two Petals to illustrate this. You might also like to refer back to Table 10.2. We begin with the Personal Mindfulness Petal, as the practice underpins all MB work. Then, we are going to focus on the Mindfulness-Based Work (Teaching) Petal as this is very often the most obvious area of content in the early stages of MBS for many supervisees who want to teach or share mindfulness.

Personal mindfulness practice

We offer an example here of how the exploration of a supervisee's personal mindfulness practice evolved over time and with their development as an MB teacher.

Example – exploring personal mindfulness practice

In the early stages of supervision, this supervisee tended to bring their teaching rather than personal practice. With encouragement, they started to feel more able to talk about their practice. As they did so, they recognized that they had a harsh attitude towards themself and had done all their life. This also showed up in relation to their way of evaluating themselves as a teacher.

Within supervision, there was gentle encouragement to bring some softening and friendliness into their practice. Finding words and ways that were okay for the supervisee wasn't easy for them. This was also explored through brief practices in the supervision session.

Over time, the supervisee felt ready to turn more actively toward befriending and compassion-based practices. The supervisor supported the supervisee in finding practices, guided some in the session, and pointed them towards books, talks, and a retreat. Supervision provided a space to continue these explorations around the implicit and explicit use of kindness within their formal and informal practice.

This was also linked with other Petals as they considered ways of incorporating an attitude of friendliness into their teaching and especially their way of viewing themselves as a teacher.

And it remains an ongoing exploration.

Mindfulness-based work (teaching)

Within this Petal there will be skills related to the developmental stage of the supervisee with their MB work. For example, a supervisee teaching an MBP, might begin with the skills needed to share mindfulness practices through to teaching different MBPs. As supervisees broaden the scope of their MB work each type of work will have its own developmental trajectory. For example, a supervisee may be a very experienced teacher and moved through different stages of learning and growth in their teaching and then move into a trainer role. Whilst they bring their existing skills with them, they also begin a new developmental learning journey, becoming more of a beginner again.

We look now at the nature of MBS at these different developmental phases within the MB work Petal.

Beginner

Supervision may begin very early in someone's training journey. MBS might help point them towards further training, support clarification of their intentions and the work they want to engage with and help them identify the skills needed and how to build them up. A supervisee may have begun a training process and want to practise their skills, e.g. guiding mindfulness practice with the supervisor and receive feedback and have the supervisor guide practice so they can learn from them too. Knowing the context of any training they are/have/wish to be engaged with is helpful in understanding their developmental journey.

Advanced beginner

The supervisee may have some experience but may not know their growing edges, so perhaps viewing clips of their teaching or bringing live teaching into supervision can be helpful, which could include the supervisor demonstrating guiding a practice and engaging in inquiry. The supervisee may be overconfident or underconfident, but either way, not so clear about the MB approach, so the supervisor may need to be more instructional, e.g. suggesting a shift from reading from a script to guiding from their own practice.

Although they may not be teaching a whole curriculum, it is often helpful for the supervisee to be anchoring into one curriculum, and whichever parts they are teaching/guiding. Gently introducing the MBI:TLC helps map out the domains and key features for the supervisee, taking care not to overwhelm them. It can also be a way to encourage the supervisee to self-reflect on their teaching, especially focusing on noticing strengths, which can also move into feedback from the supervisor. There may be times of a mismatch between the supervisor's and the supervisee's impressions, so building a trusting and safe relationship helps provide a space to navigate these more tender areas.

There will likely be a linkage with the Theory and Understanding Petal as the supervisor encourages the supervisee to understand why they are doing what they are doing and make links to the theory and their own practice, which continues to deepen through the developmental journey.

Competent

As you can see these levels flow into each other without clear delineation, so the supervisor continues to give clear guidance at times. The supervisee may be clearer about the curriculum and the *what* to do in teaching and have further capacity to extend more to the *how*, the embodied teaching. The supervisor might encourage this increasing connection with other Petals, e.g. Theory/Understanding, Group/Individual processes and Personal Mindfulness Practice and explore the link with teaching.

The supervisor is encouraging the supervisee to continue their self-reflection on strengths which might move more in the direction of self-feedback. There may be more confidence to explore growing edges and receive feedback from the supervisor to support growth. The MBI:TLC could be used as a framework at times for reflection, feedback, and dialogue together.

The supervisee may be widening their view within teaching and finding their own teacher within themself, with a balance of encouragement and pointing to where to grow. Live teaching continues with feedback/reflection to help build confidence. There may be a recognition and exploration of a range of teaching styles.

Depending on the context of the supervisee's training route, they might be preparing for assessment, so wanting to use supervision as part of that preparation. This might mean a much closer use of the MBI:TAC, alongside the MBI:TLC, viewing teaching, giving feedback, refining and polishing skills.

Proficient

This can be a stage where supervision starts to drop off now the supervisee has finished their training where supervision was likely a key component. Good practice guidelines vary in their requirements for supervision post-training; we strongly advocate continuing with supervision as learning never ceases, and the value of being in mindful dialogue adds to continuing professional and personal development. We might suggest that the more the supervisee teaches, the more they don't know; they keep exploring different layers, as each course or aspect of mindfulness work brings new discoveries and a deepening of understanding. The supervisee might still bring live guiding into the session; perhaps they are leading different practices as part of a new innovation and want some feedback. The supervisor might invite the supervisee to keep coming back to the bridge between personal practice and teaching, and the relationship with self and teaching. The mindfulness field is constantly evolving so there might also be themes and aspects of practice the supervisee is less familiar with as they trained some years prior. Supervision can be a place to explore further and consider how to bring these new understandings and skills into work that may have a very familiar and comfortable feel to it.

The supervisee may begin to teach in different contexts or curricula, including innovations they are part of developing. They may be moving into new areas of MB work, such as supervision and training others.

Advanced

This stage often extends from the previous level with many of the same needs and considerations. The scope of MB work might move even broader into supra-vision, writing, leading MB organizations, bringing in a mindful culture to the workplace, we might say more of a meta-level in the field.

The MBI:TLC and MBI:TAC as a support to developmental learning in supervision

The MBI:TLC, developed as a self-reflection tool, is particularly helpful in relation to MBS due to its reflective nature and the encouragement to see development as a continuous process.[213] It uses language which supports a reflective and strengths-based stance, giving a sense of potential with phrases such as 'No, not yet'. Since the publication of the MBI:TLC,[214] we have heard a number of creative and responsive ways that people are using the tool, along with the MBI:TAC within MBS. As one supervisor put it, *"It's a big tool, so I am exploring how to break it down into smaller pieces, more manageable steps, digestible, and relatable"*. We offer possibilities to play with in MBS:

---

213 Evans et al., 2021
214 Griffith et al., 2021

- It can be staged to offer the appropriate conditions for the various stages in the MB teacher training journey, for example:
    - In the early stage of learning, just focusing on one or more of the domains rather than any rating to have a broad map of the territory.
    - As supervisees develop in their teaching, space can be given to exploring the specifics of each domain, the key features and identifying their strengths and areas of learning.
    - Supervisees may record themselves teaching or guide a live practice in the supervision session and ask the supervisor to offer feedback.
    - At a later stage, supervisors might encourage a deeper reflection upon one domain at a time: reading about it, practising with it formally, in teaching, in life, thinking about its meaning and how it applies to their teaching, and to their strengths and learning needs.
    - If the supervisee is preparing for a competency assessment then the MBI:TAC may be used more closely, clearly identifying strengths and growing edges together.
    - Following a part or full competency assessment from a training organization, the supervisee might share their MBI:TAC assessment outcomes with the supervisor, with a view to shaping future direction within supervision.
- The supervisor and supervisee can be creative about which elements of the MBI:TLC or MBI:TAC to use in supervision depending on the supervisee's needs and preferred style of exploration, e.g. which tool, the whole tool, the strengths and learning needs table, just the words, self-created pictures, diagrams, mind maps, etc.
- The supervisor might note which domains are not often spoken about to enable further exploration and help to highlight blind spots and things that don't seem to come to the supervision agenda. This helps to broaden out and cover the whole range of what's possible within supervision.
- It can be used as part of a feedback process.
- The Belt – Contracting
    - Using it as part of the contracting stage to shape what the supervisee wants to work on within supervision.
    - Using it as part of a review within supervision, maybe once a year, helping to give structure and scaffolding, and coming back to the intention of supervision to avoid drifting.

- The supervisor might invite the supervisee prior to the supervision session to prepare by going through the domains in the MBI:TLC, using the scale if helpful, and making notes. They can either send this in advance or bring it to supervision for reflection and dialogue.
- At the end of a block of supervision sessions, the supervisor and supervisee might use the tool to summarise the supervisee's learning, strengths and growing edges to take forward.
- Explorations for the supervisor:
  - It's important to explore how you view the tool; your relationship might be communicated to the supervisee, e.g. not liking it or holding it too tight.
  - Use it yourself to reflect upon your own teaching practice and not lose sight of your own edges as a teacher.
  - Have it in mind in the supervision session, in the background to refer to but not always bring it in explicitly; you may use it implicitly, holding the domains in mind and naming explicitly when it feels appropriate.
  - Use it as a tool after a supervision session to review the supervisee's skills.
- And some cautions:
  - Use it with care; it's not the only way – it's one framework, one attempt to articulate and describe what MB teaching looks like. Watch that it doesn't reduce teaching.
  - Ensure that as a supervisor, you attune to your supervisee – is it a way they find helpful in their learning or not?.
  - A reminder that it doesn't have to be used within MBS, knowing when it is useful and when not (skilful means).
  - Consider potential cultural factors that might not be recognized through the tool and keep this in mind and as part of the supervisory dialogue.

In the MBI:TAC in supervision paper,[215] Alison and colleagues named these creative tensions and how every potential benefit of these tools is matched by a potential pitfall if the process is not held with sensitivity and care. Different dimensions are named with their opposite polarity. All dimensions are valuable and needed at different times, so the supervisor is attuning to what is needed at any one time. We have set them in Figure 10.1, showing them on a seesaw to illustrate how a supervisor might lean more into one aspect at one point in supervision and other times both are being held in balance. As a supervisor, you may also notice your own preferred style and encourage yourself to practise with the other style. Hence, you have the flexibility to use both depending on need rather than personal preference.

---

215 Evans et al., 2021

Figure 10.1 Holding the creative tensions when using the MBI:TAC and MBI:TLC within MBS

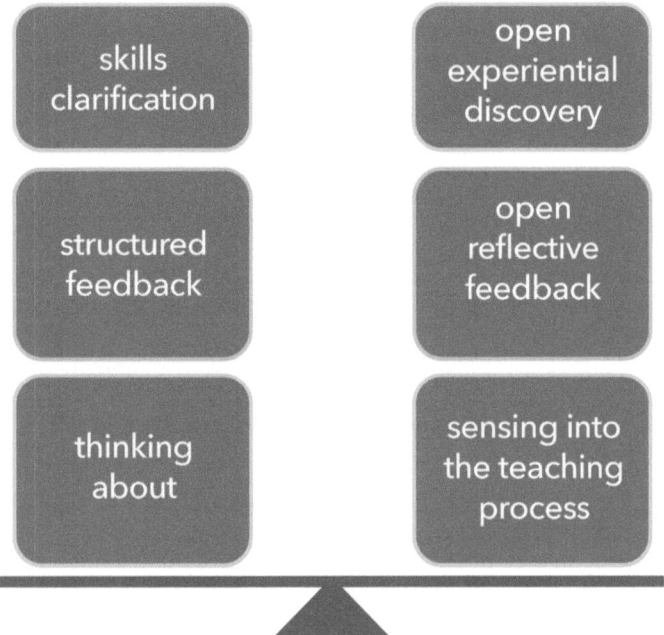

Offering and receiving feedback

The offering and receiving of feedback can be extremely valuable and a tender process. We provide some general guiding principles of fruitful ways of offering feedback within MBS based on the MBS framework.

- Build a safe and trusting environment first.
- Check in with your intention as a supervisor in offering feedback (e.g. to support, to help).
- Let it be steeped in both compassion and wisdom.
- Check out what the supervisee would like/needs from the process – a kind of contracting with each other, and knowing that there may be cultural differences in styles and expectations around offering and receiving feedback.
- Keep it as a mutual relational process: invite the supervisee to comment first, e.g. what went well, what would you do differently, checking how the feedback is landing, building on what the supervisee has already named – a spirit of collaboration.
- Remember potential power dynamics, which can be particularly activated in relation to feedback, so sensitivity is needed – the words of a supervisor can carry a lot of weight.

- Give space for the process, for the supervisee to take in the feedback, comment, and see what and how it is landing – it takes time to explore and offer feedback in meaningful ways.
- Give opportunities for growth rather than criticism, make feedback strengths-based, based on observable skills and actions, keep it as objective as possible and name preferences, being as specific as possible.
- Bear in mind the developmental stage of the supervisee which might affect how much detail and nuance to go into. Sometimes less is more – what's most important, and what to let go of for now? What would make the most difference to their teaching at this stage?
- Prioritise things that might be causing harm to participants/recipients so safety is kept uppermost.
- Possible use of the MBI:TLC or MBI:TAC, which can offer a shared language and structure, thereby removing some of the personal and bringing the observable, tangible aspects of the teaching process to the forefront – prioritising identifying skills and strengths as well as areas of development is important, especially if the teacher is critical of their teaching.

Being able to receive honest feedback can be an aid in moving through blocks in development as an MBP teacher. The combination of the supportive MBS relationship and clarity, perhaps with the use of an objective framework such as the MBI:TLC or MBI:TAC, can enable the supervisor to combine kindness with rigour.

You may like to experiment with this exercise.

Exercise – offering feedback

In our supervision training, we set up an exercise where we ask the trainees to listen to a recorded practice, imagining a supervisee had sent it to them. We invite these questions to support the process of approaching viewing/listening to teaching and offering feedback:

How did you approach it? What did you consider?

How did you draw on the MBI:TLC or not?

What might be ways you support their further development around guiding practice?

How might you feed this back to the supervisee, which might include using the MBI:TLC?

You may like to draw upon these questions/processes as a supervisor next time you are invited to view a recording of teaching.

Imagine if I had stopped supervision after my training; what might I have missed?

In short, I can't imagine not continuing with supervision. Supervision has been such an important part of my development and integral to reflecting on my teaching and practice.[216]

We feel MBS is of great value to continue through all the developmental stages, as learning never stops! We offer some responses from ourselves and our interviewees to the question: Imagine if I had stopped supervision after my training; what might I have missed?

- Seeing how I can't do this on my own, having someone to help by holding the space in a particular way. The gentle presence of a wise supervisor who offers companionship and deep listening during moments of solitude and challenge.
- Having someone with whom I can confidently share my successes and joys without fear of jealousy or sabotage. A lifelong, ever-trustworthy friend. It's lonely otherwise.
- To have someone to reflect and discuss objectively with when facing challenges and difficulties at work, to guide me through difficult times and to offer advice from a higher perspective and level. The compassionate guidance and clarity offered by supervisors when the path seems unclear or the heart feels heavy.
- Being refreshed and inspired by the dialogue, by the learning, by having different aspects of mindfulness practice and work as a focus at any one time, going a bit deeper.
- Continual learning, acknowledging there are always different perspectives that I won't discover alone.
- Keeping up to date with professional knowledge and skills, understanding new developments in the field along with reading and training; supervision as a place to learn, apply, explore, and wonder about my context.
- Having a structured way of holding accountability around MB work. *"I have my supervision booked in advance each month – I don't wait for an 'issue'. There is always something to bring."*
- Having a place to take ethical dilemmas and safeguarding concerns.
- Being able to explore habits and patterns and how they impact MB work and life. The sacred space to witness my own patterns and biases, cultivating the courage to explore them with gentle curiosity and self-compassion.
- Opportunities for transparency around my work. Someone has seen my teaching – tells me about strengths and edges. It helps me to see blind spots.

---

216 A quote from one of our interviewees for the book

- Going deeper in my exploration of my personal practice and how this supports my teaching, training and supervision practice. The nurturing ground to deepen my practice and wisdom, allowing me to share teachings with authenticity and skilful care.
- Being able to respond to my changing needs through accessing different supervision arrangements and options.
- The nourishing of my own inner trust and confidence.
- The opportunity to develop my own style and to explore new areas and to do both in such a way that I feel I have maintained my sense of integrity and professionalism.

Summary

1. We have outlined different developmental frameworks for learning:
   - Integrative Developmental Model – a supervision-based model
   - The central focus of concern
   - The MBI:TAC
   - The Conscious Competence Learning Model
   - Learning to ride a bike metaphor

   These developmental frameworks all have the intention of supporting learning, growth and competency. An understanding of developmental stages and needs helps a supervisor to meet the supervisee where they are and patiently be alongside them.

2. We outlined the characteristics of MBS at different stages of learning and experience: the nature of MBS and the role of the supervisor.

3. The warp of MBS remains as strong threads regardless of the developmental stage of learning but may have different elements emphasized and modulated, e.g. the supervisor might be holding the Container and the inquiry more to begin, which in time become more mutual and collegial processes.

4. The weft is woven in different ways to support learning and growing processes.
   - The Belt:
     - Competency is held in ways that are supportive – not too tight and not too loose.
     - Contracts need regular review to ensure they are current with what the supervisee needs as they learn.

- The Petals:
  - We offer an example of the Personal Mindfulness Practice Petal through a supervisee's developmental journey.
  - We look at the Mindfulness-Based Work Petal, specifically the development stages of teaching mindfulness and some of the common threads that come up in MBS.
5. We explore the use of the MBI:TLC and MBI:TAC as a support to developmental learning in MBS by looking at creative and responsive ways of bringing these tools into MBS, including a recognition of the creative tensions inherent within the process.
6. We outline some general guiding principles for fruitful feedback offerings. These include the supportive MBS relationship and clarity, enabling the supervisor to combine kindness with rigour.
7. We reflect upon why it's important to continue with supervision as part of ongoing learning and development.

Reflective questions

What developmental stages do you see yourself in now? There might be different stages for the varied aspects of your MB work.

Take a moment to reflect on when you began learning these different aspects of your MB work – what were the characteristics for you of being in these different stages? Do you have your own metaphor for your developmental learning? Do any of the developmental models we have presented resonate with you?

What were your supervisory needs when you first began your MB work? How have your needs changed? How has supervision changed to meet your needs over that time?

Reflect upon a time when you had the experience of receiving helpful feedback within supervision. You may like to consider what made it a helpful experience: the structure, the content, the process, the person giving it, the way it was offered, and anything else.

Reflect upon a time when you had the experience of offering helpful feedback within supervision. You may like to consider what your sense is of what made it a helpful experience for the supervisee, the structure, the content, the process, the way you offered it, and anything else.

References

Crane, R. S., Soulsby, J. G., Kuyken, W., Williams, J. M. G., & Eames, C. (2021). Mindfulness-Based Interventions: Teaching Assessment Criteria (MBI:TAC) (3rd version). https://mbitac.bangor.ac.uk/mbitac-tool.php.en

Evans, A., Griffith, G. M., Crane, R. S., & Sansom, S. A. (2021). Using the mindfulness-based interventions: teaching assessment criteria (MBI:TAC) in supervision. *Global Advances in Health and Medicine*, 10, 1-6. https://doi.org/10.1177/2164956121989949

Griffith G. M., Crane, R. S., Karunavira, & Koerbel, L. (2021). The Mindfulness-Based Interventions: Teaching and Learning Companion (MBI:TLC). In R. S. Crane, Karunavira, & G. M. Griffith (Eds.), *Essential resources for mindfulness teachers* (pp. 125-148). Routledge. https://doi.org/10.4324/9780429317880

Hawkins, P., & McMahon, A. (2020). *Supervision in the helping professions* (5th ed.). Open University Press.

Stoltenberg, C. D. (1997). The integrated developmental model of supervision: Supervision across levels. *Psychotherapy in Private Practice*, 16(2), 59-69. https://doi.org/10.1300/J294v16n02_07

Stoltenberg, C. D., & Delworth, U. (1987). *Supervising counselors and therapists: A developmental approach.* Jossey-Bass.

Stoltenberg, C. D., & McNeill, B. W. (2010). *IDM supervision: An integrative developmental model for supervising counselors and therapists* (3rd ed.). Routledge.

Chapter 11
Using the Mindfulness-Based Supervision Framework to Respond to Challenging, Complex and Sensitive Issues

In the middle of every difficulty lies opportunity.[217]

Although significantly challenging experiences do not occur very often, we consider it a responsibility of MB supervisors to give time for reflection, learning and skill development to support themselves and their supervisees in navigating times of complexity and greatest vulnerability when they do arise. In this chapter, we focus on specific themes and examples to point to particularly relevant elements of the framework in these complex situations. We offer a three-stage process and draw out general principles to act as guides within any complicated situation.

Good supervision embodies safety and challenge. The supervisor and supervisee are cultivating a willingness to turn towards the more difficult aspects of experience, including supervisees bringing challenging moments from their MB work to explore

---

217 Anonymous, often attributed to Albert Einstein. Retrieved January 13, 2025, https://quoteinvestigator.com/2021/10/07/difficulty/

in supervision, recognising times as the supervisor when you feel challenged, such as not knowing what to do and feeling in need of help, and challenges within the supervisory relationship itself. Naming and stepping into this less comfortable territory takes courage. With a tendency within MBS to focus more on the positive and avoid critique,[218] supervisors need to know how to open to challenging and searching conversations while keeping themselves and the supervisee within an active learning space, taking care that neither feels overwhelmed. Complex and sensitive issues often link to themes around Integrity and Safety and in this way, there are strong connections to the Container and the Belt.

As part of MBS training, we have developed a three-stage process to support compassionate and wise responses:

Stage one: What is your immediate reaction?

What do you notice in the body? What emotions are present? What are the thoughts arising?

To open to the supervisee, the supervisor first opens to their own inner experience, with their practice supporting a sense of steadiness within whatever is arising. This awareness of inner experience helps notice important aspects of the situation and supports emotion regulation. This links with parts of the warp; self-Inquiry and Embodied Presence.

Stage two: What do you need to consider?

Allowing time to open to the different aspects of the situation encourages taking a broader perspective: considering the urgency of the situation and the risks or potential risks, seeing it from the perspective of the supervisee, that of their participants, the context of the supervisee's life and their MB work, the broader mindfulness field, the supervisory relationship, and your own perspective, including your personal values and ethics. This has links to Intention, Integrity, and relational elements of the warp while also drawing on the Petals and the Belt.

Stage three: How might you respond?

Here, the supervisor draws on knowledge and experience to discern what is needed. Within the midst of a complicated moment, there is often a strong urge to fix and do so as quickly as possible. Although there will be times when an urgent and decisive response is required right within the moment of supervision, often there is space to respond over a period of time, allowing time or reflection and seeking support through supra-vision. Here, the Container and Mutual Inquiry will hold a central place, while drawing on relevant parts of the Petals and the Belt.

---

218 Evans et al., 2024

We continue in this chapter to explore the use of this three-stage process in relation to four themes: the supervisory relationship, safety and well-being, competency, and ethical complexity.

Each will begin with a scenario to help focus the exploration and then consider significant aspects of the theme. These examples, albeit altered to protect anonymity, are experiences we have encountered in supervision or supra-vision. We notice that these issues are not often talked about or written about. Of course, every situation is different, and there will always be specific factors or conditions that require a nuanced response. This is where the metaphor of the dance can be helpful, feeling into what is needed in each situation, when to support, when to gently challenge and when, at times, especially when safety is an issue, to take a more directive stance.

The themes are explored in a particular order, beginning with the relational element. The recommendation is to maintain a connection with this central theme as you explore the other themes of safety, competency, and wider ethical issues. Whatever the challenging issue arising, it's about tending to the relational as a foundation. The themes around safety are explored next and will be relevant to take forward into the themes of competency and ethical complexity.

With each scenario, we invite you to pause for reflection. If you have encountered an experience within one of the themes, do bring the specifics of your lived experience to mind and heart to support a connection with the nuances of your situation, and as you work through the example, see what resonates in terms of considerations and responses.

Scenario one: the supervisory relationship

The scenario
Just before the end of the last supervision session, there was a misunderstanding between you and the supervisee around an aspect of the supervisee's mindfulness work that resulted in strong emotions for you and seemed to be for the supervisee, too. There was not time to explore this within the session. There have been a few other occasions when there seemed to be tensions within the relationship. However, when you raised awareness of this, the supervisee quickly dismissed it, saying they did not notice anything and that it was all fine for them.

What is your immediate reaction?
Take a few moments to note down your experiences.

What do you need to consider?

Here are some ideas, and you may have others:

- Going back to contracting, what were the conversations and the agreements around working with difficulties and sensitivities within supervision, including within the supervisory relationship? Would it be helpful to refer back to these initial agreements and intentions of supervision?

- What are the cultural sensitivities to be aware of? How might your perception of the experience differ from that of your supervisee? What do you know about what is happening in the supervisee's life that could be connected or impacting them? What biases or assumptions might you be making, and what would support you in opening up to not knowing?

- What is the impact of the power imbalance within the relationship? Is it safe enough for the supervisee to take interpersonal risks, such as disagreeing with the supervisor? What might support a safe space for openness and honesty for the supervisee and the supervisor?

- What is the possible influence of your own habits? Watkins asserts that humility is the foundation for repair and encourages an acknowledgement that as the supervisor,[219] one has the potential to behave in ways that can cause or contribute to a rupture, make mistakes and have limitations that can impact the supervisory relationship.

- What is the stage of the supervisory relationship? Would this be a good time for a review? Have you had feedback from the supervisee on how they are finding supervision?

How might you respond?

Within this relational domain, we want to highlight the value of the warp threads: the Container, Mutual Inquiry and Space.

Taking time for practice just before the next supervision session with the supervisee will help in strengthening conditions that support an MB approach, explicitly bringing the supervisee to mind and heart, connecting with your intentions for the session and supporting a sense of embodied presence in the midst of the tenderness which may be present. Attending to the Container of mindfulness in this way can be further enhanced by beginning the supervision session with a guided practice, supporting a sense of grounding, encouraging an opening to present moment experience, and facilitating the reconnection between the supervisee and supervisor through this shared practice. The practice might include encouragement to connect/reconnect with intention, an invitation to open to all experiences, including what's not wanted or anything difficult, and an invitation to connect to specific attitudinal qualities.

---

219 Watkins, 2021

In setting the agenda for the session, there may need to be some negotiation around how to use the time to cover whatever the supervisee is bringing that's important for them while also making space to explore this theme of the supervisory relationship that feels important to the supervisor. This can be easier if there has already been a pattern of the supervisor regularly contributing to the agenda-setting rather than just being the supervisee's domain. However, in this instance, the supervisor needs to be clear about the importance of making time to explore this theme.

Drawing explicitly on an inquiry-based approach will be the cornerstone of this exploration between supervisor and supervisee, especially this movement into a more felt sense of the experience – a deliberate shift into this different way of knowing. The supervisor is tuning into what is happening in their body alongside a decentering from emotions, thoughts and urges to react, sensing into and resonating with the experience of the supervisee, and feeling into the unfolding experience within the interpersonal space as they explore the rupture and move towards repair. You may find it helpful to revisit Chapters 3 and 4.

Using the framework from Chapter 4, Figure 4.2, which illustrates the flow of the inquiry process, will help to 'unpack' the experience for both yourself and the supervisee, with a reminder that this is not a linear process but rather a moving around the cycle and a back and forth:

Then: What happened in the last supervision – the experience and what you each noticed in the body, emotions and thoughts at the time

Now: Reflecting on how it feels now – body, emotions, thoughts, urges; how are you each relating to this experience now?

Making Meaning: Reflecting and inquiring together. What does the supervisee think about what happened? What is their felt sense? What is yours? Is there any link with mindfulness theory or practice? Exploration of the body and emotions alongside the thinking element. Making space for different perspectives, moving away from a sense of there being a right answer, considering the Both/And approach. Allowing space for not-knowing. Making tentative hypotheses.

Taking Forward: What are the learning, understanding, insight, actions, and explorations to take forward? Allowing time for the supervisee to consider the learning as they may not know yet.

As part of the considerations in taking things forward, consider whether it is time for a review. Often, a more formal way of gathering feedback from the supervisee can be helpful to broaden their perspective to consider what has been helpful about supervision, as well as the more challenging and unhelpful aspects, and what they need from supervision going forward.

Remembering the importance of Space. Pauses, slowing it down, supporting yourself and the supervisee to reconnect with the body whenever needed, then opening to emotions and thoughts. Embodying the attitudinal qualities of non-judging, acceptance and patience – finding the places where there is agreement and acknowledging the places where there is a difference of opinion. Working with edges, yours and the supervisee's, holding in mind their window of tolerance, noticing when it feels safe enough to push and when not.

Allow time for practice, even if just a brief pause at the end of the session. Taking time to thank the supervisee, being specific about what you appreciated. For example, their willingness to explore this tender area, their honesty. Encourage them to take time to reflect after the session, with opportunities to pick up the conversation again next time.

Moreover, after the session, taking time for yourself to reflect, maybe journalling, and returning to supra-vision for further discussion. Interpersonal conflict can trigger feelings of guilt, shame or anger, especially if you feel you did not respond skilfully. Sometimes, in these moments of greatest challenge, we learn the most and rediscover that some learning is only possible through this experiential way. Consider what you need to best take care of yourself.

Navigating a more serious rupture – back to intention and contracting

At times of a more serious rupture, in the midst of strong emotions and tensions, it can be helpful to remember that MBS is a contracted professional relationship, so coming back to the intention of supervision, clarifying the scope of the work and the needs of the supervisee, and considering whether it's possible to resolve the conflict to be able to continue the relationship or not. The supervisor holds mutual respect and makes space for different perspectives. Is there an option to bring in a third party to help in reaching a resolution? Sometimes, within organizations, a senior person can bring an objective perspective and support the supervisor and supervisee in finding a mutually agreeable way forward.

The wisest resolution might be to conclude the supervisory relationship, acknowledging a lack of compatibility. The supervisor may be able to support the supervisee in seeking a new supervisor. Sometimes, a supervisee feels unable to have this discussion and disengages through non-attendance or drifts away without a formal closure. It is important that the supervisor marks the ending, most likely via email, to acknowledge the ending of the supervisory relationship and send well wishes to the supervisee.

Pausing for self-reflection
Interpersonal sensitivities

You might find it helpful to pause at this point in the chapter and consider your own experiences in supervision around interpersonal sensitivities. Sometimes reading about these themes can trigger memories of past experiences and these memories can come with strong emotions and body sensations.

Using the three-stage process, beginning with tuning into your reactions in the moment, and allowing your practice to support you in staying steady within your present moment experience.

Then, when, and if it feels right, working through considerations and possible responses; although you cannot alter the outcome of past events, there can be learning, healing and resolution right within these tender experiences that can have lasting impact.

Consider:

From your own experiences as a supervisee, what have you found most difficult within the relationship with your supervisor?

What have you found most challenging within your relationship with a supervisee?

What is your relationship with interpersonal conflict? What are your habit patterns? What are your personal values and ethics around interpersonal relationships and conflict?

Scenario two: safety and well-being
The scenario

Your supervisee has been managing many difficult life events for some time. They are currently in the middle of offering a short mindfulness course for participants accessing the support of a charity. They will be working with a degree of complexity in the upcoming session. You are concerned because they seem more vulnerable than in the previous supervision.

What is your immediate reaction?

Take a few moments to note down your experiences.

What do you need to consider?

Here are some ideas, and you may have others.

- What is the context of their teaching? Who is in their group? What are the vulnerabilities within the group?
- Has the supervisee experienced events in the past or that are happening now that are traumatic? How significant is the impact of these life events?
- What are the supervisee's strengths and resources?
- What is the level of competence of the supervisee? Have they taught many times, or are they relatively new? Are they teaching alone? Is there any scope for support even if they are teaching alone?
- What is the supervisee's level of awareness and insight around the impact of their well-being on their teaching practice? The fact that the supervisee has felt safe enough to name that there are difficulties in their life is important.
- When is your next supervision? How often do you meet? Is there scope to offer more supervision?
- How do you balance the restorative function of supervision with the ethical function?

How might you respond?

As described in the first scenario, approaching this from a place of embodied presence and connection, and drawing on the principles of Mutual Inquiry as the foundation.

This delicate situation requires careful balancing of compassion and kindness towards the supervisee with your duty of care for the welfare of both them and their participants. There are strong connections here with Integrity and the normative function of MBS, so drawing on the Container and the Belt.

Making a deliberate shift from the concept of a safe space to a brave space[220] supports the recognition and acceptance that difficult conversations can be uncomfortable. However, it can be approached with courage and openness. Naming this with the supervisee helps create a shared understanding of the focus and tone of the discussions. To help in setting the agenda, check in with what the supervisee would like to get from this session, perhaps suggesting that you take the first part of supervision to explore the factors to consider without rushing to a solution, then move into naming the different choices before deciding together what are the next steps. This should include clear plans for checking back with the supervisee and arrangements for the next supervision.

---

220 Arao & Clemens, 2013

It's helpful to know if the supervisee has experienced something similar in the past and what they found helpful then. If the supervisee reports that this is a new experience for them or more intense than in the past, this could indicate the need to take it more seriously.

Ask directly if they feel they can recognise when it would be best to step back from teaching. Sometimes, articulating what those conditions would be allows the supervisee to be clearer about the factors in their decision-making and helps define a benchmark around which to monitor their capacity to proceed. For many engaged in work that involves supporting others, prioritising their own self-care can be very difficult. This links to Marie Asberg's work on burn-out,[221] a key theme in session seven of many eight-week courses, which points to the good intentions behind the tendency to put others' needs before one's own. Recognizing that this is an aspect of common humanity can help to decentre from this delicate decision-making process around giving priority to self-care.

Consider all the options for drawing on help and support, including what support can be offered through MBS. Let the supervisee know that you plan to take this to discuss sensitively with your supra-visor and may come back to them if you have further reflections. Agree on a plan of action if the supervisee notices things getting worse.

Boundaries of supervision – drawing on aspects of the Belt

Within the space of Mutual Inquiry, as the supervisor and supervisee explore the supervisee's teaching practice and how this interfaces with their personal mindfulness practice and their life, it's clear that MBS can be a place of tender, deep and personal explorations. There is an emphasis on confidentiality and a focus on developing trust and safety. Supervision can be very therapeutic, yet it is not therapy. So how can the supervisor ensure clear boundaries around what is appropriate within the bounds of supervision, and when is it necessary to signpost a supervisee to therapy? This is an integral part of the duty of care towards ensuring the safety and well-being of the supervisee and their participants.

When a supervisee speaks about something happening in their personal lives, the focus in supervision is bringing mindful awareness to their direct experience rather than on the details of the event itself and exploring how their personal mindfulness practice and the underlying principles of an MB approach might support them to make meaning of their experience and begin to discern a way forward. There may be connections between what the supervisee is learning from their own experiences and practice and how this links with their MB work, such as connections to the general vulnerability of the human experience. So, one indication that therapy may be needed is when a supervisee feels the need to share more about their personal

---

221 Found in Williams & Penman, 2011

life or personal story, when there appears to be a need to have someone bear witness to their experiences and help them navigate the impact of these experiences. This may be about current events in their life or events from their past.

One of the other key factors is the intensity of emotions and when there are signs that mindfulness practice alone is not sufficient to maintain steadiness and stability. It is natural for all of us to feel overwhelmed at times in the face of life challenges, and this is often when mindfulness practice can be such a valuable resource. It may even take a little time to regain a sense of equanimity. However, if a supervisee continues to express distress, reports that their practice is not helping or may even be making them feel worse, it is essential to encourage them to talk with their doctor or healthcare provider and to consider seeking other forms of help and support which may include therapy or counselling. A basic understanding of emotional health and well-being is an important skill for supervisors, including recognising signs of common mental ill-health such as low mood or anxiety, starting a conversation and encouraging openness around emotional well-being themes, and guiding someone towards support. The supervisor's role will include discussions with the supervisee about their MB work and when it feels best to take a step back to attend to their well-being.

Part of safe practice includes being transparent about the extent and limits of confidentiality. The supervisor has a duty of care to have an open and honest conversation with the supervisee about whether anyone else needs to know about their situation. This could include the supervisee reaching out for support with their teaching, support within their workplace, support from family and friends, as well as the various organizations focusing on health and well-being. Supervisors must know and understand what is often called safeguarding (see Chapter 7). Supervisors and supervisees will work within systems with policies and procedures around promoting welfare and protecting individuals from harm. Although it is rarely needed, supervisors must know when they have a duty to act, such as when there is the possibility of harm or if there has been actual harm to the supervisee or someone connected to them.

Pausing for self-reflection
Self-care and the boundaries of MB supervision

Have there been times when you were unsure about continuing to engage in your MB work due to your own health and well-being? What is your immediate reaction in recalling this experience? What did you consider to support yourself in making a decision? How did you respond and was it the most helpful response? Did you use supervision to support you and if so, what was the learning? What learning from this would you like to take forward into your own role as supervisor? What are your personal values around self-care?

What has been your experience of supporting a supervisee navigating difficulties with their health and well-being? What learning can you draw from these experiences to help guide you next time this arises?

Scenario three: competency
The scenario

You are concerned about the quality of your supervisee's teaching around two MBI:TAC domains, which you consider to be in the beginner or advanced beginner stage. You have been working with them for some time to help them develop their teaching and understanding in relation to these two domains, but there doesn't seem to be much change. Their teaching is due to be assessed (certified) in the near future through their training organization, and you are concerned they won't pass as they need to be considered competent in all domains to pass.

What is your immediate reaction?

Take a few moments to note down your experiences.

What do you need to consider?

We offer some suggestions, and you may have others:

- Are they safe to continue teaching?
- Coming back to the intentions of supervision, what is your understanding of your role around competency? What are the edges around assessing versus supporting reflective growth? What is your responsibility to the supervisee to give your view or recommendation? This links to balancing the normative function with the restorative and formative functions of supervision.

- Does the supervisee have insight into their teaching strengths and edges?
- What has supported them in developing in other areas, in other domains of the MBI:TAC?
- What factors might specifically impact their learning and development in these two domains? What is the impact of life events or current context, their learning style, and past experiences?
- Might culture influence their learning style in ways you need to reconsider? What might you not be seeing? What assumptions are you making? Remember that the supervisor is also a learner.
- How might you modulate how you support them in supervision, such as how you offer feedback? You might return to the concept of creative tensions using the MBI:TAC or MBI:TLC outlined in Chapter 10. What's your sense of how you can support learning for this supervisee? What do you need to lean into more? Less?
- Which aspects of the Belt are relevant here? What guidelines might you draw on around good practice and safety?
- What would be the consequences if the supervisee does not pass? What would be the impact on the supervisee? On you? How might it affect the supervisory relationship? Is there an option for the supervisee to delay the assessment/certification process?

How might you respond?

Keeping the central focus on the relational nature of MBS and staying within an inquiry-based approach that encourages exploration around the supervisee's teaching skills, beginning by inviting them to share their reflections on their strengths and learning edges and their sense of their development. Watching a piece of their teaching together is one of the most effective ways of opening dialogue around their teaching skills, supporting a felt sense as you each receive their teaching. Encouraging the supervisee to explore the piece of teaching from their participants' perspective can help them recognise the impact of their teaching. When a supervisee has insight into their learning edges, this generally paves the way for a mutual dialogue around a way forward. If this is the case, offering appreciation to the supervisee for their honesty and wisdom and giving space for them to share how it is to notice and name their teaching edges. Your role might include supporting the supervisee in noticing harsh judgement of themselves and finding ways to balance an open, honest appraisal around their competency with a sense of kindness and patience.

As you continue the mutual dialogue, using the Petals as a framework for you and the supervisee to examine what might support their learning – is there a gap in understanding around the theory or the pedagogy of MBAs? Looking more closely at their personal mindfulness practice and how it links with these teaching practice domains – is there a gap between theoretical and experiential understanding? Drawing on the language of the MBI:TAC and MBI:TLC to move into a detailed examination of the supervisee's understanding of the key features of each domain and how each links with their skill development, noticing features where they demonstrate competency and where not yet.

Supporting the supervisee in recognising internal or external factors that might be impacting their competence – perhaps the assessment process itself is stressful, or other stressful life circumstances, limited time at the moment for focusing on their teaching practice, loss of confidence in themselves or the MB approach, or significant challenges within the group they are currently teaching.

Drawing on your understanding of the learning process, reminding the supervisee that learning and development are often not linear, normalising this experience of being competent in some areas and not others, moving away from comparisons, and supporting an understanding around what the supervisee needs at this time, including how you can best support them going forward. These discussions might include the supervisee asking about the possibility of an extension to their submission date for competency assessment, allowing more time in supervision to support their skill development.

Suppose the supervisee's competency is linked to challenging life events that impact their health and well-being, drawing on the previous scenario's points around responding to safety and well-being issues. The supervisee may talk with the training organization about taking a break from their studies and returning later. Supervision focuses on supporting the supervisee in completing their current group as long as it is safe to do so or guides them around how they navigate ending the course sooner if that's in the best interests of the supervisee and/or the participants.

Navigating more complexity around competence

A more challenging situation is when the supervisee does not seem to have an accurate sense of their level of competence or seems to struggle to reflect on how their participants receive their teaching practice.

The supervisor can take time both within and outside of the session to tune into and attune to the supervisee, cultivating a not-knowing attitude and a willingness to be tentative around your wonderings and taking this to supra-vision to help in recognising your blind spots. Opening to a Both/And approach, recognising that your perception of the supervisee's competence is one perspective. Be willing to examine your ideas of what competence means, especially within this supervisee's context and their teaching practice. Is the MBI:TAC or MBI:TLC all relevant in their context? Are there other ways to consider competency?

Consider what might be influencing their learning and development. For example, is it possible that, related to their past experience of education or their relationship to perceived authority, the supervisee is reluctant to name what they would see as weaknesses or failings? Explore the specifics about the aspects of the domains in question and see what you both discover. For example, suppose the areas are around relational themes. In that case, you might consider if neurodivergence or past trauma could be influencing how they relate to their participants and their ability to tune into participants' experiences – how would this inform the way you dialogue around this with your supervisee?

Reflect on your way of offering feedback and consider whether a firmer feedback style would be supportive. Dancing with edges of what supports, what is within reach for the supervisee – not too soft, not too hard. You might find it helpful to review the information on offering feedback in Chapter 10.

Acknowledging there will be times when you have a responsibility to lead the way, especially regarding safety. Again, using supra-vision as a support to determine if the supervisee's teaching practice is causing harm or potential harm, which requires a more timely and decisive response. You are drawing on aspects of the Belt, such as your duty of care and guidelines around good practice, to support you in raising your concerns with the supervisee and to discuss what action is needed. Acknowledge the tenderness of the conversation with the supervisee while naming your clear intentions that support the need for the conversation – naming a clear plan around the next steps encouraging the supervisee to be involved in the plan as much as possible for them. Sometimes, these highly complex situations result in a rupture within the supervisory relationship or a decision to end the relationship. Here, you can draw on points in the first scenario regarding the supervisory relationship.

Pausing for self-reflection

Competency

Can you think of a time when you struggled to attain competency, either around an aspect of your MB work or within another area of your work or life? What are your personal values in relation to meeting standards and competency? What was the role of supervision? What was helpful? Anything that did not help?

What has been your experience of supporting a supervisee around their competency? What do you see as the role of the supervisor in terms of assessing competency and how does this balance with your role around supporting reflective growth? What's the edge between allowing space for learning and development and ensuring safe practice?

Scenario four: ethical complexity

The scenario

Your supervisee is offering brief introductory MB courses for staff within the workplace of a public healthcare service where they are also an employee. They have been reflecting on and exploring the challenges they encounter within their primary role and within their MB work in supervision for some time. They recognise a dissonance between their values and what's possible within the pressures of the workplace, and these same themes are frequently named by the staff who attend the MB sessions. Lately, the attendance on the courses has been more sporadic, and at the end of the course, they are still reporting high levels of stress and distress in their working environment and finding it hard to cope and manage. The supervisee feels that the course in its current form is not meeting the needs of staff and is not addressing the fundamental problems within the working environment and the systems at play. They are beginning to feel more compromised of late and do not know what to do next.

What is your immediate reaction?

Take a few moments to note down your experiences.

What do you need to consider?

- What is the context – the workplace environment, structure and culture, what can be changed, what can't be changed?
- The supervisee's well-being. How can their mindfulness practice best support them in the midst of the challenges? What else is needed?
- What qualities might you draw upon? E.g. equanimity, self-care, interpersonal mindfulness.
- What can you draw on around good practice and professional practice – workplace legislation and frameworks as well as MB ones, workplace values and codes of conduct?
- How to balance integrity with innovation. The link between personal ethics and professional ethics.

How might you respond?

Firstly, acknowledge the 'size of the cloth' and its impact on the supervisee and the participants, recognising this is the system rather than the individuals alone. Reminding them this isn't all down to them in terms of how the staff feel.

Drawing on the elements of the warp, particularly the inquiry-based approach, to dialogue together around this complex situation. You might find it helpful to refer to Chapter 4, Mutual Inquiry, especially the example in the section 'Cultivation of a not-knowing stance', that explores this intuitive knowing, this 'felt' sense of the impact of events outside one's control.

Coming back to intention: supporting the supervisee to consider their intentions in their MB work and how they might balance their values and aspirations with what is possible. Supporting a balance of realism and optimism. Helping them to make decisions about self-care alongside their care for their colleagues.

Which aspects of the course might be empowering for the staff in this context? Encouraging the supervisee to look closely at feedback, asking for more specific feedback, and speaking to some of the staff on the course in more depth. As well as staff *not* finding it useful, what *did* they find helpful? These might be areas to build on more.

Looking into sources of support such as contact with peers working within similar contexts. Are there other people within the service who could offer support, or could the supervisee work in partnership with them, for example, the staff well-being service or champion? How does their MB work fit within the service's staff well-being policy and plan? Is their direct line manager supportive? Where is their buy-in with the service, especially within the senior leadership team?

Recognising in this context that the eight-week course might not be the best fit, and a discussion of innovation and change could help, pointing the supervisee towards resources and research in this area. Would further training be helpful? This comes back to the bigger picture, maybe moving from individual well-being into the broader cultural context of the workplace and the place of mindfulness within this. A shift to social mindfulness. Are leaders involved in mindfulness or compassion training?

Holding the option for the supervisee not to carry on and to take their MB work elsewhere and holding a gauge between you both of when the energy and effort to continue outweighs the benefits and joy. Do they need a break? Have they got the energy for innovation? How would they know when they could not continue, when it was enough?

Pausing for self-reflection

An opportunity to pause and reflect on your experiences around this theme of ethical complexity.

Have there been times for you when there has been a dissonance between your values and what was possible within some aspect of your work? What is your immediate reaction in recalling this experience? What did you consider to support yourself in making decisions? How did you respond and what was helpful? Not so helpful? Did you notice any habitual reactive patterns?

Did you seek support from another, such as a supervisor, mentor, or peer, and what was helpful from that, if anything? What was the learning from this personal experience?

What has been your experience of supporting a supervisee in this kind of situation? Or perhaps your experience has been witnessing the experiences of a peer or colleague when they have encountered this in a workplace environment. Did you notice any habit patterns arising in you or them? What did you see as your responsibility then and what about now? What supported/supports you in the midst of instability and potential overwhelm?

Resourcing yourself to meet challenging, complex and sensitive issues in mindfulness-based supervision

Although every situation is nuanced, there are some general principles that we believe are supportive in preparing for and navigating complex situations in MBS:

- Taking care of yourself within this process is vital – *"self-care is a non-negotiable requirement of ethical practice"*.[222] This includes time for reflection and self-care.
- Reflecting and dialoguing with others provides valuable support, e.g. regular support from a supra-visor, maybe other colleagues depending on the situation and within bounds of confidentiality.
- Cultivating equanimity within your mindfulness practice supports a sense of steadiness in times of complexity and uncertainty.
- The three-stage process provides a structured way of approaching these challenging moments and helps cultivate a compassionate and wise response.
- Being familiar with the MBS framework will help you draw on particular elements that will be most relevant to help inform your reflections and response.
- Taking time to reflect afterwards, knowing that these situations take time to process and reflect on. Often meaningful learning comes from the most challenging situations. It can highlight areas to pay more attention to going forward, such as a more robust contracting process, areas for further learning and development, such as mindful communication, offering feedback, trauma-sensitivity and responsiveness, understanding and working in neuro-inclusive ways in supervision.

---

222 Paterson & Crumlish, 2022, p. 185

Summary

1. Being open to and responding to the more challenging and complex aspects of supervision and the supervisory relationship is a responsibility of taking on the role of MB supervisor.

2. We used four themes to highlight aspects of ethical and safe practice, including the more serious and complex side of these situations. Integrity within the supervisory relationship is held as central in all situations.

3. We offer a three-stage process to support a reflective and responsive approach:
   - What is your immediate reaction?
   - What do you need to consider?
   - How might you respond?

4. We encourage reference to the MBS framework to decide which elements are the most important to draw on in each situation. Integrity and safety are key themes.

5. Supra-vision supports the supervisor in caring for their well-being and offers guidance around what to consider and options for responding with compassion and wisdom.

6. Although each situation has its nuances and requires moment-to-moment responsiveness, we offer general principles to hold in mind.

7. Taking time to reflect on and consider how you might respond to challenging and tender moments that might arise is part of the supervisor's learning and development. This also supports the development of personal and professional values and ethics.

Reflective questions

What are your strengths and growing edges in responding to the most challenging moments that arise or might arise in supervision?

Revisit any of the reflections offered throughout the chapter.

Using the three-stage process, take some time to reflect on a challenging moment from any of the themes named above or any other theme alive for you now in your supervision practice or one that you have encountered in the past. This could include challenging experiences you have had as a supervisee and in the supervisor role. What is your learning here? You might also choose to take this to supra-vision.

What would support your ongoing learning and development in navigating complexity within supervision? Is there specific training, such as mindful communication, that could be helpful?

References

Arao, B., & Clemens, K. (2013). From safe spaces to brave spaces: A new way to frame dialogue around diversity and social justice. In L. M. Landreman (Ed.), *The art of effective facilitation* (pp. 135-150). Routledge.

Evans, A., Griffith, G. M., & Smithson, J. (2024). What do supervisors' and supervisees' think about mindfulness-based supervision? A grounded theory study. *Mindfulness*, 15, 63–79. https://doi.org/10.1007/s12671-023-02280-8

Paterson, M., & Crumlish, L. (2022). *Group supervision: Notes for beginners*. Institute of Pastoral Supervision and Reflective Practice.

Watkins, C. E. (2021). Rupture and rupture repair in clinical supervision: some thoughts and steps along the way. *The Clinical Supervisor*, 40(2), 321-344. https://doi.org/10.1080/07325223.2021.1890657

Williams, M., & Penman, D. (2011). *Mindfulness: A practical guide to finding peace in a frantic world*. Piatkus.

Chapter 12
Using the Mindfulness-Based Supervision Framework in Group Supervision

Group supervision lets in more light and air.
More light helps us see more.
More air helps us breathe more freely.[223]

In this chapter, we examine the benefits of supervision in a group and how the MBS framework can guide the supervisor and supervisee about their roles and responsibilities within this supervision format. We point to two strands of theory as a resource for the group supervisor: group theory and frameworks from the MB teaching context, and group supervision theory and frameworks from clinical practice. We illustrate how these two strands connect with elements of the MBS framework, in particular, examining the role and style of the supervisor, contracting as part of the Belt, attending to group process, and exploring the three warp threads: the Container, Mutual Inquiry and Space. We start with supervisor-led group supervision and then discuss peer groups.

---

223 Paterson & Crumlish, 2022, p. 82

The value of supervision in a group

Michael Paterson encourages looking beyond the obvious economic benefits (time, cost and availability of supervisors) to the value of a greater range of perspectives and possibilities within group supervision.[224] He advocates that in supervising groups, the supervisor commits to exploring their relationship with groups and embracing all the joys and challenges of being part of a community. This resonates with what we hear from participants on MBS training when we examine the benefits of group supervision and from supervisees who have been part of group supervision sessions. We hear statements such as *"a supportive atmosphere with others who share the same concerns and issues"*, *"a place to check intuitive, emotional responses with others"*, *"connecting with common humanity"*, *"liveliness"*, *"companionship"*, *"reduces loneliness and isolation"*. It also provides an opportunity to learn about group processes in action, mirroring what happens within MBPs and other groups we are all part of. Groups are often described as more than the sum of their parts; our colleagues Trish Bartley and Gemma Griffiths state, *"The process of groups – their chemistry, connectivity and social potential – is fascinating"*.[225] In a time when there is a greater need than ever for pro-social behaviour, coming together in community with increased opportunities to welcome and work within a greater degree of diversity, group supervision has the potential to broaden the scope of learning. It offers experiential opportunities for supervisor and supervisees to examine being part of a collective and how this might inform their intra- and inter-personal worlds.

Let's pause for a reflection.

Pausing for self-reflection
Your experience of group supervision

Taking a few moments to drop into a comfortable posture and then recalling an experience of being in supervision in a group, perhaps for MB work or in a different modality – either as a supervisee or a supervisor. Feeling into this experience.

How did it feel different from individual supervision? What was your relationship with the other participants? What qualities was the supervisor bringing/were you bringing if you were the supervisor?

Are there any ways the group had strengths or advantages? Is there any way that group supervision extended the scope of learning?

---

224 Paterson & Crumlish, 2022
225 Bartley & Griffith, 2022, p. 18

Then turning to the less supportive aspects? What were the disadvantages? Things you missed from individual supervision. What were the challenges for you as a supervisee or supervisor?

When you consider group supervision now, what do you notice arising? Emotions, thoughts, or body sensations? What are you curious about? Do you have questions?

What is happening in a mindfulness-based supervision group

Of course, the primary purpose of an MBS group, the task, is the same as in individual supervision, so the fundamental role of the supervisor is the same. In terms of process, the supervisor will be attending to the relationship between themselves and each supervisee whilst also attending to the group process. Paterson[226] draws parallels between group supervision and Adair's leadership model,[227] which proposes that group leaders need to attend to and balance three needs: the task, the group and the individuals within the group. Holding these three needs in mind can provide a helpful map for preparation, during the supervision session and post-supervision reflection. On the MBS training, after experiential opportunities to explore group supervision, trainees frequently describe group supervision as even more like a dance than individual supervision: movement between task, individual and group, movement between letting go and holding the space, feeling into what 'step' is needed next. Peter Hawkins and Aisling McMahon created a model that represents different styles of group supervision. They suggest that the group follows the style the supervisor models, especially in relation to how the supervisor responds to what is brought to the supervision space. We use a slightly adapted version of their model. (Figure 12.1).[228]

---

226 Paterson & Crumlish, 2022
227 Adair, 1984
228 Hawkins & McMahon, 2020, pp. 185-186

Figure 12.1 Group supervision styles

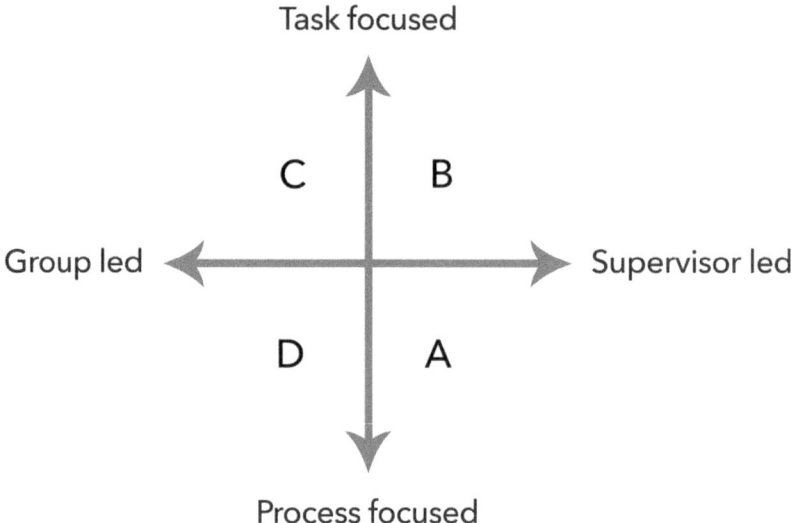

When a group first forms, they are likely to start in quadrant A, with the supervisor guiding the group process and supporting the creation of group guidelines, assisting each supervisee in identifying their needs and encouraging the identification of shared goals and intentions. The focus then moves more into the task, quadrant B, exploring what each supervisee brings to supervision. Over time, the group might move towards quadrant C, with a more supervisee-led exploration of the themes. Once a stronger sense of safety has been established, the group may begin to move into quadrant D, looking at processes. Groups may move through different quadrants at different times, and when a group is going well it will attend to both task and process, with the supervisor ensuring that the group does not get stuck in one style.

We reflected on the MBS groups we have facilitated with this model in mind and offer a glimpse into what is happening in these groups within these four quadrants. In the example we name some of the processes we have witnessed and name aspects of the MBS framework we draw upon. We find that quadrant A is where all groups begin and then they move to quadrant B as they turn to the Petals, the content. As facilitators, we hold an intention for all MBS groups, even those meeting for a short-term group, to move into quadrant D. In our experience quadrant D becomes increasingly accessible the longer a group meets or in times of challenge. The supervisor is supporting this dance around the quadrants, holding a sense of what is needed at any one time.

Example – what is happening in an MBS group

Quadrant A

Focus on process of group as it is forming. Attention to contracting and safety. Guidelines established. Getting to know each other. Sharing intentions and hopes, including supervisor's intentions for the group and the proposed structure. Naming themes and questions that are on supervisees' minds. Establishing a mindful Container. Bringing in practice. Inviting an inner and outer awareness. Inviting each member to contribute encourages mutuality.

Quadrant B

Bringing in content, the Petals. Supervisees choosing which Petal to bring. Maybe focused on the more immediate aspects of their MB work. Mutual inquiry is often more between supervisor and each supervisee at this stage. The supervisor is encouraging finding space and exploring ways of finding space within a group, encouraging embodied presence, drawing on the attitudes of mindfulness.

Quadrant C

Increased interactions with each other during the inquiry process. Mindful communication when speaking and listening. Listening with the whole being, feeling into the words and what resonates. The group embodying the attitudes and within the relationships. Petals are still a focus but maybe more nuanced, going deeper into topics, more movement around all the Petals. Might be more vulnerability expressed in the group. Not always needing a consensus, creating room for different perspectives.

Quadrant D

Times when the group turns more to process. Recognising the process with the group in the here and now. Making links with other aspects of MB work. The group might also turn more to its own process if there are challenges or boundary issues. The supervisor might help the group to not forget the MB work and the participants – keeping them in mind as well.

Let's look more closely now at how elements of the MBS framework can support the supervisor in attending to and tending to the tasks and processes within group supervision.

Using the weft of the mindfulness-based supervision framework: the Belt

Contracting

Bartley and Griffith propose that there are two key enablers within groups: safety – *"establishing a safe process within the group"* and inclusivity – *"supporting respectful interconnections between group members"*.[229] In the context of MBS, the process of cultivating safety and inclusivity begins at the contracting phase. Alongside the themes explored in Chapter 7 around contracting with individual supervisees, supervisors will also be contracting with the group. This includes a written contract and having contracting conversations with group members (for short-term groups, these may be email conversations), which may include individual conversations first and then talking with the whole group. It's essential to be clear about supervisees' responsibilities for their self-management within the group and how they offer respect and care to each other. The process will include inviting supervisees to reflect on what skills and attributes they will be drawing on in being part of group supervision, considering how it will feel to explore their MB work in the presence of their peers, how able they are to offer and receive feedback within a group and what agreements there will be about this process, how they might make use of the group context, what do they need from the group, and how will they navigate challenges that may arise within the group. Checking for pre-existing relationships and being transparent with the individuals and the whole group is helpful.

These individual and group conversations help develop a shared understanding and agreement around intentions, structure, and how the group will be together – the conditions that support community and a sense of belonging. So, the supervisor is encouraging each supervisee to consider their own goals for supervision alongside what they may learn from being part of a group, what they need to feel safe and welcome in the supervision space, and what's required to support healthy stretch and growth. The co-creation of guidelines as part of the contracting stage supports the move towards 'we', outlining the collective responsibilities and sense of shared ownership. It's important to distinguish the boundaries between supervision and therapy as with individual supervision. Within group supervision, the group process will likely be part of the discussion at some point, but it's not group therapy.

Sometimes, group supervision is arranged through an organization, perhaps for economic reasons or as an integral part of a teacher training programme. It's essential to be clear about how the needs and wishes of the organization might inform the contracting stage. One way I (Pamela) have noticed this influence is around group size and duration of the sessions. Often, organizations request larger

---

229 Bartley & Griffith, 2022, p. 94

groups and less time than I would recommend, so there may need to be some negotiation required to find the optimum balance of group size and length of sessions. In our experience, three to four group members seems the most effective size, and allowing 90 to 120 minutes per session, ensures everyone has space to bring their issues for reflection, and the session is not too long.

Agenda setting

Agenda setting within group supervision is worthy of some attention at the initial contracting stage and then continuing to explore what works best for each group as they begin to meet. Especially for newly formed groups or those just meeting for a small number of predetermined sessions, having a clear agreed structure around agenda setting can be incredibly helpful in supporting the flow and spaciousness of the session. In some groups, especially at the start, it may be that the time will be divided equally amongst the group members. Sometimes, there might be an agreement to focus a whole supervision session on a particular theme that all of them will find beneficial. Agreeing to send supervision issues and questions to the supervisor before the session allows the supervisor to draw out common themes and consider if there is a natural flow between themes that might influence the order of the agenda. This can be particularly helpful for newly formed groups.

Another way to support the group process is to agree on a simple structure to guide supervisees in preparing for group supervision. Paterson suggests three questions to guide agenda setting: What are you bringing for reflection today? What do you hope for by bringing it? How would you like to explore it in this group?[230]

Some groups find their own way of making the most of being in community. For example, one group of more experienced practitioners each share their agenda items at the start of the session and decide together, with the support of the supervisor, the order and time allocation for each item. There have been times when someone has brought up an issue that has some urgency, such as around safety. Another group member will decide that their issue can wait until next time to allow more time to explore the more pressing issue in greater depth. This group strongly believes that all can learn from a more in-depth inquiry around specific themes and that being together and sharing is as important as discussing their own issue.

The unique characteristics of each group cannot be anticipated. It's important in group supervision to allow space for adjusting group guidelines and agreements once the group sessions get started, allowing time for the group to find its own way and create its own group culture. Returning to the working agreements after one or two sessions can help fine-tune the process and strengthen the sense of co-creation. I (Pamela) can recall an experience early on as a group supervisor of feeling discouraged when there were initial tensions and confusion within a new

---

230 Paterson & Crumlish, 2022

group around the structure and responsibilities despite exploring this before the first session. However, having been clear that we would review the process now that the supervisees had a better understanding of what they needed, this allowed space for refining our shared agreement and created a much stronger sense of ownership by the whole group than was possible beforehand.

Planning regular review sessions is also vital. Within individual supervision, it is often quite organic to make adjustments as needed for one supervisee's particular needs, but within a group, it's a more complex process. Supervisees need the opportunity to offer feedback outside of the group, and the supervisor can then reflect on the feedback from everyone and support the group in negotiating how best to meet the needs of individuals and the group.

Using the warp of the mindfulness-based supervision framework

Space

Space is interesting to consider within group supervision. There is often a different energy within a group, and it can be more challenging to find and create space – a trainee on MBS training described it as more stimulation for both the supervisor and the supervisees.

The supervisor may be more explicit about the importance of space and invite the group to consider collectively how to create space. For example, ensuring there is always time to begin and end with a brief practice, inviting a pause between themes/agenda items, pausing to invite a tuning into resonance, *"What's coming up for you as you are listening/speaking?"*, encouraging the group to make decisions around using the time and what's most needed, *"We still have a few things on our agenda. Can we take time to consider how to spend the remaining time today?"* There can also be more space for individuals within group supervision – when other group members are talking, the spotlight is not so intensive on others, who may have time to breathe and pause. The supervisor can encourage group members to tune into their own process during these non-speaking moments, connecting with the body, feelings and thoughts with their whole being, mindfully listening.

The Container and Mutual Inquiry

Relational inquiry is at the heart of group supervision, held within the Container of mindfulness. Drawing parallels with group-based MB programmes, frameworks from MB teaching can be a valuable resource for group supervisors, supporting awareness and appreciation of the unique contribution of engaging in Mutual Inquiry within a group context. We point to three resources with overlapping features and illustrate their relevance to group MBS.

1. In the MBI:TAC, group learning is one of the six domains of teaching competency. Supervisors might hold the different aspects of this domain in mind within their group supervision work, reflecting on their knowledge and skills and identifying areas for development.

    - **Creating a learning container** – Facilitating group agreements and boundaries that support the establishment of a safe space where active learning can occur, where each group member feels able to share their own experiences and respects the contributions of others.
    - **Group development** – The supervisor attends to the group's different needs at different stages of its lifespan and responds to challenges that might impact the group process.
    - **Personal to universal learning** – The supervisor invites the group to notice shared experiences, which is especially helpful when a supervisee describes a vulnerability or a struggle within their MB work. The supervisor acknowledges the uniqueness of the individual's experience and the sense of common humanity.
    - **Leadership style** – The supervisor demonstrates authority, balancing the tasks and process of group supervision. They convey confidence in the process, encouraging Mutual Inquiry rather than the supervisor as an expert.

2. We touch on the three capacities within Bartley and Griffith's Inside Out Group (IOG) model: reading the group, holding the group, and befriending the group.[231] Their model emphasizes embodying which we have covered in other parts of this book. Here, our focus is how the capacities might inform group MBS.

    - **Reading the group** is about how we make sense of or interpret what is happening in the group from moment to moment. It entails a combination of intuitively sensing the atmosphere within a group, drawing on particular group theory, and drawing on one's own experience of being in and leading groups. As part of reading the group, the supervisor acknowledges that the collective experience is influenced by the presence of each group member, including themselves, who will bring their own patterns into the group space. This includes understanding the impact of personal histories, past traumatic experiences, and social constructs. Here the supervisor will be drawing on their own work and learning in developing cultural awareness.
    - **Holding the group** is the process of caring for and responding to the individuals within the group, the group as a whole, and oneself as the supervisor. In the MBS framework, this would draw on all the elements of the Container of mindfulness to build a solid foundation that supports the Mutual Inquiry around the different Petals.

---

231   Bartley & Griffith, 2022: Griffith et al., 2019

- **Befriending the group** speaks to the attitudinal qualities the supervisor is cultivating towards the group, the individuals within it, and themselves. The supervisor is bringing a sense of friendliness and compassion to all that arises. This includes knowing when a stronger response is needed, such as upholding a boundary to protect the group's safety, taking time to appreciate a moment of joy, or pausing to connect with the resonance within the group. Befriending oneself as the supervisor may include taking time for reflection and using supra-vision as a support. These qualities link to Embodied Presence and Compassion/Wisdom within the Container of the MBS framework.

3. Donald McCown, Diane Reibel and Marc Micozzi's concept of stewardship[232] offers another way of considering the role of the group supervisor. This involves holding the space and acting as a catalyst to support co-creation. In turn, this helps to take care of what the authors call the three treasures: *freedom, belonging* and *resonance*. So, in the context of the MBS framework, the Container is how we hold the space – this attention to the qualities and attributes that hold the whole process, and co-creating is expressed through the process of Mutual Inquiry. From this foundation, the supervisor can take care of the three treasures, which are described as interdependent:

- **Freedom** is about the supervisor encouraging supervisees to be themselves, showing up authentically without the need to conform to what they think is expected of them as an MB practitioner, actively encouraging the expression of different experiences and opinions, and offering equal space to each supervisee.

- **Belonging** supports shared responsibility and accountability, with the supervisor supporting each supervisee in being aware of their place, contribution, and impact on the group.

- **Resonance** within the group. The supervisor encourages the supervisees to be open and receptive to different viewpoints and to trust their own perception and wisdom; the supervisor also does the same for themselves. They sense the emotional tone within the group, are attuned to the felt sense, and see what's needed, if anything.

So, within the MBS framework, the elements of the Container provide the conditions for holding, tending, or stewarding the group process. The supervisor is embodying and encouraging mindful awareness of inner and outer process, leaning into the attitudinal qualities, and bringing mindfulness right into the heart of speaking and listening when in relationship with each other. They have the integrity of the relationships within the group in mind, taking care of safety. At the same time, the qualities of Mutual Inquiry give the conditions for exploring, reflection and learning. Space supports the conditions for these processes to thrive.

---

232 McCown et al., 2010

The role of the supervisor

While there is much to be drawn from the MB group process, since the task within group supervision is distinctly different from that of an MBP, group supervision models from other disciplines can provide further maps as a guide. Brigid Proctor, whose work was developed for the clinical context, outlines three styles of supervisor-led group supervision, and we explore how each of these styles might inform the inquiry process.[233] Linked to our metaphor of the dance, Proctor describes the role of the group supervisor as moving between leadership, receptivity and assertiveness, these moment-to-moment choice points and flexibility and responsiveness.

1. Authoritative – Supervision *in* a group

When we explore this within MBS training, invariably, the group discusses other words that sit easier with them than the term *authoritative* – terms such as *more hands-on*, *directive*, and *stronger leadership* may help articulate this style of supervision. So, it's not about being authoritarian but rather about taking a more active leadership role while offering supervision to each supervisee in turn within the presence of the other supervisees. The supervisor still needs to be aware of the group, but the Mutual Inquiry process is between the supervisor and each supervisee. This might be likened to the process of vertical inquiry within MB group teaching. Proctor points out that it is important in this group style that supervisees know their role and that there is an explicit working agreement. The supervisor ensures fairness regarding time and quality of attention given to each supervisee. So, the leadership skills are strong, setting up and managing a clearly defined structure, with moderate receptivity as the supervisor stays in touch with both individual and group, and minimal assertiveness required as there is a clear structure established without much room for negotiation. In terms of the three needs, the supervisor's main priority is attending to the task and the individual.

Although the initial sense may be that this style does not lend itself well to MBS, perhaps it does. For example, elements of a more directive leadership role might fit at the beginning when working with a newly formed group of new practitioners, or with a group who are meeting for just a few sessions, while the supervisor is attending to the group forming. Even within these conditions, we sense that supervisor-led group MBS is often more akin to Proctor's description of Participative and Cooperative styles.

---

233 Proctor, 2008

2. Participative – Supervision *with* the group

In this style, the supervisor is more aware of and responsive to the group as a working system. They are actively engaged in group facilitation, considering the task of creating a reflective space and considering what the group needs to foster a safe, reflective learning environment. The supervisor will demonstrate a balance of the three roles: still an active leadership role but also receptive to the flow within the group, trusting that they can be assertive when needed to reset a boundary or negotiate with the group. They are also balancing task, individuals and the group. This might be likened to horizontal inquiry, where the supervisor is making moment-to-moment decisions about when to stay with the individual supervisee and when to open up to the wider group. Here, the metaphor of dance helps capture the sense of what's taking place; within the inquiry process, the supervisor is listening, attuning, and becoming aware of choice points.

The supervisor will actively promote co-supervision, drawing on the wisdom of the group members. As the supervisor gains experience within group supervision, there may be a growing trust in the different learning that comes from being in community, which then, in turn, supports the supervisor to emphasise this collegial aspect of group supervision. At the end of a recent group supervision session, one of the supervisees stated, *"I didn't have much to bring today, and the particular things others wanted to talk about didn't seem that relevant to me, so I wondered at the start if the session would be helpful for me or not. However, now I've learned different things that I wasn't expecting – things I didn't know I didn't know, as well as just space to share without any answers."*

3. Cooperative – Supervision *by* the group

Proctor highlights that in this style of group supervision, it may be unclear to an observer who the supervisor is: the supervisees will be more proactive, being clear about what they want from supervision and taking turns at moving into a leadership role, with the supervisor more likely to contribute later rather than sooner. The group will be strong enough to hold vigorous discussions, including disagreements. The supervisor still has a leadership role in the overall process but increasingly shares this responsibility with the other group members. It is a complex role – we might say a more complex dance – discerning when to trust the group, for example, working with difficulty or vulnerability, and when they need to step in to more actively guide the process. For instance, if the supervisor saw that one supervisee was taking a lot of time within the session and others were missing out on opportunities to speak, it would take some courage for the supervisor to name this within this group that is otherwise primarily autonomous. So, in terms of the three roles and how they compare to a participative style group, there will be less leadership, the same level of receptivity as they stay open to listening and attuning, and higher assertiveness to hold the agreed boundaries when it's necessary for the supervisor to step in.

If the group members are more experienced practitioners, a cooperative style group may be established from the beginning, with the supervisor supporting the group to contract together around the more complex group agreements. In our experience, more often what happens is the supervisor and the supervisees initially set up agreements to form a participative style group, and then over time, as the group moves towards a higher degree of participatory style, at the following review of supervision there may be discussions and agreements around adopting guidelines that are more akin to a cooperative style.

Supervision of supervisees who are co-teaching

Supervision in a pair is, of course, a form of group so everything in this chapter is relevant. We also want to name a few points specifically about this unique group as there are factors to consider during contracting and working together that help support a safe learning space for co-teachers. Meeting each supervisee individually as well as coming together for contracting conversations and continuing to have periodic individual supervision alongside the paired supervision, allows each supervisee space to name and explore issues they may be reticent to share in the presence of their peer, including tender topics or themes around co-teaching. It also allows the supervisor to really tune into each supervisee and their needs, fine-tuning their responses.

It's essential to know about the co-teachers' relationship outside of MB work, particularly if there is a hierarchical relationship, and to consider their respective levels of experience in MB teaching/work and how this might influence their work together. Making it clear that their co-teaching experience and relationship will be part of the agenda supports a sense of transparency, clarifying that supervision is a space to share the joys and challenges of co-teaching. Initiating discussion around offering feedback with sensitivity to their fellow teacher will also help build a sense of a safe and open learning space. It's pretty common for supervisees to have very different perspectives about what took place within their MB teaching. If one supervisee is critical of themselves or their teaching, having the other supervisee's perspective can be really helpful, as it tends to be more balanced and point to strengths as well as learning edges. The supervisor may also balance differences in other ways – different communication styles and goals, where the focus is placed, the range of themes brought to supervision, various degrees of vulnerability, and skill levels. Just as in other forms of group supervision, the supervisor is balancing the task alongside the needs of each individual and those of the small group as a whole.

The Container as a resource to hold complex processes

Alongside the benefits of coming together in a community, group supervision also brings a greater complexity with meeting different minds, bodies and hearts, as each group member brings their own lived experience, opinions and ideas, and communication patterns and habits into the shared space. Some of the ways this complexity could show up are:

- a supervisee showing or sharing considerable vulnerability within the group
- misunderstandings or disagreements between group members
- an ethical issue around safety or professional conduct
- straying from the group agreements

Here, we point to a few principles about working with challenging or sensitive moments within a group. Firstly, it's helpful if the supervisor can embrace challenging moments and conflict as part of the process, seeing it as drawing attention to important issues and recognising that turning towards difficulty and working with it in a particular way is a central aspect of MB practice.

Coming back to the MBS framework, the Container offers a way of staying steady in the midst of difficulty, opening to what is here, and can support the supervisor as they guide themselves and the group to open to and work with challenging moments and issues:

- Recognising and naming within the group when a tender or challenging moment arises supports the whole group in seeing it as part of the process.
- Coming back to Intention supports a reconnection with group agreements and guidelines as needed, such as agreements around respect, non-judgement and valuing diversity.
- Intention can also help point to the different functions of supervision and the need to balance all three – for example, linking ethical issues to the normative function can be helpful while also holding in mind the need for this to be addressed in a supportive (restorative) and gradual (formative) way.
- Compassion/Wisdom will guide the supervisor in balancing the needs of the individual supervisee and the whole group. For example, considering to what extent it's possible to explore vulnerability in the presence of the group, recognising that it can feel exposing to share and examine one's vulnerability or ethical edges in the presence of peers, and when it will be more helpful to discuss on a 1:1 basis. Supra-vision can be extremely helpful here.
- To support a sense of mutuality, the attitudinal qualities and the principles of skilful feedback can guide supervisees in sharing their perspectives while reminding them that MBS is not about advice giving or fixing.

How can you resource yourself as a mindfulness-based group supervisor?

- Reflective practice: reflection on your own experience of being part of a group, your relationship with groups, and what learning can be taken forward from these experiences.
- Being part of a group supervision yourself.
- Knowledge and experience of working with group and individual processes. Supervisors need to know the richness and challenges that can arise within group supervision *and* have the necessary skills in group facilitation to apply that knowledge to facilitate a reflective space.
- You may like to follow up on the references and models we have drawn upon in this chapter.
- Taking care of yourself: space for reflection afterwards. Use of supra-vision as a space to discuss group process. Taking time to reflect on each supervisee – who are you drawn to, feel a connection with, and who not so much?
- Acknowledging that as one moves from individual to group supervisor, there is likely a shift back to apprentice, new territory, new learning, new skills. Bringing in attitudes of beginner's mind and patience with yourself.
- Learning and skill development in interpersonal mindfulness.

Peer groups

In our discussions with colleagues, supervisors and supervisees, the meaning and understanding of the word 'peer' in relation to supervision always raises many different opinions, with various terms used with quite different interpretations. We believe that clarity of meaning is important, so we wish to encourage reflection and discussion around the details and characteristics of these gatherings rather than just what they are called. Of course, we have had to give them names to distinguish one from another, aware that some readers might disagree with our chosen names.

We make a clear distinction between three types of peer groups:

Peer-group supervision: We refer back to the definition of supervision in Chapter 1 and suggest that the same elements need to be present in peer supervision for it to have the term *supervision* in its title. So, all members need training, knowledge, and skills in MBS. This ensures that each member can step into the three central roles of the supervisor – restorative, formative and normative. This will include the ability to hold a reflective learning space safely, offer skilful feedback, and challenge when needed. Using the MBS framework in contracting supports members in understanding the intentions, structure, and responsibilities.

There are different ways of organising peer supervision: in a pair, each person takes a turn in the role of supervisor and then supervisee; in a group of three, there may be an addition of an observer role; in a group of three or more, there may be more co-creation, with the group more akin to Proctor's cooperative group supervision,[234] with one person hosting or facilitating and the others engaged in co-supervision.

Sometimes, this type of peer supervision is called reciprocal supervision, which means that it is experienced equally by all members. So, the space is held safely and with care while ensuring rigour around professional practice.

Peer-group reflection: Here, group members come together to reflect on their MB practice and work without the necessity of having knowledge and skills as a supervisor. There are still clear agreements around the structure and responsibilities, with mutual accountability, including each group member taking on various roles within the session – facilitating the space, presenting a theme for reflection/discussion, and offering reflections. So, within the co-created and non-hierarchical space, there is still clarity around who holds that space.

We occasionally hear from supervisees or supervisors that there can be trickiness in peer reflection groups, such as, collusion where the group prioritizes consensus over critical discussion and reflection, blind spots, interpersonal tensions between group members that are not addressed. This is one reason all MB practitioners need access to what we define as supervision.

Peer meetings/connections: In addition to the descriptions above, practitioners will likely meet up with peers for more informal connections, conversations, and reflections, which, too, have their place in one's ongoing development.

We believe the distinction between these types of peer groups is important regarding professional issues, offering clarity and guidance to supervisors, supervisees and those tasked with defining good practice. We recommend that good practice advocates for a certain amount of supervision, a combination of individual, group or peer supervision. This can be supplemented with peer-group reflection/peer meetings and connections.

Summary

1. MB supervisors make a definite choice when entering the arena of group supervision: they appreciate the value of community and embrace all the joys and challenges of being part of a group process. We illustrate what is happening in an MBS group, pointing to aspects of the MBS framework.

---

234 Proctor, 2008

2. Drawing on a combination of two strands of theoretical models provides a helpful framework to support awareness and understanding of the task and process of MB group supervision: theory from MB teaching and pedagogy and theory from group supervision within other modalities.
3. Taking adequate time for contracting is essential in developing foundational conditions that support a sense of trust and inclusivity, which will contribute to a wholesome group experience. Groups can take time to find their way, all its members shape the group culture, and each group will be unique.
4. The warp threads provide a strong foundation to hold the complexity of working within groups.
5. Group supervision highlights the metaphor of dance with the supervisor feeling into and making choices moment by moment. The supervisor role is balancing the task, the individual and the group, and moving between leadership, receptivity and assertiveness.
6. Different interpretations of peer supervision exist. We encourage dialogue around the different characteristics rather than the name per se.
7. We advocate that all MB practitioners need supervision, which can be supplemented by peer-group reflection and more informal connections with peers who resource and support MB practitioners.

Reflective questions

You may wish to revisit the reflection at the beginning of the chapter.

Does the contracting phase include attention to all three elements of the task, the group and individuals within the group?

Reflecting after a group supervision: What choices did you make to prioritise one element of task or process over another? Who or what did you not see during the session?

Are you aware of each supervisee's goals, and how aware are you of each supervisee during the supervision session?

Within the supervision session, are you aware of what is happening within the group? Is there space for everyone? In what ways do you attend to the group as a system?

Is the group formation stable enough to support a focus on the task?

What knowledge, skills and experience do you/will you draw on to support you in offering group MBS?

Of the different theories presented, which elements resonate the most with you? How might you bring this into your experience of being a supervisee or supervisor within a group?

What do you find challenging/anticipate would be challenging in offering group supervision? What could resource you in navigating this?

What are the strengths that you bring/could bring to group MBS?

How do you/could you celebrate the joys and delights of being in community within group supervision?

Do you see a difference between what we are defining as group supervision and peer-group reflections? How might this inform your work as an MB supervisor?

References

Adair, J. (1984). *Action centred leadership.* McGraw-Hill.

Bartley, T., & Griffith, G. (2022). *Teaching mindfulness-based groups: The inside out group model.* Pavilion Publishing.

Griffith, G. M., Bartley, T., & Crane, R. S. (2019). The inside out group model: Teaching groups in mindfulness-based programs. *Mindfulness,* 10, 1315–1327. https://doi.org/10.1007/s12671-019-1093-6

Hawkins, P., & McMahon, A. (2020). *Supervision in the helping professions* (5th ed.). Open University Press.

McCown, D., Reibel, D., & Micozzi, M. S. (2010). *Teaching mindfulness: A practical guide for clinicians and educators.* Springer.

Paterson, M., & Crumlish, L. (2022). *Group supervision: Notes for beginners.* Institute of Pastoral Supervision and Reflective Practice.

Proctor, B. (2008). *Group supervision: a guide to creative practice* (2nd ed.). Sage Publications.

Chapter 13
Using the Mindfulness-Based Supervision Framework within Supra-vision

In this chapter, we begin by describing what supra-vision (supervision of supervision) is. We explore supra-vision in relation to the fabric of MBS, the warp and weft, and refer to the use of the MBS framework within supra-vision. We intend this chapter to be relevant for receiving and offering supra-vision, with the main emphasis on receiving supra-vision. In the next chapter, we explore ongoing development as an MBS supervisor, and as there are many overlaps, the two chapters can be read in close conjunction with each other.

It can get very confusing who we are referring to once we speak about supra-vision, so let's clarify how we will be using the terms within this chapter. We are calling it (mindfulness-based) supra-vision because the content is MBS. We will refer to the supervisor as the supra-visor and the person receiving supra-vision as the supervisor, as this is the role/work they are bringing to supra-vision. The person they are supervising we are calling the supervisee and the people they are working with are the participants/recipients. In practice, you may use the terms supra-visor and supervisee (the supervisee within supra-vision is an MBS supervisor).

Chapter 13 Using the Mindfulness-Based Supervision Framework within Supra-vision

What is supra-vision?

A small group of supervisors within the Mindfulness Network[235] met as a working party in 2018 to explore aspects of supra-vision as a common area of interest. We draw upon their reflections and add our own to outline the principles and application of supra-vision.

In many ways, supra-vision is very similar to supervision. The principal difference is that supra-vision adds another layer to the process; perhaps we might say it holds a meta-perspective, i.e. it has the responsibilities and tasks of the supervisor in their work with their supervisees, rather than having the teacher and their participants as the focus. This is illustrated in Figure 13.1.

Figure 13.1 The people 'present' and who is being held in mind during supra-vision

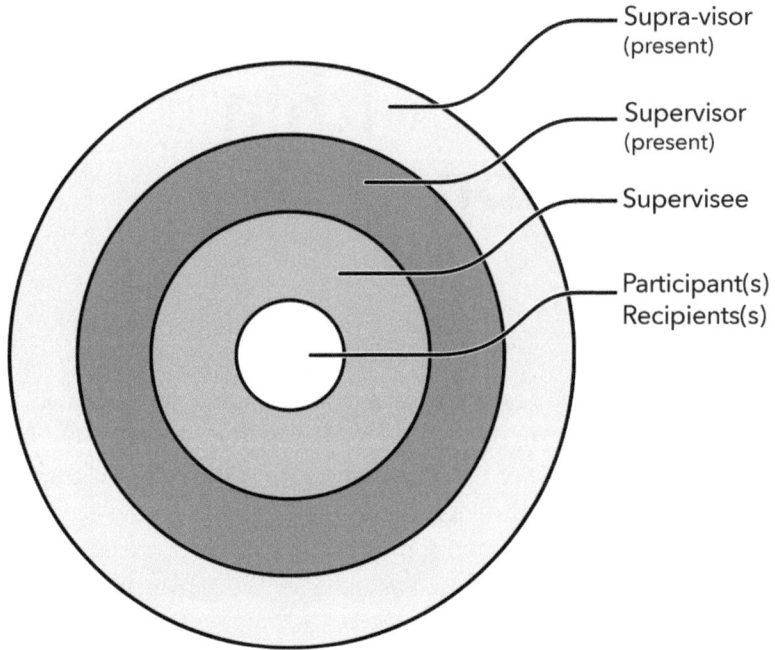

Key features of supra-vision

As with MBS, supra-vision has the same three functions: formative, restorative and ethical. It specifically emphasizes supporting the supervisor's supervisory skills, experience and development.

---

235 Thanks to the supra-vision working party in the Mindfulness Network https://home.mindfulness-network.org/reflections-on-supra-vision-for-mindfulness-based-supervisors/

Supra-vision:

- **Is a co-creative process of deepening understanding** of how to apply the principles and perspectives of MBS to the different situations and contexts of supervisees' MB work.
- **Provides a supportive and collaborative context** for sharing the responsibilities of supervising, including ethical and educational issues.
- **Helps the supervisor find support and encouragement** to be more courageous in raising potentially challenging issues with supervisees.
- **Helps develop and maintain a breadth and depth of perspective** in relation to MB work.
- **Helps remind supervisors about threads, themes and issues** that may have been forgotten, rekindling curiosity and learning.
- **Provides live and interactive modelling** regarding MBS whilst acknowledging different styles of supervising.
- **Provides a restorative function** as supervising can be tough at times and a supervisor can feel as if they have a lot on their shoulders in terms of responsibility so having a place to resource and check responsibilities with another is important.
- **Can act as a checking and monitoring process** for supervisors, a reminder of the core values, intentions, skills base, and mindfulness practices that need to be returned to; their work as a supervisor is monitored, as referred to by a research participant: *"That's why I want supervision of supervision because otherwise, nobody knows what I'm doing in this little room in my home."*[236]

If we hold developmental models in mind, supra-vision can help newer supervisors develop their skills in this role. With any role, learning is crucial, and it cannot be assumed that one knows what to do and how to do it just because one has been working in other areas of MB work. As Cal Stoltenberg and Brian McNeill put it, *"… careful supervision of supervision is necessary for anyone to become familiar with the intricacies of a given model and effective implementation."*[237] Peter Hawkins and Aishling McMahon also speak to the importance of ongoing supra-vision: *"we would contend that receiving good quality supervision and going on a supervision training programme is not sufficient to become a good supervisor, and that supervision of supervision, sometimes called supervision consultation, is a critical ingredient."*[238] Over time, supra-vison can support supervisors in various ways, e.g. continuing to develop and grow their skills in more nuanced ways, identifying further training needs, seeing habits and tendencies and exploring different ways of supervising.

---
236 Evans et al., 2024, p. 74
237 Stoltenberg & McNeill, 2010, p. 212
238 Hawkins & McMahon, 2020, p. 176

Using the mindfulness-based supervision framework within supra-vision

Since supra-vision is a form of MBS, the warp elements described in Part Two are all the same for supra-vision. The supra-visor–supervisor relationship is likely to be highly collegial, given that the supervisor will already be an experienced MB practitioner. We find that the MBS framework can be held more explicitly in mind within supra-vision.

Aspects of the weft are woven a little differently as the content is MBS. We offer some examples of these ways that aspects of the Belt and Petals are woven into the fabric of supra-vision.

Using the weft of the mindfulness-based supervision framework: the Belt

Contracting will happen in much the same way as for MBS, but the details will be around a supra-vision context. If a supervisor has supervision and supra-vision from the same supervisor, they will need to discuss the logistics and include this within their contracted way of working together.

The supervisor may not be used to the level of responsibility involved in providing MBS. There are many ethical dimensions that come into supervision which touch on aspects of integrity in the Container, and good practice, safety, and diversity and inclusion in the Belt. For example, the supervisor may bring to supra-vision how to approach supervisees around themes of well-being and safety. This might be the supervisee's well-being or safety or that of their participants/recipients. This more meta, we might say 'senior', position in the field brings responsibility in assisting the holding of ethical issues, which often raises many questions and wonderings about the best course of action in the role of supervisor.

We offer an example of a supervisor finding themselves in a supervisory relationship where they were unsure how to proceed. This illustrates how the supra-visor held each of the layers from Figure 13.1 and the MBS framework.

Example – holding the layers

A new supervisor brought to supra-vision a dilemma they had with a supervisee. The supervisee who was very new to teaching MBPs was working in a corporate setting with groups of large numbers. They had little experience of the setting and size of the group. They were under a lot of stress in their life for a range of reasons and did not feel able to set boundaries or discuss the situation with the organiser in the corporate setting.

Within the supra-vision, the supra-visor and supervisor used the MBS framework to explore this dilemma.

Supra-visor – the supra-visor could hear the complexity of this scenario. Various aspects of the MBS framework stood out as immediate areas to inquire further into: Integrity – of what was being offered, whether they could stay true to the MBP programme or needed to make some adaptation; Safety – and well-being of the supervisee and also the participants; Good Practice – was this supervisee adequately equipped and experienced to work in this context, which also linked with the Contexts Petal.

Supervisor – the supervisor concurred with these observations and noticed how they felt affected by the content of this dilemma, as it tugged at ethical concerns. They felt acutely aware of how new the supervisee was to teaching. The supervisee's questions aligned with several of the Petals – how to teach inquiry in this context, how to work with such a large group online, how to get people to turn cameras on. The supervisor was very aware of the supervisee's stress levels and concerned that this work was exacerbating the situation.

The supra-visor and supervisor kept the supervisee very much in mind and considered the participants' safety and the quality of the MBA they were receiving.

Within supra-vision, the supervisor was able to zoom further out from the Petals and the supervisee's skills development to the bigger picture. It made more sense why they were feeling so uneasy about this situation. Priorities around safety seemed to be uppermost which guided how to proceed next within supervision with this supervisee. This included the supervisee's well-being, how to manage the remainder of this course (or not), empowering the supervisee to have conversations with the organization about future work, and making decisions about the well-being and safety of the participants, e.g. bringing in a more trauma-sensitive approach with lots of choices, signposting ways of getting help if things were difficult within practice. A decision was made to work more specifically with skills building in their next group, which was a more standard eight-week programme with 12 participants.

Using the weft of the mindfulness-based supervision framework: the Petals

In supra-vision, the supervisor brings in aspects of their work with one or a range of supervisees, which can be touching on any of the Petals that the supervisee is bringing to MBS, e.g. working with a supervisee who is questioning the need for personal practice or struggling to practise, how to offer feedback to a supervisee, working with supervisees in challenging contexts, helping supervisees to adhere to curricula, working with supervisees stepping into new and innovative areas of work, supporting supervisees to understand the underlying theory and intentions behind their work, and how to work with a group.

The Petals within the supra-vision session relate to the supervisor's skills and needs. There will be times when the focus is on the supervisor's teaching/MB work experience to support their skills and interventions as a supervisor. I (Alison) can think of many occasions where a supervisor has wanted to explore an aspect of MB work to check their understanding so they are not 'misleading' their supervisee. However, the focus will more generally be on the skills, knowledge and experience of MBS.

- **Contexts** – Some of the themes we have encountered in this Petal are supervisors working in contexts where MBS is not recognized or fully valued, how to help the supervisee into the culture of MBS, how to become the person of the supervisor, being an ambassador for supervision, knowing the supervisees' and the participants' cultural contexts, remembering all these different layers.
- **Theory and understanding** – One obvious way that this Petal is woven differently in supra-vision is that there is a focus on understanding the theory and practice of supervision, including using the MBS framework to aid an understanding of what MBS is. It might also lead to discovering further training needs, books, and research papers about supervision to read/digest and reflect upon.
- **Group and individual processes** – This might include understanding developmental models of learning in relation to the supervisor themselves and their supervisee, and working with individual and cultural differences. If the supervisor is offering MBS in a group it will include how to work with a group process. And if supra-vison is within a group, it might include how to be a group member and recognising the group processes.
- **Personal mindfulness practice** – This could be supervision specific, relating directly to the role of a supervisor, e.g. how practice supports an embodied dialogue, bringing compassion and other heart-based practices into the role of being a supervisor.
- **Mindfulness-based work** – Within this Petal, the work here is MBS, so the focus will be on learning supervision skills. Each supervisor will have their own developmental and cultural needs so the supra-visor will be attuning the inquiry

and way of working. Although the supervisor is an experienced practitioner, they may be new to being a supervisor, so be keen to learn and develop. We offer an example here from a supra-vision group where the group were interested in developing their skills as a supervisor to support their supervisees with their inquiry skills. All of these supervisors knew inquiry well from their MB work but were less sure about how to support another to develop these skills.

Example – from a group supra-vision exploring how to support supervisees in developing their inquiry skills

This question arose on several occasions during the group, so it was decided to dedicate a session to this topic. The format for the session was plenty of time for reflection, sharing experiences and ideas, and listening to others (Mutual Inquiry), with the supra-visor providing some guidance and ideas. Pauses (Space) allowed the supervisors to step back from their knowledge and experience of inquiry and consider how best to support another's learning, knowing that different people have different needs.

The group pondered the sorts of questions/issues supervisees were bringing, such as: How to interrupt? How to judge their 'performance'? How to weave in the themes? What is layer two of the concentric inquiry circle model? When to stop? What is a mindfulness inquiry, and when is it therapy? How do I get people to share when they are reluctant to do so?

Ideas arose through this creative inquiry within the supra-vision session, about supporting supervisees' learning and skill building in the MB teaching/work Petal, such as:

- Lots of boosting confidence and taking away the pressure of getting it right.
- Normalising that it is an area many people find hard.
- Keeping it experiential and working with specific examples.
- Bringing embodied listening and speaking into MBS explicitly as part of supporting this mode of being during inquiry.
- Using small clips of recordings or transcripts to tease out aspects of inquiry, watching them together, pausing regularly to explore.
- Working with strengths; what is already there?
- Having live moments of guiding and inquiry within supervision, a sort of role play but keeping it real.
- Exploring understanding and possible misunderstanding of frameworks in relation to live material/examples.
- Sharing their own experience and any 'tips and tricks'.

The session finished with group members considering what they would take forward into the next supervision sessions, knowing that they had a whole bank of other possibilities for future occasions.

Using recordings within supra-vision

Viewing/listening to recordings of supervision may form part of supra-vision from time to time. As with MBS, recordings can be a great aid to learning. We are not suggesting doing this within each supervision session, but it could be helpful periodically to dive into a session, not just a troublesome one but also ones that are going well. You may view a whole session or just 10-20 minutes. We offer an option for reflecting on the supervision session using the MBS framework. It is based on a set of reflection questions used within one of our MBS training courses.

Example – reflecting on a recording of supervision

When watching the video or listening to an audio tape, have a copy of the MBS framework to hand and bear questions 1-3 in mind. You may do this in supra-vision together or both do this separately before you meet up, and then continuing the reflection and dialogue around questions 1-3 before moving onto question 4 and 5.

1. What aspects of the MBS framework were observable in this supervision? Implicit and explicit
2. What was missing? Where were there gaps? (fine to be things missing, might not all be there in each session but maybe things missing that could have been there)
3. What were the choice points? Could also use this as a moment to reflect and consider intentions: What was underneath that choice, what other choices were available?
4. Are there any changes I/the supervisor could make with this supervisee? Any areas to lean more into? Intentions for the next session, or direction of travel with this supervisee?
5. Are there any broader learnings as a supervisor, recognisable patterns, strengths and edges?

As with all recordings, written consent needs to be obtained. It can be challenging to record sessions, so great care needs to be taken and lots of options for supervisees to be able to say no. It is often an intimate space where recording may not be welcome. We offer a sample of information to be provided to a supervisee about recording (Appendix C) and, if they agree, a sample consent form (Appendix D). Feel free to use these samples as a starting point to consider your context and develop your information and consent form.

Using the mindfulness-based supervision framework explicitly during supra-vision

The MBS framework can be used more explicitly in conjunction with supra-vision. We offer some practical examples here, based on our own experience, often instigated by supervisors we are supra-vising:

- The supervisor can use the framework in pre-supra-vision preparation as a lens to reflect upon the MBS they are offering and guide their agenda setting and topics for reflection within supra-vision.
- Reflecting together during and particularly at the end of supra-vision, on which aspects of the framework have been explored in the session, and how to take that forward into their supervision work.
- Both have a copy to hand in supra-vision to refer to as needed and to keep it alive in the background.
- For the supervisor to use it to review their own development: Which aspects of the framework are more present? less present?
- Discussions about how to use it during supervision, e.g. to help a supervisee see the breadth of what they could bring to supervision.
- Supervisor and supra-visor using it for their post supra-vision reflections.
- Using it in conjunction with recordings as already outlined.
- Using it to review supra-vision as part of contracting.

Forms of supra-vision

Supra-vision might take various forms.

Supra-visor and supervisor are the same person

In principle, an existing supervisor can become a supra-visor when their supervisee becomes a supervisor themselves. There might be advantages in being supra-vised by someone with whom trust and understanding have already been established.

However, factors to bear in mind would be:

- Does the existing supervisor have sufficient experience to be a supra-visor?
- Does the existing supervisor have enough experience and understanding of an MBS framework for supervising (depending on what is needed)?
- Does the existing supervisor have a sufficient understanding of the contexts of the supervisor's supervisees?

There would need to be clear contractual boundaries and sufficient time allocation to ensure that neither supervision nor supra-vision is squeezed out.

Separate supra-visor for an initial period to closely guide new supervisors

When learning new skills, having more intense supra-vision can be helpful. There are often lots of questions, wonderings, and feeling your way into this new role. It can be helpful to have supra-vision from an experienced MBS supervisor, and you may want someone familiar with the framework and this MB way of working within supervision.

Separate supra-visor and supervisor – ongoing

This might depend on how much supervision you are doing. For instance, if you are engaged in a lot of MBS work, then regular monthly supra-vision would be helpful. This allows you to have dedicated time to focus on this work and your development. If you are engaged in supervision work less frequently, you may have supra-vision just when you actively supervise others or you may choose to periodically join a supra-vision group.

Group supra-vision

Group supra-vision can be a really helpful way of learning with all the benefits of being in a community. The format we tend to offer is based on 1.5-hour sessions held monthly with three to five people. We contract in blocks of four sessions, so people do not need to overly commit. It allows supervisors to dip their toes into group supra-vision, which some choose to complement with 1:1 either simultaneously or spaced out.

Reciprocal peer supra-vision

This could be in dyads or triads with other trained and experienced supervisors (see also Chapter 12 on group supervision). We offer an example of a form that comes from supervisors within the Mindfulness Network for working in peer triads for supra-vision.[239] It is important to note that all the participants are experienced supervisors. The formality of the structure helps to hold the session and keep it from sliding into a peer discussion.

---

239 Thanks to supervisors within the Mindfulness Network for developing this format

Example – peer supra-vision format

This is an example for a 1.5-hour peer supra-vision session with three experienced MBS supervisors. Approximate timings are given in brackets in minutes.

Welcome – brief check-in (5)

Arrival practice (8)

There are three roles: Supra-visor, Supervisor, and Observer. Each session has three rounds, so each person has an opportunity to inhabit each of the three roles. Decide who will begin in which role.

Round 1 (each round 22 minutes total)

A. Supra-vision session (12-15)

B. Reflection/feedback (7-10)

- Supra-visor shares and reflects on their process of supra-vision
- Supervisor shares and reflects on receiving supra-vision, giving explicit teaching and learning points
- Observer shares and reflects on their observations of the supra-visors approach, giving explicit teaching and learning points

This is repeated three times, and roles are swapped, taking a moment to transition/pause/move the body between each round (3)

Closing practice and setting future dates (5)

We are often asked, *"how much supra-vision do I need?"* It's a difficult question, and whilst we could come up with some figure based on the ratio of supervision work you are doing, we prefer the approach proposed in the IMI integrity framework. It places ethics first, which points *"to the very spirit of this work, which holds compassion, inclusion and ethical behaviour as the primary impulse for our mindfulness practice."*[240] Supervisors are experienced MB practitioners, who we feel can bring an ethical stance to these decisions about how much supra-vision is needed. You will likely need more supra-vision when you first begin supervising as everything is new. We think that 1:1 supra-vision can be very useful here. Over time you might reduce the amount of supra-vision a little and explore group supra-vision. We suggest engaging in your own ethical practice and reflections, checking in with your own values and integrity, and aligning with good practice guidelines. We are not currently aware of anything specific stipulating supra-vision requirements. In short, never let your supervision work go unsupervised.

---

240 International Mindfulness Integrity Network, 2024, p. 3

Becoming a supra-visor: offering a guide

All this chapter is relevant for you if you are taking on the role of supra-visor and here we offer a few additional reminders/pointers:

- **Required skills and experience** – We would recommend that as well as meeting good practice guidelines for supervisors,[241] you have longstanding and ongoing experience of offering MBS to a diverse range of supervisees in different contexts, receive your own ongoing supervision and supra-vision, have a clear knowledge of supervisory models and frameworks and a heartfelt and engaged involvement with supervision.

- **The focus in supra-vision is supervision** – The skills someone might need as a supervisor, and their existing supervision skills, helping them see their supervision strengths and edges. The actuality of their supervision sessions is what they bring to supra-vision – the things they are encountering, questions they have, and problems they are encountering.

- **Using the MBS framework** in the ways suggested throughout this chapter: you need to know more about MBS, the framework and the structure to supra-vise.

- **Holding the bigger picture** – You are helping supervisors with their responsibility in their role as a supervisor – the responsibility for the field, the bigger picture. There might be cultural variations around how the field is and what dilemmas arise around ethics and professional issues.

- **Sharing experience** – You are sharing your experience of supervising, to help build a picture of what it's like to be a supervisor – there is less written and articulated about supervision, so you are guiding people.

- **Agenda setting** – In this highly collegial relationship, the supervisor generally sets the agenda. Although it is rarer for the supra-visor to bring things to the agenda, they may offer an agenda item, such as a reminder of something from the last session.

Summary

1. Supra-vision (supervision of supervision) is a form of MBS. It has the formative, restorative and ethical functions as found in all supervision.

2. Two differences between supra-vision and supervision are:
   - It adds another layer to the people involved and takes a more meta-perspective.
   - The focus of the sessions is MBS, supporting the supervisor's skills, experiences, ways of working with their supervisees and their development as an MBS supervisor.

---

241 E.g. BAMBA Good Practice Guidelines for Supervisors of Mindfulness-Based Teachers guidelines https://bamba.org.uk/good-practice-guidelines/

3. The warp of MBS remains as strong threads, the relationship between supra-visor and supervisor is highly collegial, and the MBS framework is more explicit.
4. The weft is woven in different ways to support the supervisor's skills:
   - The Belt:
     - Supervisors often bring ethical issues to supra-vision – it is a place to explore how to hold safety and good practice in mind and act skilfully.
   - The Petals:
     - Supervisors are learning how to work with the varied Petal content that their supervisees bring.
     - The Petals are also the content of supra-vision and have a supervision focus, e.g. developing the skills of being a supervisor, understanding the theory behind supervision, bringing practice into the role of being a supervisor, understanding the cultural context for the supervisor, supervisee and participants/recipients.
5. We offer ways of bringing the MBS framework into supra-vision, such as reviewing recordings as a way of reflecting pre, post and during supra-vision, and reviewing your strengths and growing edges as a supervisor.
6. Supra-vision can take different forms: supervisor and supra-visor are the same person, a separate supra-visor, group supra-vision and reciprocal peer supra-vision with other supervisors (we offer a format for this form of supra-vision).
7. We offer some pointers and reminders about stepping into the role of being a supra-visor.

Reflective questions

If you are supervising and don't have supra-vision yet, what are you noticing after reading this chapter? Is there a form of supra-vision that might work for you? What steps can you take to set this up?

How can you make the most of your supra-vision? Perhaps reading this chapter has sparked some new ideas of inspiration around supra-vision for you? How might you communicate this with your supra-visor?

Are there any ways you would like to bring the MBS framework more into supra-vision? For example, you might like to use the reflective questions we offered in relation to viewing recordings more generally to reflect on a supervision session and take to supra-vision: What aspects of the MBS framework were observable in this supervision? What was missing? Where were there gaps? What were the choice points?

References

Evans, A., Griffith, G. M., & Smithson, J. (2024). What do supervisors' and supervisees' think about mindfulness-based supervision? A grounded theory study. *Mindfulness,* 15, 63–79. https://doi.org/10.1007/s12671-023-02280-8

Hawkins, P., & McMahon, A. (2020). *Supervision in the helping professions* (5th ed.). Open University Press.

International Mindfulness Integrity Network. (2024). Ethics and standards document. *A framework for the integrity of mindfulness-based programs. A living document* (3rd ed.). https://iminetwork.org/

Stoltenberg, C. D., & McNeill, B. W. (2010). *IDM supervision: An integrative developmental model for supervising counselors and therapists* (3rd ed.). Routledge.

Chapter 14

Using the Mindfulness-Based Supervision Framework with *You* as a Mindfulness-Based Supervisor in Mind

> *My growth as a supervisor is supported by the opportunity to develop my own style and explore new areas and to do that in such a way that I feel I have maintained my sense of integrity and professionalism.*[242]

Stoltenberg and McNeill remind us that "*... the training* and development *of supervisors is an area of professional development that requires focussed and systematic procedures*",[243] which requires an investment of time and energy to thoroughly understand a particular model and way of supervising. We, too, believe it to be vitally important to pay attention to training and ongoing growth in this MB supervisor role. Whilst the role draws on many existing skills you have in your MB work, along with your own experience of being supervised and your personal mindfulness practice, it also has its unique and distinct skills to be learned, attended to and cultivated.

---

242 Quote from one of our interviewees
243 Stoltenberg & McNeill, 2010, p. 199 (non-italics added by us)

This chapter begins by looking at the developmental stages of learning to be a supervisor. We explore *You* as an MB supervisor in terms of what you bring to the role on a more personal level, e.g. embodiment, your cultural history, your insights from your mindfulness practice and how this influences MBS. We turn to the Belt, good practice within MBS and offer a variety of ways that skills, competency and confidence can be grown using the MBS framework, along with honing compassionate attitudes. We include a Mindfulness-Based Supervision Self-Report Competency Checklist (Appendix E), which identifies competencies around the different elements of the MBS framework, to support your reflection and growth as an MB supervisor. We describe ways of approaching using this checklist. We finish with recommendations to resource your growth.

Developmental stages of being a supervisor

In Chapter 10, we presented the developmental stages of supervisees. Here, we turn to the developmental stages of being a supervisor. Within the therapy field, the Integrative Development Model outlines a parallel process for supervisors, with learning taking place over four stages.[244] The model assumes that anyone training to be a supervisor has passed through the stages of learning to be a therapist. So, suppose we translate this into MB work. In that case, we are speaking about experienced MB practitioners who are at least proficient, if not advanced, in their area of MB work. However experienced they are in their other MB work, when they begin supervising, they will likely start at Level 1 or 2 in the model for supervisors. We use the level of the model to describe the characteristics of an MB supervisor at various developmental stages.

- **Level 1** – The supervisor may be anxious, with a focus on 'doing the right thing', wanting to take a structured approach to the supervision, wanting to provide appropriate guidance for their supervisees; this often brings a high motivation to supervise well, they might be anxious about providing feedback so a structured approach to giving feedback can be supportive (such as using the MBI:TLC), early ventures to supervise rely on their own experience of being supervised. As one new supervisor said, *"I felt out of my depth. I had a moment where in my mind, I called upon my supervisor – what would … say now?"* They often begin by supporting supervisees who are new to MB work. This helps them as supervisors to find their feet in the role. Supra-vision is an essential support in these early forays into supervising.
- **Level 2** – The supervisor views the process of supervision as more complex and multidimensional, which brings interest and curiosity, as well as possible confusion and doubt. They might focus on the supervisee and need some support

---

244 Stoltenberg & McNeill, 2010

to keep objectivity. If doubt is present, the supervisor might need support to work with this and build their confidence in their skills and abilities. They may be widening the scope of the supervisees they work with. The structure may be loosened, and they find more freedom to work with the emerging moment in supervision. Regular supra-vision continues to be essential.

- **Level 3** – The supervisor will likely feel more stable in their skills now and able to have a balanced, honest appraisal of their own strengths and areas for growth. They often highly value supervision and enjoy this aspect of their MB work; they continue to use supra-vision as needed. They are aware of the supervisee, self, the recipients, and context.

- **Level 3i (integrative)** – The supervisor is mastering the art and craft of supervision. They can work equally well with supervisees new to MB work right through to very experienced supervisees and may not have definitive preferences. They can adapt supervision accordingly, so this attuning we have been speaking about is an increasingly natural process. They can integrate ideas and skills across all of the domains of MBS with increasing fluidity and with supervisees with a range of backgrounds and experiences. It is essential for them to keep learning and keep the work of supervising fresh and alive.

Using the warp of the mindfulness-based supervision framework with *You* as a mindfulness-based supervisor in mind

Let's return to the figure from previous chapters, with two people, the supervisor and the supervisee, bringing awareness to their own bodies and experiences and what is happening between them (Figures 3.1; 4.3). There is a process of attunement; they stay in contact with each other, give and receive, and develop potential for change. So within this practice of relational mindfulness we might ponder the question: What do *You* bring as the person of the supervisor? We see two broad elements:

- Your skills and knowledge which includes different aspects of the weft, such as: MB teaching, underpinning theories, relational mindfulness, supervision skills, the other terrain of the Petals, and the themes articulated in the Belt.

- Yourself – *You* as the MB supervisor which includes all the different aspects of the warp, such as:
    - embodying (staying present and open, responsive, authentic)
    - your self-awareness and 'other' awareness
    - your cultural history and experience, vulnerabilities, attachment style, beliefs and values

- your inner sense of safety/ability to regulate your emotions and capacity to facilitate a sense of psychological safety for another
- your qualities of compassion and wisdom

So, all these aspects of *You* as an MB supervisor are part of the weave of MBS and can be nurtured and cultivated. Fiona Adamson and Jane Brendgen remind us about the idea of *"self as instrument"*[245] an idea used in coaching, supervision and therapy literature. The premise is that we bring who we are and how we are relationally into the MBS space. It is important to appreciate that what you bring as the 'self as instrument' will influence the learning and development of your supervisees as much as having knowledge and skills. So, how do you bring the self-awareness and insights from personal practice into this relational realm and consider the influence on the learning environment between yourself and your supervisee?

You can explore ways in which MB practice and reflection support you in inhabiting the warp. Let's look at some examples from the Container:

- Reflecting on your intention to become a supervisor and repeat this regularly (see the reflection in Chapter 3).
- Working with the body in stillness and movement in relationship with your environment and other people to support Embodied Presence.
- Practising the different heart qualities introduced in Chapter 3, including practising them explicitly in relation to supervision.
- As part of integrity and authenticity, knowing the framework you are working within, knowing your style and limitations, and working skilfully with all of this.
- Exploring the three functions of supervision, formative, normative and restorative (see Chapter 3), investigating those you are less familiar/comfortable with through a practice-based lens.
- Bringing awareness to your personal and professional cultural identity and how this influences you in relationships, e.g. in relation to the power dynamics within different relationships, including supervisory relationships – feeling into this exploration in the body, feelings, thoughts and the urges to act.

These are a few possibilities, but the point we want to make strongly here is that *You* as a Supervisor are broader than skills development. The warp is supported through mindfulness practice, awareness, reflective processes, exploration and dialogue, and embodying particular qualities and attitudes in life. Within the Mindfulness Network, we developed retreats specifically for MBS supervisors to develop the warp and contemplate the practice of MBS through a practice environment.

---

245 Adamson & Brendgen, 2021, p. 91

Using the weft of the mindfulness-based supervision framework with *You* as a mindfulness-based supervisor in mind: the Belt

Good practice

Ethical best practice codes. These codes have different names, including codes of conduct, ethical standards, codes of ethics, etc. You may have a code of conduct from an existing non-mindfulness-based profession and/or an MB code you adhere to.[246] It's important to know the codes you adhere to and use them as a supervisor to reflect upon your supervision work.

Training and ongoing good practice. We use the BAMBA supervisor guidelines as a benchmark for training and ongoing good practice.[247] The components include MBS training, ongoing supervision training and development, learning from experience, personal reflection and supra-vision.

As an overarching principle, we refer to the document "A Framework for the Integrity of Mindfulness-Based Programs", *"The IMI network encourages all participants in our growing field to consider the work of sharing practice, studying methods, and training instructors as a matter of responsible stewardship of human potential."*[248]

Competency

We have developed a Mindfulness-Based Supervision Self-Report Competency Checklist (see Appendix E). The checklist outlines an MB supervisor's experience, knowledge, understanding, skills, and qualities, and encourages self-reflection and dialogue.

The first draft was developed in 2022, using the BAMBA Good Practice Guidelines for Supervisors as a starting point. We piloted the checklist on three occasions within MBS training. We received feedback that it provided a valuable tool for developing as an MB supervisor, mirroring the processes supervisees are engaged in with their MB work. Supervisors noted that it takes time to reflect thoroughly and needs space. They found after reflecting alone on the checklist that a conversation with an experienced supervisor helped to reflect deeper, clarify actions to take forward and re-invigorate learning.

---

246 E.g. International Mindfulness Integrity Network's Ethics and Standards document, 2024, accessed on the home page www.iminetwork.org
247 https://bamba.org.uk/good-practice-guidelines/
248 International Mindfulness Integrity Network, 2024, p. 2

The latest version of the checklist included in this book aligns coherently with the current MBS framework. The checklist includes three sections and finishes with space for overall reflections and identifying strengths and growth areas. Here is an outline of key points of each section:

Section 1 – mindfulness-based supervisor training and development. Section 1 is based on the Good Practice element of the Belt. This section invites you to review the essential MBS training requirements and what we would call additional or aspirational; we recommend that you engage in all these aspects of training at some point in your journey as a supervisor. The essential gives a beginning point. We have based this on the MBS training pathway developed within the Mindfulness Network.[249] We also acknowledge that you may have alternative ways you have trained or are training as an MBS supervisor, which hopefully would map onto this pathway. It may be helpful to refer to Chapter 13 about supra-vision as you complete this section of the checklist.

In Chapter 2, we named the theory, research, and practice of supervision within other modalities as one influence we can draw upon within MBS, so we included this in the checklist. We had a personal experience of this when, early in writing this book, Pamela attended a workshop about cultural sensitivity within clinical supervision, and we realized how much we could relate to this within MBS. This workshop sparked off reading, research and conversation between us. We have drawn upon this learning and woven these theories, research and practice into the book.

Section 2 – mindfulness-based approaches, practice and supervision experience. In section 2, we invite you to reflect upon ongoing good practice using all the Belt and the Petals elements. Keeping yourself up to date in all areas helps to be able to turn towards these different Petals within MBS. The ongoing commitment to your personal mindfulness practice also supports developing and maintaining the qualities of the warp, e.g. Embodied Presence and Compassion/Wisdom. The 'ongoingness' of keeping up to date is important, and some things need to be refreshed. Using video/audio of supervision can be a great way of learning. We offer guidance for using recordings in Chapter 13.

Section 3 – specific competencies for mindfulness-based supervision. In section 3, we invite reflection, using a rating scale to indicate where your competency in this aspect of MBS lies at this moment in time. This section covers the whole of the MBS framework, offering a headline competency or two for each element. It is not an exhaustive list, and we give space for you to add further competencies.

We offer some tips for using the checklist.

---

249 The Mindfulness Network Supervision Training https://supervision.mindfulness-network.org/supervision-training/

Ways of approaching the Mindfulness-Based Supervision Self-Report Competency Checklist: Attitude

- As in the words of the poem 'Growth'[250] *"Growth is measured by gentleness and awareness ..."* can you come from this spirit of compassion and care? Holding this way of being with your growth can feel palpably different from a comparative, critical attitude about what is not here rather than what is.

- You may want to check what sort of mood you are in and if it is one that supports reflection. One trainee shared, *"My observations of doing this after receiving criticism and harshness coloured the whole thing, leaving me feeling 'I am a s... supervisor."* So, the mood you are in can impact how you process and what you see, so take care.

- You might know your tendencies when it comes to scoring. Do you lean toward high or low scores? Holding the scoring aspect lightly or letting this part of the process go if it's not helpful for you.

- For those areas where you feel less competent or even feel things have not gone so well, coming to the sentiment from the lines of the poem 'Growth' again: *"the art of falling down"*, and the way *"with which we once again pick ourselves up, the lightness with which we dust ourselves off, the openness with which we continue and then take the next step."*

Ways of approaching the Mindfulness-Based Supervision MBS Self-Report Competency Checklist: Practicalities

- It may be helpful to review Part Two of this book to remind yourself of the MBS framework.

- When you come to complete the checklist, give yourself time to reflect and make comments. The comments could be on the checklist or in a separate diary or document.

- You can bring mini practice moments and space into the process. It doesn't all have to be completed at once.

- Decide what to do with it next, which includes taking it to supra-vision for further exploration, conversation with MBS peers, further self-reflection, viewing through different lenses, e.g. a more compassionate lens, and what your supervisees might see in you.

- Complete the final sections, stepping back for overall reflections on your growth and identifying at least five strengths, emphasising a strengths-based approach. Consider areas for growth, which might include further developing a strength or widening how you apply it. Growth is not always about gaps or places of lack.

- Add in a review process, ideally annually. And if this is not possible, what might you be able to commit to? E.g. an annual self-reflection and take to supra-vision every other year?

---

250 'Growth' by an anonymous poet, found in Lakey, 2010, p. 255

Using the weft of the mindfulness-based supervision framework with *You* as a mindfulness-based supervisor in mind: the Petals

The Petals include all your skills and knowledge in relation to your area of MB work (such as teaching MBPs, conveying mindfulness through other forms, or 1:1 MB work), and your skills and knowledge in relation to the MBS aspect of your MB work (see the Petals section in Chapter 13 for a detailed description). The Mindfulness-Based Supervision Self-Report Competency Checklist (Appendix E) touches upon each Petal of *You* as a supervisor.

Resourcing your ongoing growth as a mindfulness-based supervisor

We emphasise the importance of MBS training at different levels, which includes the theory of MBS, opportunities to practise with fellow learners, supra-vision when you begin to extend and apply that training into the practice of MBS, ongoing updating through reading, talks, further training, and attending retreats that specifically build the warp competencies.

We have found that learning with MB supervisors, receiving feedback from supervisees, considering the range of supervisees you supervise, and ongoing supervision-based reflection can also assist growth. We offer a few words for each of these.

Learning with mindfulness-based supervisors

For example:

- Setting up a peer triad with fellow MB supervisors so you can offer and receive supra-vision and feedback for yourself as a supra-visor/supervisor (see Chapter 13).
- Joining an MBS community.[251]
- Attending a specific MBS supervisors' retreat or practice days.

Feedback from supervisees

We have already spoken about reviewing supervision with supervisees and incorporating a feedback process into those reviews. Here, we are emphasising how that feedback can be a lens through which to explore *You* as a supervisor. Perhaps you invite your supervisees to offer feedback at the end of a block of supervision or as part of a regular review process if you are in an ongoing relationship. Then, take time to reflect on the feedback, which could be within supra-vision. We offer an example.

---

[251] International Supervisors SiTT group https://www.sitt.community/; Mindfulness World Community (Supervision in Mindfulness Interest group) https://www.mindfulnessworld.community

Example – reflecting on feedback of MBS

A new supervisor brought their first experience of supervising using a mindfulness-based approach to supra-vision. At the end of supervising their supervisee, they evaluated how it had gone and felt unsure how it had landed for the supervisee. The supra-visor suggested they reach out to the supervisee and ask for feedback.

In the next session, they explored this feedback together. It was very positive and didn't include any suggestions for change. The supervisor could see their tendency to brush off the positive and not spend any more time reflecting on the feedback. Therefore, they asked the supra-visor what they could see in the feedback. Together, they viewed the feedback through two lenses:

1. **What were the strengths the supervisee was pointing out?** Which MBS supervisor skills/competencies did these relate to? E.g. there were several references to the supervisee learning and developing skills they took forward into their MBP.
2. **Through the MBS framework:** Looking at which aspects of the framework the supervisee had commented on, e.g. the supervisee had recognized the space that was offered, alongside guidance, the supervisee felt the supervisor was embodying mindfulness.

The supervisor used this to start building a list of their strengths alongside their own reflections, which they could build on and see where there were gaps and areas for growth in the next round of supervising.

Considering the range of supervisees you are working with

We have already suggested that when starting as a supervisor, you begin supervising supervisees who are also early in their journey. Give yourself time to learn and develop the warp and weft of MBS. There will then come a point in your development where you feel competent to expand and diversify. This might be done with different modes, e.g. individual, group, or pair, or to supervisees with more experience. It might be within different contexts while taking care to still stay within your limits. Each aspect of newness gives opportunities for learning.

Personal mindfulness practice

If anything is named mindfulness-based, it requires an underpinning mindfulness practice. As a supervisor, we feel this needs to be a regular and sustained practice, which feeds into your work as a supervisor. You can tailor your practice at times to support *You* as a supervisor. For example, we explore aspects of the MBS framework through mindfulness practice in retreats for supervisors. This includes the different ways we can be in our body in our physical working environment, in relation to others, and in relation to our computer (as a lot of supervision occurs with online platforms). We can bring and embody mindful attitudes and heart qualities such as compassion, joy, friendliness, and equanimity in many ways. We are exploring aspects of supervision through relational mindfulness practice using different elements of mindful communication.

Ongoing supervision-based reflection

Throughout this book, we have been inviting reflection. All the reflections at the end of each chapter are there to support your growth. Here, we offer ways of reflecting on *You* as a supervisor. We have already set out the Mindfulness-Based Supervision Self Report Competency Checklist (Appendix E) as an annual or periodic reflection tool, and here we outline some routine ways of reflecting, beginning with an example.

Example – reflective supervision diary

I (Alison) have several reflective diaries, including one specifically for supervision. I like it being a physical book, and I like to use an ink pen, which slows the process down (I acknowledge this won't be right for everyone). I regularly take time to pause, reflect, and make notes on processes and learning, about the supervision I receive and give, dialogue with other supervisors, and anything else around supervision that has been of interest.

For my own supervision and supra-vision, I reflect before and after the session. The process supports me in dedicating time to reflection. Through writing, I find ways to clarify and articulate what I am experiencing and often any learning or actions to take forward. It helps to set intention and direction.

As a supervisor, my diary is separate from my notes about my supervisees. In my diary, I don't write about each supervision. Still, I will take time to reflect on a particular supervisee (anonymously), a particular moment, or an incident that stood out in some way. Often, I focus more on the process and use it as an opportunity to reflect on myself as a supervisor, with all the aspects of the MBS framework in mind. I often use a set of questions such as: What went well? What was disappointing? What would I like to change?

Revisiting my reflections can be something I forget in the midst of life. I need to take myself somewhere other than my usual working spot, whether out in the garden if it's warm or cuddled up by the fire with a cup of tea. This shift supports a more open and receptive approach to taking in these reflections.

In Chapter 13, we offered a way of reflecting on a supervision recording that utilizes the MBS framework. We are not suggesting you do this after every supervision, but you could set an intention to periodically reflect in this kind of way. A version of these questions could also be used for your self-reflections on a supervision session without the recording. It would be helpful to have the framework to hand as you reflect.

- What aspects of the MBS framework were evident in this supervision?
- What was missing? Where were there gaps?
- What were the choice points? What other choices were available?
- Are there any changes I want to make with this supervisee? Any areas/intentions I want to lean more into for the next session or direction of travel with this supervisee?
- Are there any broader learnings for me as a supervisor, such as patterns that I recognise, or my strengths and edges?

Other ways of using the MBS framework as part of your reflections could include delving into one aspect of the framework in detail and considering your own skills and strengths/learning-growing edges. We encourage you to be playful and find out what structures and approaches support self-reflection for you, including the practicalities of when, where, and how.

You as an ambassador of mindfulness-based supervision in your context

In our experience of supervising and meeting other supervisors, we hear time and time again about how MBS (and mentoring) is often not valued, not included, forgotten, or misunderstood. In our discussions, we see that this could be part of the opportunity and responsibility of the role of supervisor. We see that we have been in these roles of ambassadors advocating for MBS for some years (along with others) and wish to bring this more explicitly to light so it creates opportunity and not just frustration.

So, what do we mean by the term *ambassador*? One meaning is a person who represents, speaks for or advertises a particular organization, group of people, or activity. We also looked up the word advocate and like the definitions around publicly supporting or promoting an idea, development, or way of doing something. Both terms fit with what we are inviting in this section, so we will use the term *ambassador* for *You* as the person and advocating for the action.

There are many ways you can step into this role of ambassador and advocating for MBS in your context. One obvious way is with your supervisee where you are supporting them to understand what MBS is, feel into the process and see the value.

We also suggest that you become an ambassador in your working context. Stoltenberg and McNeill have this aspirational wish, *"We can only hope that these individuals* (supervisors) *are valued and well utilized in the settings in which they work."*[252] Whilst we agree with this sentiment, our experience is often that the importance of supervision is easily forgotten and needs active advocation to be kept in the limelight and valued. You might be that person or one of a few people in your context who can do this. So, to get down to the minutiae of what we might be talking about here, we give some examples from our experience in workplace settings:

- When new MBP groups, MBA work, or mindfulness research are being set up, reminding your manager/team/peers about including supervision provision.
- Speaking about the value of MBS whenever you can, showing how you learn and benefit from MBS.
- Putting up a case for receiving your own supervision, sometimes having to 'fight' quite hard.
- Whenever supervision seems missing from documents/plans, suggesting it's added and explaining why.
- Pointing to good practice guidelines about the need for ongoing supervision.
- Speaking about MBS with your line manager regularly and in any review meetings, evidencing its part in your competency as an employee.

Many supervisors either work or do their supervision work in a freelance/self-employed capacity. As a supervisor, you are also influencing the messages you give about *You*, as a supervisor, and who comes to you for supervision. This gets communicated through conversations you have with others in the field, your website (if you have one), social media profiles and posts, blogs, newsletters, etc. Areas to consider could be:

- How you communicate what you can offer in relation to supervision.
- The way you describe MBS and your experience.
- How you portray the difference between coming to an MBS supervisor and another supervisor.
- The contacts that you make and foster.
- Your connection with the wider MBS community.

Your context may afford you other opportunities to be advocating and supporting best practice in this field. It is often on our radar, keeping open the question: How can we best be in service of spreading the word about the delights and importance of MBS, and anything to change to keep it relevant? Finally, we acknowledge that this is not always an easy role, and takes courage, often meaning we step out of our usual habits and comfort zone.

---

252 Stoltenberg & McNeill, 2010, p. 207 (non-italics added by us for clarity)

Summary

In this chapter we have discussed ways you can support your growth as an MB supervisor.

1. There are different developmental stages of growth as a supervisor, and we describe the characteristics of four levels.
2. Developing the warp includes cultivating embodied presence, openness and responsiveness, deepening your awareness of self and others, and bringing in your cultural history and experience.
3. The weft of *You* as an MB supervisor is woven in different ways:
   - The Belt:
     - Good practice is held through ethical codes, training and ongoing good practice activities.
     - We have developed a Mindfulness-Based Supervision Self-Report Competency Checklist (Appendix E) that covers your MBS training and development and ongoing good practice in MBS. We offer guidance on ways of using the checklist.
   - The Petals:
     - This includes all the specific competencies in supervising, many of which are named in the competency checklist.
4. We suggest other ways of supporting your growth using the MBS framework, such as connecting with other MB supervisors, reflecting on supervision, receiving feedback from supervisees, your personal mindfulness practice, and the range of supervisees you work with.
5. We encourage you to explore ways to be an ambassador, advocating the value and importance of MBS.

Reflective questions

Take some moments to reflect upon your own experience of receiving supervision.

What did you notice in good supervisory role models? Skills, the way the supervisor was, and the process?

What did you notice in less helpful supervision role models? Skills, the way the supervisor was, and the process?

What do *You* bring as the person of the supervisor?

Your skills and knowledge in a range of aspects of MB approaches (the Petals)? And your skills and knowledge as an MB supervisor (also the Petals)?

And *You* (the Warp), e.g. your embodiment, self-awareness, cultural background, vulnerabilities, values, and ability to be in a relationship with another?

Take some time to recall moments in supervision when you were supervising that went well. What were your strengths? And recalling a time it didn't go so well: What growth is needed? What support do you need?

Which ethical code(s) do you refer to/adhere to as an MB supervisor? Take time to consider how they relate to your work as a supervisor. Is there anything new for you in this reflection? Anything to take forward into your work as a supervisor?

How are you feeling about the MBS Self-Report Competency Framework (Appendix E)? How might you use the MBS competency framework, if at all? When would be a good time and way to do this? Do you want to do this with another or others?

Are you receiving the supervision you need for your work and being a supervisor? Are there other ways of supporting your growth that you feel moved towards after reading this chapter?

Are there any ways, in your current context, you could step more into this ambassador role, advocating for MBS? These steps can be very small. How does it feel to be more in an ambassador-type role? What support do you need?

References

Adamson, F., & Brendgen, J. (2021). *Mindfulness-based relational supervision: Mutual learning and transformation.* Routledge. https://doi.org/10.4324/9781315161280

Lakey, G. (2010). *Facilitating group learning: Strategies for success with diverse learners.* Jossey-Bass.

Stoltenberg, C. D., & McNeill, B. W. (2010). *IDM supervision: An integrative developmental model for supervising counselors and therapists* (3rd ed.). Routledge.

International Mindfulness Integrity Network. (2024). Ethics and standards document. *A framework for the integrity of mindfulness-based programs. A living document* (3rd ed.). https://iminetwork.org/

Appendices

The resources to accompany this book can be downloaded by visiting the link or scanning the QR code

www.pavpub.com/mindfulness-based-supervision-and-mentoring-using-an-embodied-dialogue-to-support-learning-and-reflection-resources

Appendix A
Mindfulness-Based Supervision Contracting Conversation Checklist

Intentions

- Begin to know each other and to get a sense of compatibility.
- Find out what the supervisee's needs are.
- Help the supervisee to understand what mindfulness-based supervision (MBS) is through explanation and through embodying the process.
- Complete the more formal written contract after discussion with the supervisee.

Possible areas to cover

(In addition to going through the written contract)

Introductions

(These might lead into background information)

Background information

Supervisee's experience:

- MB training and previous MB teaching and work.
- Previous supervision experience.
- Mindfulness practice.

Supervisor's MB experience and work

Cultural background: both sharing what feels relevant around cultural background

The nature of MBS

Purpose of supervision – formative, normative, restorative

Structure and process of supervision – might share a copy of the MBS framework

- including how mindfulness supervision covers all the different Petals
- use of inquiry and pauses
- all held in a mindful container

Supervisee's needs

Supervisee's expectations/aims/intentions/needs – spend time on this – short reflective practice

Learning style – including any learning needs it would be helpful for the supervisor to be aware of

Anything else the supervisee needs the supervisor to be aware of, e.g. communication needs, physical conditions that could affect the supervision

Confidentiality

Clarify the bounds of confidentiality, including recognising any dual relationships and how to handle them. Also, clarify exceptions, e.g. supervisor's supra-vision, safeguarding issues, and agreeing on any evidence/reports needed for employers or training organizations.

Ways of working

- Preparation for supervision sessions
- Structure of sessions
- Contact between sessions
- Recordings/live teaching
- Use of tools such as the MBI:TAC and MBI:TLC
- Ways of offering feedback to each other
- Ruptures

Practicalities and responsibilities

Go through the practicalities in the contract and basic ground rules, e.g. frequency, fees, payment, cancellations, missed sessions, reviewing

Responsibilities, e.g. safety, confidentiality, data protection, insurance

Specifics

Anything else specific to this supervision relationship

Appendix B
Sample Mindfulness-Based Supervision Contract

Agreement between _____ (Supervisee)

address: _____

phone: _____

email: _____

And: _____ (Supervisor)

address: _____

phone: _____

email: _____

Content and process of the sessions

Supervision is set in a framework of adherence to Good Practice Guidelines. As a supervisor, I agree to adhere to good practice guidelines for supervisors and teachers (*insert the guidelines you adhere to here …*), and I encourage all my supervisees to adhere to specific good practice guidance.

The supervisee will primarily determine the content of subsequent sessions and will be responsible for deciding what material to bring to supervision and how to apply the learning gained. The supervisor may wish to be emailed in advance with a provisional agenda for the next supervision session to facilitate the best use of the time available.

The supervisor will be responsible for offering mentoring, guidance and support; this may include bringing an issue to the session agenda and/or suggesting a practice of teaching and inquiry during the sessions. The supervision process will aim to encourage a mindful inquiry and exploration around the issues brought to supervision or arising in the session. This is a two-way learning process, though advice and guidance may be offered as appropriate.

The content of supervision will depend on the specific aims and objectives of the supervisee, but is likely to include:

1. development of personal practice, including exploration of how this underpins professional mindfulness-based work
2. development of mindfulness-based work, such as teaching practice/1:1 client work, by supporting the supervisee's reflective practice to enhance their understanding and refine their skills in specific aspects of conveying mindfulness, leading practices, inquiry, group and individual processes and so on
3. aiding the supervisee in explorations about how they can integrate mindfulness within their professional role and context, whether in relation to specific healthcare or therapy settings or other applications of mindfulness-based approaches such as commercial organizations

Please note: mindfulness-based supervision does not:

1. provide clinical supervision. We may discuss the application of mindfulness in any clinical work you do, but you need to have a separate clinical supervisor to hold responsibility for your clinical work
2. incorporate personal counselling
3. provide monitoring or evaluation of the supervisee's work, unless contracted specifically for such monitoring or evaluation

Confidentiality

Discussions in the sessions will normally be held in complete confidence.

If audio or video tapes are used as part of the supervision process, the supervisee will ensure that the participant(s) of the course or client(s) are explicitly aware of this and gain their written consent(s) to record material being used for this purpose.

It is understood that the supervisor may take any appropriate matters arising from this supervision to their own supervision process. All reasonable care will be taken to ensure the supervisee's anonymity.

If the supervisor is sufficiently concerned about a matter with serious criminal, ethical or personal implications told to them by the supervisee, they reserve the right to break confidentiality by discussing this with another responsible person. Every effort would be made to discuss this with the supervisee in the first instance.

Safeguarding

The supervisor will work with the supervisee to ensure that the supervisee is aware of their own responsibility and duty of care in safeguarding course participants and those associated with them, as well as anyone else the supervisee comes into contact with through their MB teaching, 1:1 or other MB work. This includes accessing relevant training, in order to comply with good practice.

The supervisor has a safeguarding duty to the supervisee and is required to raise any concerns about risk of harm, neglect or abuse to the supervisee.

Therapeutic executor

In the event of a serious accident, sudden illness, or death of the supervisor, their appointed therapeutic executor (*insert the name of your therapeutic executor here ...*) will inform the supervisee and support them in making other arrangements for supervision.

Data Protection

The supervisor will comply with Data Protection Regulations. The supervisor is not obliged to but may keep process notes of the supervision sessions to act as an aide memoire. Notes will be kept securely and destroyed at the end of an agreed period of time. The supervisee is responsible for complying with the relevant requirements for Data Protection for their mindfulness-based work.

Insurance

The supervisor has their own professional indemnity insurance for their mindfulness teaching and work, including supervision and supervisees are expected to have their own for their mindfulness-based work.

Arrangements for the sessions

The supervisor and supervisee will arrange the supervision agreements as suits the needs of the supervisee in terms of length and frequency of the sessions and frequency of reviews. It is suggested that there be a review after the first three to four sessions and then regularly at an agreed time frame. The supervisee is encouraged to offer feedback at any time. If any marked changes need to be considered (i.e. the nature, aims and expectations of supervision have changed) then a new contract has to be negotiated.

Supervision can be arranged in hour long or half-hour long sessions.

The times of the sessions are to be negotiated between the supervisee and supervisor.

The format of supervision, e.g. Zoom, Teams, phone, and who will set up the call, is to be agreed upon.

The supervisee agrees to inform the supervisor if they intend to end supervision before the agreed time period. Unless there is prior agreement, if the supervisor has not heard from the supervisee within 6 months, they will assume this contract has concluded. If the supervisee makes contact at a later date, a new contract will be set up.

Cancellation

Cancellation of sessions should, wherever possible, be made in a reasonable time (48 hours); otherwise, the supervisee may be liable for payment in full.

Cost and invoicing procedure

£ _____ per half hour

£ _____ per full hour

The supervisee will be emailed an invoice for this payment after each session or after a suitable number of sessions to be agreed between supervisor and supervisee.

To be completed by the supervisee

Statement of the supervisee's aims for and expectations of the supervision:

Time of sessions:

Duration of each session:

Frequency of sessions:

Number of sessions planned before review:

Any other agreed arrangements:

| Name of supervisee | Date | Signature |

| Name of supervisor | Date | Signature |

Note
Both parties should complete and sign this agreement and retain a copy for their records.

Appendix C

Sample information sheet for recording supervision

Request to record one of our supervision sessions

With good practice and learning in mind, I think recording myself as a supervisor is a good idea. I am aware that for myself and many other teachers, being able to view yourself teaching and have others view you can offer interesting insights and possibilities for useful feedback. It seems that this process could equally be of help for mindfulness-based supervision. Therefore, I am emailing all my supervisees to see if this would be possible. I imagine there will be reasons why this would not feel okay, as supervision can be experienced as a confidential and intimate space, so please do not feel obliged to say yes. If the possibility doesn't land well with you, then there is no need to let me know or explain.

How I would wish to use the recordings for my development as a supervisor

- To view the recording myself and reflect upon strengths, edges, and areas for development.
- To show small clips to my supra-visor for reflection and feedback in supra-vision.

Consent to record could be given for either or both ways of using the recordings, and this is outlined on the consent form.

Practicalities

- To use the record function in Zoom. If you did not wish to be in the recording, I could spotlight myself; please let me know.
- When sharing the recording with my supra-visor to do so through a password-protected link or by showing the recording from my own computer during the supra-vision.
- To store the recordings for a maximum of eight weeks and to delete as soon as they have been viewed.

- If, after the recording, you change your mind, the recording would immediately be deleted.
- There would always be an option to pause for sections of the supervision/supravision, for instance, if there was a theme that felt too sensitive to be recorded.

Many thanks for taking the time to read this and for your consideration. Let me know via email or in our next session together if this interests you now or at some point.

Warm wishes,

Appendix D

Sample consent form for recording supervision

(to be adapted as needed, adding in your details and information)

Consent to recording supervision session(s)

I have read the information about the practicalities of these recordings and have been able to ask any questions I have.	**Yes/No**
I confirm that I consent to the recorded session to be viewed by _____ for their development as a supervisor.	**Yes/No**
I confirm that I consent to the session being recorded and shown to _____ 's supra-visor _____ (*name of the supra-visor*) for reflection and feedback in supra-vision.	**Yes/No**
I understand that I can withdraw at any time without prejudice.	**Yes/No**

Name of supervisee   Date   Signature

Name of supervisor   Date   Signature

Appendix E
Mindfulness-Based Supervision Self-Report Competency Checklist

You as a mindfulness-based supervisor: Reflecting on your experience, skills and competency

This checklist offers a way of reflecting on the skills and competencies you hold as a supervisor to support your continued learning and growth. You can use it as a tool for self-review/reflection and as part of a dialogue with another mindfulness-based (MB) supervisor, e.g. your supra-visor or experienced peer.

Sections 1 and 2 check in with experience and continuing good practice. Section 3 invites you to reflect on your strengths and learning edges around specific MB supervisor competencies. For further guidance, see Chapter 14 in the mindfulness-based supervision (MBS) book.

Date of review:

Date of last review:

Key learning and growth since the last review:

Appendix E

Section 1 – Belt: Good practice
Mindfulness-based supervisor training and development

Note: we have based this on the mindfulness-based supervision training pathway developed within the Mindfulness Network – you may have alternative ways you have/are training as an MBS supervisor

	Completed (date, training organization)	Notes
Essential:		
MBS foundational training which includes working within an inquiry-based framework		
Supra-vision: receiving supra-vision as part of your learning once you begin supervising; discussing with your supra-visor how much is needed to best support your learning needs		
Additional:		
Further MBS training which builds on skills, which might include working with groups as well as individuals		
Specific retreat for MB or other retreat that specifically supports the warp aspects of the MBS framework		
Familiarity/training with the use of the MBI:TLC and the MBI:TAC as an aid to supervision		
Further supervision-related trainings/ workshops (MB or from other modalities)		

Section 2 – Belt: Ongoing good practice
Mindfulness-based approaches, practice and supervision experience (covering the Petals and Belt)

	Up to date	Notes
To continue to teach MBAs or be engaged in the MB work you are supervising others in		
If supervising MBPs, to be a proficient teacher of mindfulness-based courses – as assessed by experienced colleagues and ideally using the MBI:TAC		
If not supervising MBPs, discuss with your supervisor what 'proficient' looks like in your area of MB work, using the MBI:TAC domains and definition of proficient as a guide. This will include your MB work being assessed/reviewed by another experienced professional in your field or by your supervisor		
To stay up to date with the curriculum/curricula in which you are teaching or the area of MB work you are engaged in		
To be in a regular mindfulness supervisory relationship in relation to your MB teaching/work (recommended monthly when actively working)		
To attend regular retreats (five to seven days) which facilitate mindfulness practice in depth (or equivalent ways of having extended periods of practice)		
To have ongoing study and guidance to support a deepening of personal mindfulness practice, including meetings with a teacher on teacher-led retreats, ongoing dialogue with a meditation teacher, or an experienced MB supervisor		

To explore the interface of personal mindfulness practice with your MB work and MBS, via personal reflection and in super/supra-vision		
To have a deep familiarity and up-to-date knowledge of the theoretical underpinnings of the mindfulness approach being taught/delivered and its aims and intentions, e.g. through reading, workshops, etc.		
To stay up to date with the current and developing evidence base for MBAs, with a particular emphasis on area you supervise in		
To be familiar with the principles that influence learning and development of individuals and groups		
To understand the scope and influence of 'contexts' such as: the supervisee's training, work and personal context, organizational context, cultural context, wider mindfulness field, and more global issues		
To receive supra-vision individual and/or group when actively supervising		
To periodically use recordings of supervision (which could include peer supervision) for self-reflection and within supra-vision so your supervision work is viewed by another		
To keep updated and refreshed with supervision, e.g. through reading supervision-based books and supervision-based research papers, talks, and further supervision-related training		

Section 3 – Specific competencies for mindfulness-based supervision

Suggested Scale	
1 Strength .... **Growing Edge 4**	
Clear strength	Clear growing edge
Consistent	Inconsistent
Clear evidence of skill/ability	Less evidence of skill/ability
Deep understanding	Limited understanding

	Scale 1-4	Reflective Notes
Warp – Container		
Integrity: ability to develop and maintain a trusting and supportive supervisory relationship		
Intention: ability to balance the educative, supportive and ethical aspects of supervision as required		
Embodied presence: ability to have an embodied presence that is open, responsive, and authentic during the inquiry process within MBS to facilitate the supervisee's learning		
Compassion/Wisdom: ability to bring both compassion and wisdom into the supervision space, e.g. balancing holding vulnerability and knowing when and how to challenge		
Warp – Space		
Ability to take pauses, and create space within the supervision session in a variety of ways		

Warp – Mutual Inquiry

Ability to work with an inquiry-led framework of mindfulness-based supervision

Ability to work collaboratively, which includes working skilfully with any power dynamics

Ability to enable the supervisee to reflect, inquire and use the supervision session effectively

Weft – Belt

Contracting: ability to set up a supervision contract, identifying, adapting and considering:

- the nature of the work, context and specialist skills required
- the cultural and organizational context
- the supervisee's mindfulness practice and mindfulness teaching developmental needs
- ways of supporting the supervisee to present appropriate supervision material

Safety: having knowledge and understanding of ethical and professional practice and ensuring this is a regular topic of conversation in supervision. This includes knowledge and understanding of relevant frameworks around safety and trauma sensitivity related to the supervisee's teaching

Diversity and inclusion: ability to work and practice in accordance with key principles of equality, diversity and inclusion within the supervisory relationship and your MB work, and to support the supervisee in bringing these principles into their work		
Competency: ability to reflect on your own work as a supervisor to identify strengths, learning edges and training/supervisory needs		
Weft – Petals		
Contexts: ability to facilitate exploration and discussion around cultural competency within the supervisee's work		
Personal mindfulness practice: ability to supervise the development of the supervisee's personal mindfulness practice, relating this to the supervisee's work and life		
Mindfulness-based work: ability to support the supervisee in identifying both their strengths and learning needs, which might include using the MBI:TLC as a framework, but is not limited to this		
Mindfulness-based work: ability to incorporate direct observation into supervision, through live teaching or recordings of the supervisee's work		
Mindfulness-based work: ability to give accurate and constructive feedback that facilitates new learning and to challenge poor practice where necessary (also competency and integrity)		

Appendix E

Group and individual processes: ability to conduct supervision in different formats, e.g. individual, group, pair of co-teachers		
Group and individual processes: ability to work with different learning styles and needs of individual supervisees		
Group and individual processes: competence in group facilitation if offering group supervision. This includes knowledge and understanding of group process, ability to contract with a group, and ability to balance the needs of the group, individuals within the group and the task of providing effective MBS		
Theory and understanding: understanding the different theories underpinning MBS (e.g. see Chapter 2) and knowing when and how to draw on a particular theory		

Any other competencies that you wish to add

Appendix E

Overall reflections

Key strengths identified

1.

2.

3.

4.

5.

Areas for growth and development over the next 12 months
(being as realistic and specific as possible and naming what you might need to support you)

1.

2.

3.

Planned date for the next review process

Afterword

Our intention in offering this book is to inspire and share our passion for MBS, enhance the art and craft of it, and bring alive the content and process. Rebecca Crane's words from the foreword to the book echo our sentiment around the place and value of MBS:

> *"The range of possibilities for bringing mindfulness alive in the world is vast and growing as the field continues to innovate. MBS is an anchoring thread of consistency through this diversity, offering a reliable relational space to reflect, resource and build skills and understandings."*

A central thread running through this book is defining *mindfulness-based* supervision as distinct from mindfulness-informed supervision, emphasising that to be called mindfulness-based, it needs a personal mindfulness practice underneath, alongside and around it; the supervisor is making a commitment to cultivating mindfulness within their practice and their lives, and so the mindfulness-based approach is part of the fundamental fabric of MBS. One of our interviewees pointed to the value for them as a supervisee of this integration within MBS of work and the personal:

> *"The opportunity to grow as a person – quite surprising and wonderful realisation that supervision has added greatly to my unfolding life journey in the broadest sense."*

We offer the MBS framework as a way of conceptualising the various elements of content and process of MBS and to illustrate their interconnectedness. Within the confines of a two-dimensional representation of the framework, it is hard to show its full nature, and in our minds, we imagine it in a three-dimensional form. We find that using the metaphors of the warp and weft and the dance also helps to convey the dynamic sense of MBS.

Afterword

Future directions

The MBS framework is the fruit of much collaboration, shaped by the contributions and experiences of those within the mindfulness field and the broader field of supervision.

As best we can, we have tried to widen the applicability of this mindfulness-based way of working. It began its life with MBSR/MBCT teachers, and now includes supervisors and supervisees in many kinds of MB work in a multitude of settings. As we have been writing, we have been aware of the overlaps with mentoring – a vast term that means many different things to people. We envisage that the warp in particular is relevant to many mentoring relationships and could be a supportive framework.

Our hope is that others will adapt and use it in different ways according to their culture and context. We imagine adaptations and new iterations will be shaped by this grassroots knowledge and experiences alongside the varied theoretical frames of reference. It will be important to also keep abreast of shifts and developments within the underpinning theory and research, particularly future research into supervision.

We hope this widening continues and will be fascinated and heartened to feel that organic adaptations happen as it meets diverse people, professions and conditions. We encourage You, as a mindfulness-based supervisor, to take your place in advocating for MBS, in whatever ways are possible, however large or small.

We do know that cost can be a barrier to people receiving ongoing MBS. We sincerely hope and urge the field to find ways for innovative solutions, such as sliding scale fees, bursaries, and services and projects costing-in supervision as part of mindfulness provision.

We bring an awareness that our cultural background will have influenced this book in ways that are beneficial and ways that hinder. We offer humility and apology for any unintended offence or lack of understanding. There are limitations within the scope of a book, for example, it is not focused on MBS from the perspective of the MB supervisee – maybe another book!

Final words

As we conclude this book and our contribution to the conversation, we touch into our love of MBS and its potential. We look forward to further connection and conversation with supervisors and supervisees around the world – you have been in our hearts as we have crafted the words, pictures, metaphors and stories in these pages.

We encourage you to:

> *Keep on pausing, keep learning, keep wondering.*

You can find us at:

Alison   https://www.vividmindfulness.co.uk/
https://www.linkedin.com/in/dr-alison-evans-b79230276/

Pamela   https://www.pameladuckerin.com/